PREHISTORIC
FLINTWORK

PREHISTORIC FLINTWORK

Chris Butler

First published 2005

Reprinted in 2008 by
The History Press,
The Mill, Brimscombe Port,
Stroud, Gloucestershire, GL5 2QG
www.thehistorypress.co.uk

Reprinted 2011, 2012

© Chris Butler, 2005

The right of Chris Butler to be identified as the Author
of this work has been asserted by him in accordance with the
Copyrights, Designs and Patents Act 1988.

All rights reserved. No part of this book may be reprinted
or reproduced or utilised in any form or by any electronic,
mechanical or other means, now known or hereafter invented,
including photocopying and recording, or in any information
storage or retrieval system, without the permission in writing
from the Publishers.

British Library Cataloguing in Publication Data.
A catalogue record for this book is available from the British Library.

ISBN 978 0 7524 3340 0

Typesetting and origination by Tempus Publishing.
Printed and bound by TJ International Ltd, Padstow, Cornwall

CONTENTS

List of Illustrations		6
Acknowledgements		9
Preface		11
1	An Introduction	13
2	Human use of Flint	23
3	Common Tool Types	49
4	The Palaeolithic Period	57
5	The Mesolithic Period	83
6	Early Neolithic Flintwork	119
7	Neolithic Flint Axe Production	139
8	Later Neolithic and early Bronze Age Flintwork	155
9	Later Prehistoric Flintwork	179
10	Analysing Prehistoric Flintwork	193
Glossary of Terms		202
Bibliography		210
Index		218

LIST OF ILLUSTRATIONS

TEXT FIGURES

1	Seams of flint showing as horizontal bands in the chalk.
2	Examples of nodular and tabular flint.
3	Schematic section of Sussex.
4	Flintknapper Allan Course at work.
5	Knapping strategies.
6	Replica hafted flint knives.
7	A polished flint axe from a probable ritual pit deposit at Seaford, Sussex.
8	An example of a conchoidal fracture.
9	An example showing a flake removed from a single platform core.
10	Knapping technology.
11	Cores.
12	The basic attributes of a flake.
13	Platform preparation.
14	Examples of struck flakes, blades and bladelets.
15	Hard and soft hammer-struck flakes.
16	A punch being used to remove blades from a core.
17	An example of pressure flaking.
18	Retouching.
19	Common tool types.
20	Lower Palaeolithic handaxe typology.
21	Lower Palaeolithic Mode 1 flintwork.
22	Lower Palaeolithic Mode 2 handaxes.
23	Lower Palaeolithic Mode 2 implements.
24	Levallois technology.
25	Middle Palaeolithic Mode 3 implements
26	Middle Palaeolithic Mode 3 flintwork.
27	Earlier Upper Palaeolithic flintwork.
28	Later Upper Palaeolithic flintwork.
29	Final Upper Palaeolithic flintwork.
30	Mesolithic bladelet cores.

List of Illustrations

31	Mesolithic flake cores and core debitage.
32	Examples of hafted microliths.
33	Microlith production using the microburin technique.
34	Microlith debitage.
35	Clark's microlith classification scheme.
36	Jacobi's microlith classification scheme.
37	Hengistbury Head microliths.
38	Kettlebury 103 microliths.
39	Hermitage Rocks microliths.
40	Tranchet adze production.
41	Examples of Mesolithic tranchet adzes.
42	Mesolithic picks and adzes.
43	Mesolithic scrapers.
44	Mesolithic implements.
45	Star Carr piercers.
46	Other Mesolithic tools.
47	Early Neolithic cores.
48	Early Neolithic leaf-shaped arrowhead typology.
49	Leaf-shaped arrowheads from Hurst Fen.
50	Examples of early Neolithic end scrapers.
51	Examples of Neolithic end scrapers.
52	Other early Neolithic scrapers.
53	Examples of Neolithic scrapers.
54	Early Neolithic tools.
55	Early Neolithic tools.
56	Neolithic tools.
57	Neolithic axe production.
58	Examples of axe-thinning flakes from Cissbury.
59	Neolithic axe types.
60	Polished axes.
61	Large Neolithic flaked axe and Scandinavian axe.
62	Mineshaft 21 at Harrow Hill 1924-5.
63	Section through a typical flint mine.
64	The Curwens' excavation 1924-5 at Harrow Hill.
65	Later Neolithic/early Bronze Age cores.
66	Later Neolithic arrowhead typology.
67	Examples of later Neolithic arrowheads.
68	Barbed-and-tanged arrowhead typology.
69	Examples of barbed-and-tanged arrowheads.
70	Later Neolithic and early Bronze Age scrapers.
71	Later Neolithic and early Bronze Age implements.
72	Later Neolithic and early Bronze Age implements.
73	Sickle and daggers

74 Later Bronze Age cores.
75 Later Bronze Age scrapers.
76 Later Bronze Age flintwork.
77 A nineteenth-century gunflint.
78 Example of the measurements of a flake for length/breadth analysis.
79 Four refitting flakes.

COLOUR PLATES

1   Flint raw material.
2   Flint seams in the chalk cliffs and a shingle beach near Birling Gap, Sussex.
3   Nodules of the distinctive Bullhead flint.
4   A prehistoric flintknapper at work.
5   A selection of flint cores.
6   A modern flintknappers kit.
7   Various natural pieces of flint.
8   A selection of different scrapers.
9   The Boxgrove excavations.
10 *In situ* knapping debris from handaxe manufacture at Boxgrove.
11 An Acheulian handaxe.
12 A Mesolithic tranchet adze.
13 A section through a pit at the Streat Lane Mesolithic site.
14 A reconstruction of a Mesolithic tent structure.
15 A reconstruction of a Mesolithic rock shelter.
16 Replica hafted arrowheads.
17 Neolithic axe roughout, polished axe and flaked axe.
18 A polissoir on Fyfield Down near Avebury.
19 A modern example of a flaked axe hafted into a wooden handle.
20 A Neolithic flaked axe.
21 Grimes Graves, Norfolk.
22 Antler pick, with axe roughout and axe-thinning flakes.
23 The excavation of a Neolithic flint mineshaft at Harrow Hill, Sussex in 1982.
24 A flint quarry excavated at Harrow Hill in 1986.
25 An early Bronze Age round barrow.
26 Modern replica one-piece sickles.
27 The Amesbury Archer.
28 Crowlink Barrow, Sussex.
29 Richborough Castle, Kent.

ACKNOWLEDGEMENTS

I would like to thank Robin Holgate who was responsible for first introducing me to the delights of prehistoric flintwork. I am grateful to David Field, Robin Holgate, Matt Pope and Caroline Wells for reading drafts of the text and making many helpful comments and suggestions. Roger Jacobi read an early draft of the Mesolithic flintwork chapter and made many useful suggestions and provided some helpful direction. Any mistakes or inaccuracies that remain are solely my responsibility. Claire Goodey has done a superb job in illustrating all of the flintwork examples, and has been very patient with my requests and changes of mind. All the remaining drawings are my own. I would like to thank Allan Course for allowing me to photograph some of his repli-cated flint tools and flintworking equipment. Many others have helped with comments and support, for which I am very grateful. I would especially like to thank Liza who has supported and encouraged me throughout.

This book is dedicated to my mother
Valerie Butler

PREFACE

There is currently no guidebook or manual available to help archaeologists and others recognise and interpret prehistoric worked flint in the British Isles. This book aims to fill that gap by providing a guide to the technologies and types of prehistoric flintwork used by Palaeolithic and Mesolithic hunter-gatherers through to later prehistoric farmers, and what this can tell us about how past societies exploited the landscape.

The book begins with an introduction to the human use of flint, which explains how to identify worked flint and describes the various techniques used in flintknapping and the making of implements. This sets out the groundwork for the remainder of the book, which looks at flintwork in a traditional manner, period by period.

The Palaeolithic, Mesolithic, Neolithic and Bronze Age periods are examined in turn, describing the different diagnostic flint implements used in each period and how they were produced. Against the background of the change from hunter-gatherer societies to farming communities, the changes in flintworking technology and the types of flint implements produced are discussed. For each period, the book explores what the analysis of flintwork can tell us about society and human use of the landscape. The flintwork from a number of case studies is reviewed to help us understand how and where flint was procured; the types of tools found on settlements, manufacturing and ritual sites; and the eventual decline in the importance of flint. Having considered the flintwork from each period of prehistory, the final chapter describes some of the methods archaeologists can use to analyse flintwork to help answer questions about our past. Finally there is a glossary of all of the terms used in the book.

This volume is intended as a summary of current knowledge on prehistoric flintwork. There are many gaps in current knowledge, and different specialists have their preferred terms and methods for analysing flintwork. I have tried to bring together all of the terms and definitions currently used by lithic specialists, and illustrate as many examples of the different types of tools and other pieces of flintwork as was possible. It was not my intention to create any new classifications, although some might argue that this is long overdue.

Prehistoric Flintwork

NOTE ON THE ILLUSTRATIONS

The flintwork has been drawn at 1:1 and reduced to 50% for publication, except for some smaller pieces, such as microliths, which were drawn at 2:1 and reduced to actual size for publication. A small number of very large pieces has been drawn at 75% and subsequently reduced by 50% for publication. Some of the Neolithic axes have been reduced to 40% to allow them to fit on a page. Scales are included on all the pages of flintwork. The following standard conventions were used in the illustrations (after Martingell and Saville 1988).

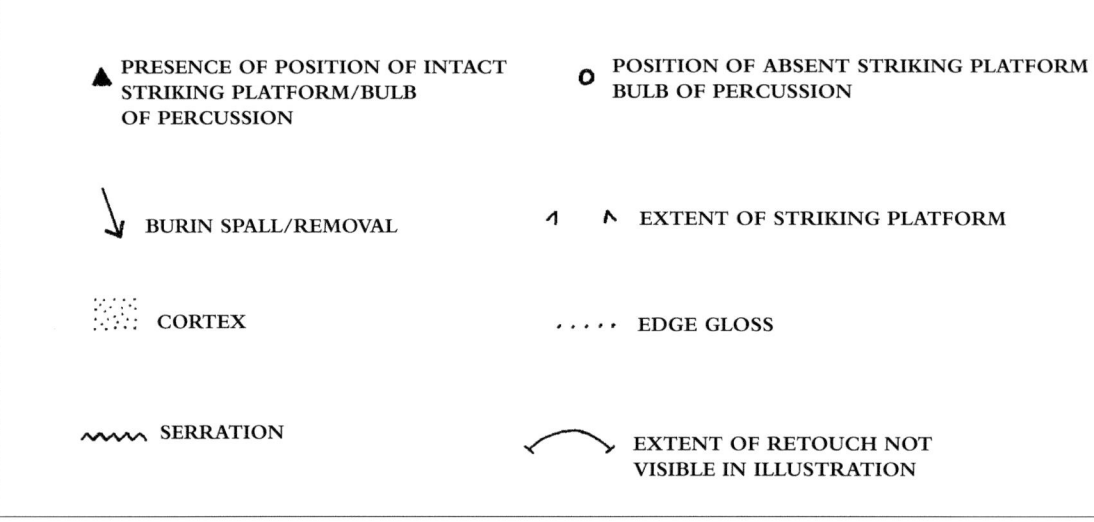

1

AN INTRODUCTION

Ever since becoming interested in prehistoric flintwork I have been frustrated at the lack of any reference guide or manual to aid the identification of worked flint. For those studying other types of artefacts such as Roman pottery or Saxon stirrup mounts, there are reference guides available, but if you study prehistoric flintwork the only way you can locate reference material is to wade through specialist excavation reports. Whilst teaching the identification of worked flint over the last ten years numerous people have jokingly suggested that I should write a guide myself. Laughing it off I have nevertheless kept the idea in the back of my mind, and when the opportunity arose to write a book on prehistoric flintwork I thought 'well, why not give it a go?'

This book is aimed at individuals who are interested in prehistoric flintwork and want to be able to identify worked flint, and know more about what they have found. It is written for the non-specialist; however it will also be useful for those archaeologists who, whilst interested in flint because they find it during the course of their work, only have a basic understanding of the technologies and processes by which flint artefacts were made. Students of archaeology at all levels should also find this book useful in their studies.

To start, we need to understand what flint is, where it comes from, why it was important to prehistoric people and why it remains important to archaeologists studying the past. For each of the periods of prehistory, I intend to look at the technologies that were used to work flint and produce tools. I will look at the different types of diagnostic flint tools and waste produced in each period, and then move on to show how the analysis of pieces recovered during excavation and surveys can help to interpret past land use and the activities that were being carried out. In doing this I intend to concentrate on the flintwork of southern Britain, and especially that of Sussex from where most of my examples have come. As will become evident, there are regional differences in the technology and flintwork in some periods of later prehistory and where it is relevant I will highlight these. An important aspect of this book is to provide a concise, detailed guide to the different types of flintwork that can be found, and to that end I have included drawings of many different pieces,

Prehistoric Flintwork

so that it can be used as a reference when trying to identify pieces of worked flint. This is not to say it is exhaustive because there were as many different types of some flint pieces as there were people making them. A good example of this would be the numerous different sizes, shapes and styles of Neolithic and Bronze Age scrapers: in cases like this I have tried to illustrate as many different types as possible to give an idea of the range.

Although it is essential to understand how flint is knapped to be able to understand the technology and strategies employed in producing flint tools, this book does not explore flintknapping in any depth. There are other books currently available that cover this subject; for example the books by Whittaker and Lord.

WHAT IS FLINT?

Before moving on to look at prehistoric flintwork in detail, it is useful to understand exactly what flint is and how it was formed, although there is much uncertainty and disagreement amongst geologists as to the exact process.

1 Seams of flint showing as horizontal bands in the chalk

An Introduction

2 Examples of tabular or sheet (top) and nodular (bottom) flint.

Flint was formed in the calcareous chalk deposits that are found in southern Britain and elsewhere in the world. Chalk is a sedimentary rock formed from microscopic marine creatures, rich in silica, which died and were laid down as a calcareous mud in the bottom of shallow tropical seas. Between 70 and 100 million years ago, the seabed became dry land, and rainwater percolating down through the chalk dissolved the silica molecules until they collected in strata contained within the chalk. These strata comprised concentrations of larger fossilised sea creatures, such as echinoids and brachiopods, which had collected here. Over many millions of years the build up of silica in these strata has formed the layers or seams of flint that are found in the Upper Chalk of the South Downs and elsewhere (*1*). Much of this process is poorly understood, and there is a view amongst some geologists that the formation of the flint may have started while the chalk was still being formed beneath the sea. The flint that is found in these seams frequently takes the form of irregularly shaped nodules or Nodular flint (*2* and *colour plate 1*), sometimes in the shape of the fossilised sea creatures it has replaced, or as cylindrical nodules, which may be hollow. It can often be found in the shape of the larger fossilised sea creatures. The flint can also be formed in sheets, called Tabular flint or simply Sheet flint. Humans have exploited both these types of flint in the past.

Chert is a very similar material to flint, although it has a greater density and a coarser crystalline structure. It can occur in some limestones and sandstones, as well as in secondary deposits (see below), and has been utilised by man for making tools in the past. In North America the term 'chert' is used frequently to describe all forms of chert and flint. Other stones, which can also be fractured in a similar way to flint, were frequently used as a raw material for the manufacturing of tools, especially in areas where flint is not available. The stone that was most commonly used was obsidian; this is a glass-like volcanic rock found in the eastern Mediterranean and in parts of the New World, which fractures in exactly the same way as flint, and produces a very efficient range of tools. Obsidian tools are not found in the British Isles, although there are other fine-grained volcanic rocks in Britain that can be knapped in a similar way to flint. Whilst flint is probably the most important type of stone used in British prehistory, during the Neolithic period ground axes were produced in Cornwall, Wales and Cumbria and other locations where there were any suitable stone types that could be flaked or pecked. These axes were distributed through a trading or exchange network across the whole country (Malone 2001). Other axes made from exotic stones like jadeite, that have a mainland European source, also came into the country at this time.

WHY IS FLINT SO IMPORTANT?

Flint is one of the most durable rocks available, being sharper than a metal razor and second only to diamond in hardness, and it can be found in many parts of the British Isles. It is useful because it fractures conchoidally (see Chapter 2). The knowledge that a nodule of flint would break, or fracture, in a certain way when it was struck, meant that it could be worked predictably and could be used to produce tools of defined type and shape and for a variety of different tasks.

Flint can be easily worked into tools; almost anyone can make basic and functional tools with a minimum of tuition. Before the introduction of metal, it was the best material for a multitude of tasks, and even after metal tools were introduced, flint continued to be an important source of basic tool manufacture for another two thousand years in Britain.

Flint continued in use after the Roman occupation, although not for tool manufacture, but as a construction material. Most Roman villas and many other buildings in southern Britain were built with flint walls, and this use of flint continued through the Medieval period, up to the present day. Roman roads were frequently metalled with flint, and much later there are records of flint being taken from Roman roads to provide material for the construction of later turnpike roads. Flint was also used in the manufacture of glass, and for gunflints. The Brandon flintknappers in Norfolk made their gunflints from the same seams of flint that had been used by Neolithic flint miners five thousand years earlier. The ability of flint to produce a good spark also meant it was used as a firelighter or strike-a-light from prehistory to the Medieval period.

The importance of flint to archaeologists is enormous, again because of its durability. Our ability to understand the actions of past societies, and their use of the landscape, relies on our finding the places they lived and the evidence of their activities. For most periods of prehistory, especially those before the introduction of pottery and metals, the only things that survive for us to find are stone tools and the residue from making those stone tools. Without flint we would understand little about our past. We therefore need to appreciate how prehistoric people used flint, where they obtained the raw materials, and how tools were made and used. Only then can we start to piece together how the landscape was exploited throughout prehistory.

SOURCES OF FLINT

A range of different sources has been exploited in the past for flint raw material. This can be illustrated by looking at Sussex as a case study. Figure 3 is a schematic section through Sussex showing the different places that flint could be obtained as a raw material. We can split these sources into primary (where the flint is found naturally), and secondary (where it has been re-deposited due to erosion and geological processes).

Primary sources
Flint can be obtained directly from the chalk itself. During the Neolithic period flint was mined directly from seams in the chalk. Quarrying of flint from seams exposed on the upper slopes of the chalk Downs also took place in the Neolithic period. It is likely that quarrying also occurred during the Mesolithic and the Bronze Age, but there is little direct evidence for this.

Secondary sources
As well as occurring within chalk, flint can frequently be found in what are known as secondary deposits. These are deposits formed by the effects of weathering and mechanical action on the primary seams of flint within the chalk. Glacial action has changed the shape of our landscape, and in doing so has gouged away the chalk, redepositing the flint in gravel beds.

The weathering and erosion of chalk cliffs has resulted in the flint eroding out and collecting in the beach shingle below (*colour plate 2*). Prehistoric people could easily have collected freshly fallen nodules from cliff falls, or pebbles from the beach. In some parts of the country the only source of flint may be beach pebbles washed up onto beaches by longshore drift that moves nodules along coastlines, sometimes many miles from their original

Prehistoric Flintwork

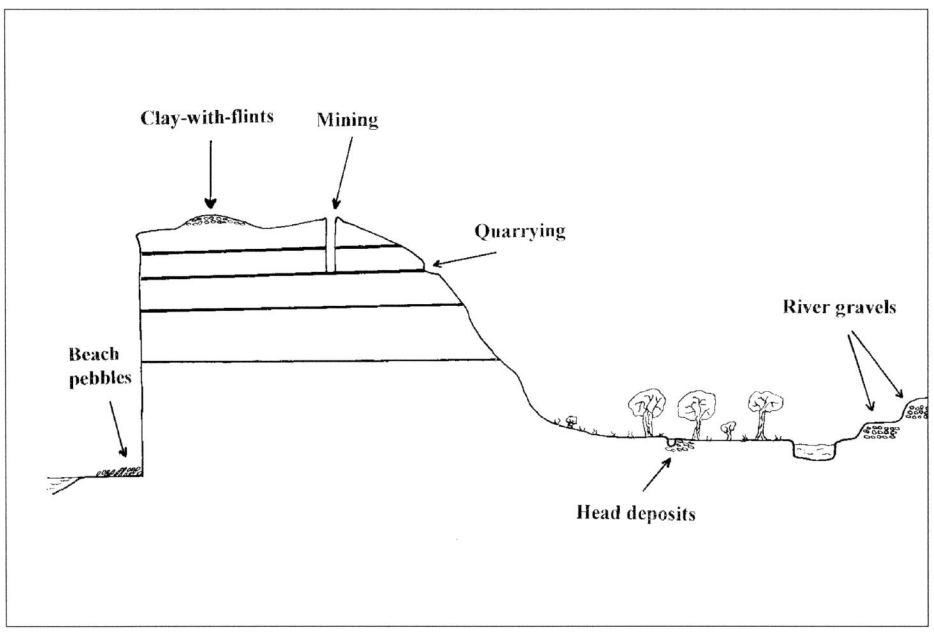

3 Schematic section of Sussex showing the sources of flint that were exploited by prehistoric people

source. On the Sussex Coastal Plain there are ancient beaches and river estuaries, which now exist inland as buried flint gravels. Where these gravels have been exposed by later coastal erosion, flint nodules could have been collected or quarried.

On the top of the chalk Downs there are deposits known as Clay-with-flints. The formation of these deposits is a matter of debate, and current thinking is that they formed either as a residue from solution of the chalk, or as periglacial deposits during the last ice age. Different deposits of Clay-with-flints in different parts of the country may have formed in different ways. Clay-with-flints, as is suggested by its name, comprises a matrix of clay and flints (both Nodular and Tabular flints can be found in the same deposit), and was used as an important source of flint raw material throughout prehistory. At East and West Hills, Pyecombe, in Sussex (just to the north of Brighton) a systematic survey and excavation of a Clay-with-flints outcrop has shown that it was a source of flint from the Mesolithic through to the Bronze Age. During the Mesolithic period tranchet adzes were being made from this flint, whilst during the Neolithic period the manufacture of polished axes took place. Chalk flint has also been moved from its original location by glacial action, for example from Northern Ireland to north-west England and north Wales.

In the river valleys of southern Britain, river terrace gravels have provided a further source of flint material. In the Sussex Weald, Head deposits or solifluction gravels can provide a source of flint. These are probably relic gravels, and can be found where streams have re-exposed them, or as natural exposures. These deposits are the probable sources of the weathered flint nodules that can be found almost anywhere in the Weald.

THE CHARACTERISTICS OF FLINT

Although flint from chalk, preferably taken directly from a seam, is normally the best quality for knapping, most of these other sources can provide adequate flint. However, when flint has been exposed to weathering, extreme variations in temperature, and frequent battering and rolling, it can lose some or all of its moisture content. This can introduce weaknesses and flaws,

4 Flintknapper Allan Course at work, removing the outer cortical flakes from a flint nodule with a hard hammer. *C. Goodey*

making the flint less suitable for knapping. Even flint taken directly from chalk can have in-built flaws resulting from minute inclusions incorporated during its formation. In later prehistory when there was less concern over the quality of the flint raw material, or in parts of the country where flint was scarce, any nodule of flint could be selected irrespective of its quality. A skilled flintknapper could use most types of flint to produce a basic range of flint tools, by removing the weathered outer parts of a nodule or parts containing flaws, before attempting to manufacture a tool (*4*). However, for the more specialised and better-made tools, the selection of good quality flint was essential.

Flint is covered with an outer skin called cortex. This varies in thickness from a few millimetres to a couple of centimetres, and is generally off-white to buff in colour (*colour plate 1*). On beach pebbles the worn outer surface of the pebble is frequently pitted and battered, and where the cortex has been removed it is often stained or discoloured to a grey or buff-brown colour. The cortex is softer than the flint itself, but it fractures in a similar way. As with other aspects of flint, cortex is not fully understood, however, it is thought that it could be an intermediate stage of flint formation, or decomposition of the nodule. The identification of whether cortex is present or not, and how or where it was removed, is helpful during the analysis of an assemblage of flintwork, as it enables us to understand the initial working of flint nodules, and the process used by prehistoric people to produce tools.

The colour of flint can be a helpful indicator in attempting to source its origin. Its natural colour is normally grey or black, but due to the ability of flint to absorb moisture once it comes into contact with surrounding soils and minerals, it will begin to attain an ochreous/olive/black/yellow colour over its surface according to the soil it is in.

As well as this staining, the surface of flint can change colour due to weathering. The beginning of this process (called patination) can be seen when freshly struck flint looks glossy, but within minutes it will begin to dull. Flint that has been struck more recently or which has been buried in neutral conditions will not have any patination, and will therefore retain its grey or black colour. In peaty or waterlogged conditions a glossy patina is attained. Frequently flint contains inclusions, which will show as small white flecks (called intraclasts) or as a mottled effect within the grey or black colour. When worked flint is found which contains these small inclusions, they can be used as a method of identifying where the flint raw material might have come from.

Some typical patination and staining colours and their probable origins are shown below (Table 1), but this is only intended as a general guide, as there are many variations.

TABLE 1 PATINATION AND STAINING

COLOUR	PROBABLE SOURCE
Patination	
White/light grey	Chalk Downland
Light blue	Chalk Downland
Staining	
Orange, buff, brown, yellow-green	River terrace gravels
Black/grey	Clay-with-flints and Head deposits
Dark/mottled blue	Clay-with-flints
Olive/dark grey/black	Rivers and Peat

There are few distinctive deposits of coloured flints in the UK, with probably the most recognisable one being Bullhead flint from the Thames Basin, which has a distinctive thin orange layer below a greenish-black cortex (*colour plate 3*). Another distinctive type is Portland chert, which is a dark grey-blue in colour, from Portland in Dorset.

2

HUMAN USE OF FLINT

THE BASICS

From the earliest times, the process of making a tool from a nodule of flint has required a strategy. The strategy starts with the selection of a piece of raw material, when some basic questions need to be asked. Is the nodule the right size? If it is too large it will be difficult to manage and hold whilst making the tool, or it may be too small for the tool that is going to be made. Is the quality of the flint good enough for the knapping process? If it has flaws the flint might break awkwardly or shatter whilst being knapped, but perhaps that may not matter if the tool being made is a simple scraper on a thick stubby flake.

Once a suitable nodule has been selected the next stage of the strategy comes into play. Is the nodule carefully prepared (or trimmed) prior to making the tool itself, perhaps by removing all of the cortex from around the outside; or is the requirement simply for any piece of sharp flint that can be knocked off the nodule? The process of making a tool (called the *chaîne opératoire*) requires planning and forethought (*5*). Each piece that is removed performs a role in the careful reduction of the nodule. Many pieces may need to be removed sequentially to get to the point where an important defining piece is removed. But even this may only be part way through the strategy. The knapper will be thinking two or three steps ahead, knowing exactly where he or she is going to strike the nodule in working towards the goal (*colour plate 4*). It may be that it is not the nodule itself that is being made into a tool, but pieces are being deliberately removed from it so that they can be made into smaller tools. A number of pieces may need to be removed from the nodule before a piece the right size and shape is detached which can be taken onto the next stage.

Having got the shaped nodule or a small removal that is to be made into a tool, it will now need careful finishing (called retouching) to refine its shape and create its working edge so that it can be used to carry out its intended task. The flintknapper has a model of the finished item in his or her mind, something that he/she is aiming towards. It may have to be fitted into a wooden handle or shaft, either alone or with other similar pieces (*6*). This gives

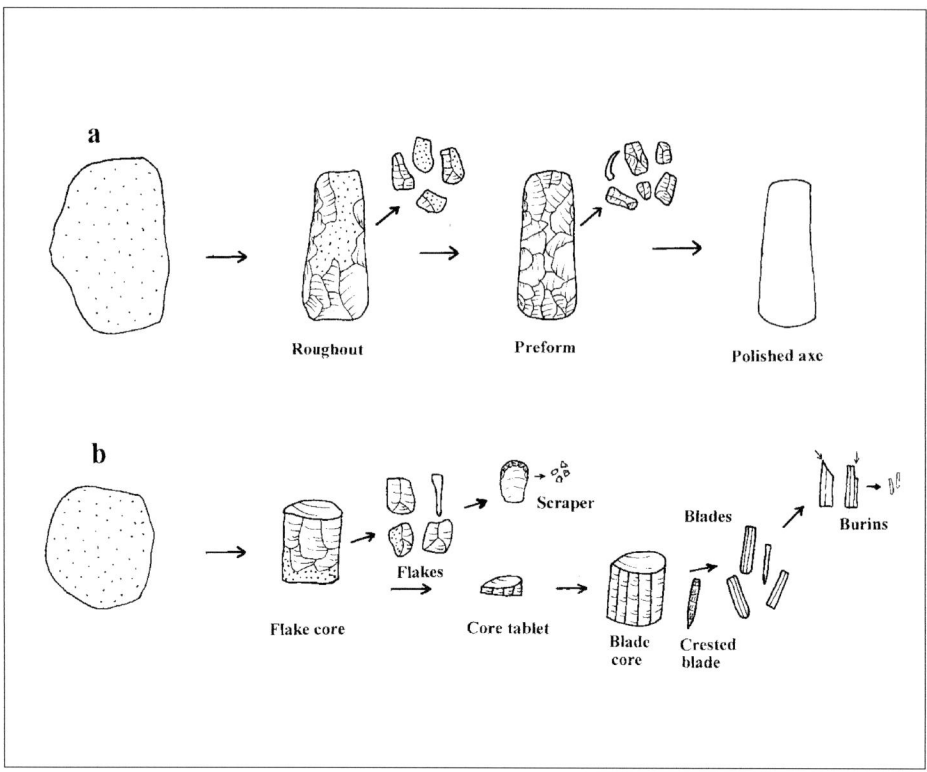

5 Knapping strategies: a) Core tool technology – transforming a nodule into a polished axe; b) Flake tool technology – using the flakes and blades removed from cores to make different types of tool

us the finished tool, perhaps to be kept for some time as part of a tool kit, being brought out whenever needed, or perhaps simply used for the immediate task, and then discarded.

HUMAN USE OF FLINT

Flintknapping techniques developed and altered over time as the requirement for hunting equipment and other tools changed in response to changes in use of the landscape. The introduction of other raw materials, such as metals, also affected the flintknapping technologies used. During the Mesolithic period for example, the use of microliths to make composite hunting equipment required the production of bladelets from which the microliths were made. To produce bladelets a good quality flint was required, and a very controlled process was needed to remove bladelets from the core consistently. As we will see later, lithic specialists can follow this process all the way through from the selection of the flint to the use of the microlith in its finished form as a piece of hunting equipment. When hunting equipment changed in the early Neolithic

Human Use of Flint

period, and microliths were replaced by leaf-shaped arrowheads, the knapping strategy changed, as bladelets were no longer required. Because bladelets had become redundant, the process by which they were made was no longer fully relevant, and we begin to see changes in the knapping strategy used in the early Neolithic period. This process continues as the types of tools evolve through the Neolithic period. We do not fully understand the reasons behind these fundamental changes in tool type, but they are probably in response to the slow transition from hunting and gathering to farming that was taking place at this time. The changes meant that less care and skill was needed to produce flint tools, and this affects the process right back to the original selection of raw material. The transformation becomes even more apparent in the Bronze Age, when metal begins to replace flint for some types of tool. This leads to a

6 Replica hafted flint knives made by Allan Course

Prehistoric Flintwork

general decline in flintworking skills, with a much smaller range of tool types, and some quite crude and expedient tools being produced.

We should remember that sometimes flint tools were not being produced for use as functional items. There are many prestigious items made from flint that have been found unused and in mint condition in burials and other ritual deposits, such as in pits or ditch terminals (7). An increase in these deposits, which frequently included finely made axes, knives and arrowheads, occurred during the Neolithic period and early Bronze Age, just at the time when

7 A polished flint axe from a probable ritual pit deposit at Seaford, Sussex

general flintworking skills appear to be on the decline. Perhaps there were now specialists making these items for the 'ritual market', whilst the day-to-day tools could be made by almost everybody.

Flint had uses other than as a raw material for tools. Burnt or fire-fractured flint is frequently found on excavations and during fieldwalking and can be a useful indication of past activity. When flint is heated and cooled rapidly in water, it turns a light grey colour and cracks, looking like a miniature piece of crazy-paving. There are various theories as to why flint was heated. The first is that it was used in cooking, either being added to water in vessels to bring it to the boil, or used in primitive steam ovens. Examples of its use for cooking have been found on sites ranging in date from the Mesolithic period to the Bronze Age, and there are ethnographic examples of such activities. Fire-fractured flint was also frequently crushed (having been weakened by the heating) and added as a temper to pottery, especially during the Bronze Age. Finally, some people think that the enormous piles of burnt flint sometimes found near streams and settlements may have been primitive saunas.

Flint was also used as a building material. An early example of this is the use of natural flint nodules to hold down hides around the Mesolithic shelter at Streat Lane (Butler 1998). The Romans used it for building the walls of their villas and other buildings, including the Saxon Shore forts and town walls in southern Britain. It was also used as a metalling for roads and yards. Only rarely were nodules knapped to square them off for building purposes, and occasionally the flakes from this knapping can be found in the wall footings of these buildings. In the Medieval period buildings were frequently built of flint (Dawson 1998). Until the late thirteenth century natural unknapped nodules were used, but after that date nodules were frequently knapped so that they could be fitted more closely, and frequently the freshly exposed black flint was used as a decorative feature. The flakes removed in this process were sometimes used to fill gaps between the flint nodules in the wall, being pushed into the mortar before it dries; this process is called 'galleting'. Today flintknapping is being carried out by a new generation of knappers, who are building and restoring buildings in the traditional manner.

FLINTKNAPPING

There are a number of very good books on how to knap flint, with those by Lord (1993) and Whittaker (1994) being the most useful. It is however useful to understand how flint is knapped before we start to look at how to recognise pieces of worked flint.

When a nodule of flint is struck, it fractures conchoidally. This means that at the point of impact a conical fracture develops, and continues until the force of the blow has dissipated. The size and type of cone depends upon the area of

Prehistoric Flintwork

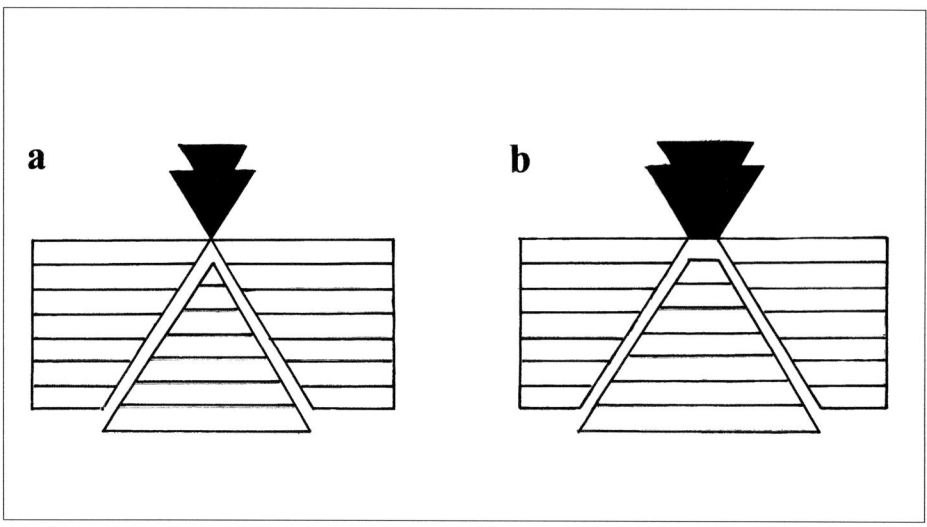

8 An example of a conchoidal fracture: a) where the hammer has a small point of contact with the core, the result would be a pointed cone; b) a hammer with a broad point of impact would produce a broader flattened cone. After Lord

contact with the hammer, so that a small area of contact will result in a pointed cone, whilst a large area will result in a flattened cone (*8*). The features that result from the conchoidal fracture provide us with some of the recognition points that help us to identify a piece of worked flint.

The nodule of raw material from which pieces are being removed is referred to as a 'core', and the pieces that are being removed are called 'flakes' (*9*). The other important component that is required for knapping is something to detach the flakes with. Referred to as a hammer, this might be of wood, bone, antler, stone or metal, and all of these have different properties, which are discussed below.

Cores
A core is a nodule of flint from which flakes have been removed, some of which may have been selected for modification into tools. Lithic specialists recognise many different forms of core, and classify them depending upon the type and manner of flake removal (e.g. flake, blade or bladelet), the number of platforms that can be identified and their shape. These different types will be covered in detail when we look at the relevant periods.

To remove flakes successfully from a core you need to have a flat surface on the core, which is called the 'striking platform'. This platform can be created either by simply removing part of the nodule with a sharp blow from a hammerstone (called 'quartering'), or sometimes a suitable natural platform may be found on the nodule. Having found or made a suitable platform, simply hitting the platform with a hammerstone will result in frustration, few flakes and frequently bloodied hands! To successfully remove flakes, the platform must have an angle of less than 90° (to the face of the core), and the angle at which it is struck must also be less than 90° (*10*). If the angle is at or greater than 90° it will tend to crush the platform and create incipient cones below its surface, which can spoil the platform for further flaking (*10g*).

So to recognise a core, first of all look for the platform(s), i.e. a flat surface on the core, which has been struck to remove flakes. Running diagonally away from the platform you will see a number of negative flake scars; these are the scars left by the flakes that have been removed. If you look carefully at these scars you can see the ripples left by the shock wave travelling through the flint, and by their curvature, you can determine in which direction the flake was removed. Second or third platforms may frequently be found at the opposite end to the first, or at 90° to it, or frequently at irregular angles. If the core has been well used (i.e. many flakes have been removed from it) then it may not be very large (*11*). Occasionally, on a well-used core, an earlier platform may have been removed, and you may only have the remnants of some of the negative flake scars to hint that there once had been another platform.

When a flake is removed from the core it leaves a negative scar on the face of the core. Because the cone fracture has created a bulb on the flake at the point of impact (see below), this leaves a negative impression at the top of the flake scar near the platform, and also two projecting 'overhangs' on the edge of

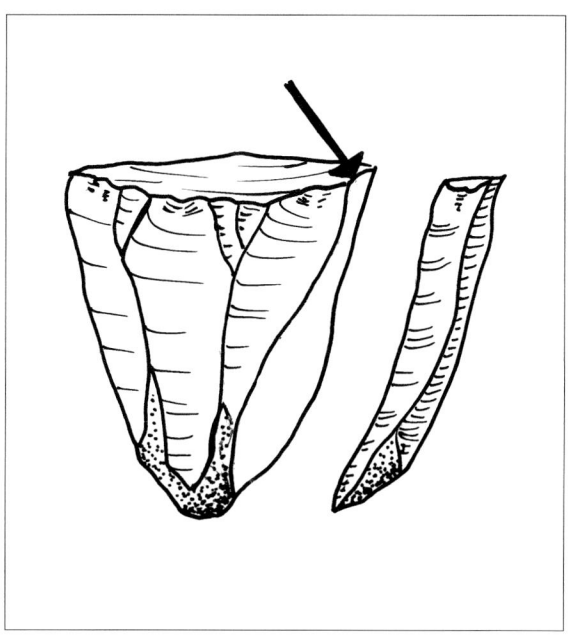

9 An example showing a flake removed from a single platform core. The arrow shows the point of impact of the hammer on the platform

Prehistoric Flintwork

the platform. These overhangs can mean that it is difficult to strike the platform accurately, close to its edge, to remove longer flakes, so in some periods of prehistory the edge of the platform was trimmed or abraded to remove these overhangs. This is called platform preparation. Rubbing or lightly striking along the edge of the platform with a hammerstone results in this abrasion, and leaves a very distinctive edge to the platform comprising small flake scars and abrasion along a straight platform edge. When the next flake is removed from this platform, it will also display those traits on its distal side at the butt or proximal end as that part of the platform edge will be removed as part of the flake (see below).

Many cores will have been abandoned at different stages of use, and this can be a good indicator of the period that they date from. In the Mesolithic and early Neolithic periods, cores tended to be fairly well worked out, and so are quite small when found on archaeological sites (*colour plate 5*). In later periods of prehistory, especially when less care was taken in the selection of raw material and during the knapping process, they were cruder, with irregular platforms and were sometimes discarded after just a few flakes had been removed. Occasionally a nodule might be found which has just one

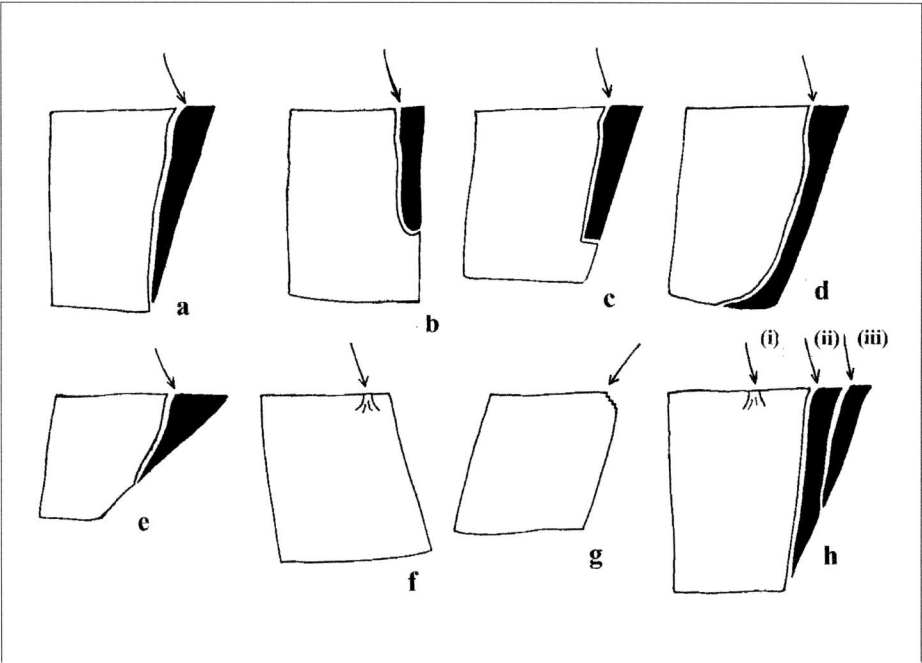

10 Knapping technology: a) Feather termination; b) Hinged termination; c) Step termination; d) Overshoot termination; e) Smaller flaking angle – short and thick flake; f) Flaking angle over 90° – no flake produced; g) Incorrect angle of blow – no flake and crushed edge; h) Depth of blow into platform i) too deep – no flake; ii) correct position; iii) too close to edge – short flake. *After Whittaker*

Human Use of Flint

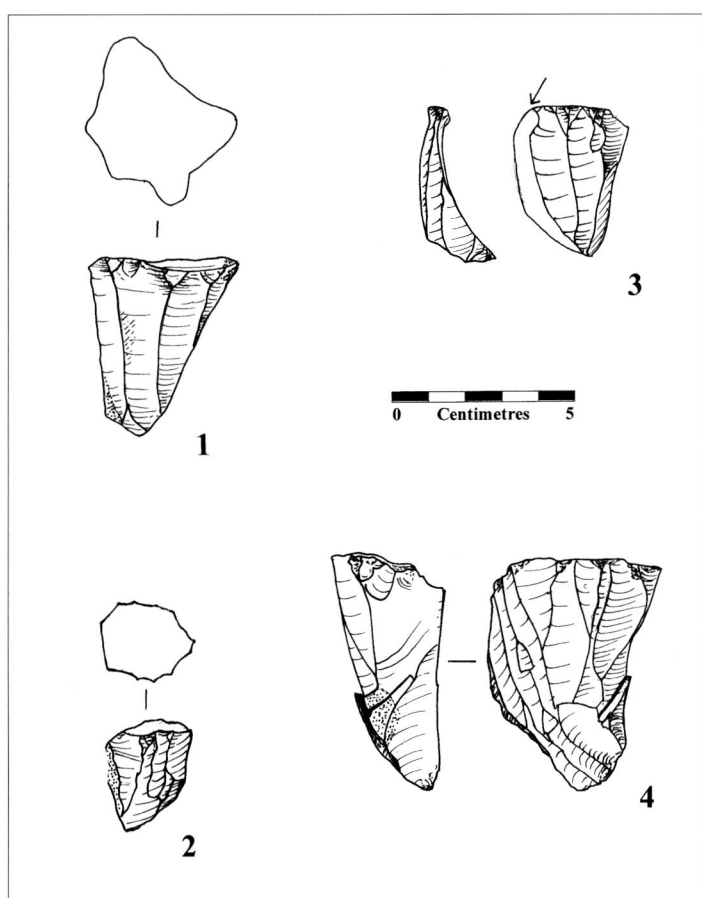

11 Cores: 1) An unprepared core; 2) A worked-out bladelet core; 3) A plunging blade on a core; 4) A step fracture on a core with two opposing platforms

or two flakes removed from it. Rather than classifying this as a core, it may well have been what we call a 'tested nodule', i.e. a nodule of raw material from which one or two flakes had been removed to test whether the nodule was suitable for knapping. Finding tested nodules on a site is useful because it suggests that the people knapping were being selective in their choice of raw material.

When a core platform had become exhausted, and no further flakes could be removed from it, a number of things could happen. Firstly, it could simply be discarded; this is likely to happen where either there is a plentiful supply of raw material, or simply the core was no longer needed. Secondly, the core could be rotated until another suitable platform was found, or a new platform could be created. Finally, the existing platform could be rejuvenated. This was usually achieved by directing a blow at 90° to the edge of the platform, which removed the old exhausted platform and in doing so created a new platform from which flaking could then recommence.

31

Prehistoric Flintwork

The technique of rejuvenation was normally performed during periods of prehistory when greater care was being used in knapping or when cores were being curated (carried around by the knapper who then removed flakes from the core as and when they were needed). There are examples of cores being curated in parts of the country where flint was not a natural resource and so the most had to be made of each piece. Rejuvenation was practised in these areas many centuries after the technique was no longer being used elsewhere.

When considering cores, allowance needs to be made for the size of the original nodule that was being used. For example, it is stated above that small cores were a potential distinguishing feature of the Mesolithic period. But if the original piece of raw material was itself quite small, as might be the case where beach pebble or gravel deposits are being exploited, then the cores resulting from that will also be quite small, even if just a few flakes had been removed. The size of the core and amount of care taken in removing flakes can be the result of a number of things in addition to the size of the raw material. It could be due to the scarcity of the raw material, or due to the type of tool that was being produced.

Flakes

To recognise a humanly struck flake we need to look for the features that result from the conical fracture, and the negative scars left by other flakes that have already been removed from the same core. Figure 12 shows a typical flake, but many flakes will have been broken during or after knapping so may not display all of these features.

Lithic specialists describe the front or interior surface of a flake (the surface that would have been on the inside of the core) as its ventral side, and the back or external surface is called the dorsal side. At the top of the flake (called the proximal end) there should be some surviving part of the striking platform from the core. This is the part of the platform that the blow fell upon and is generally called the butt. Immediately below the butt on the ventral face of the flake is a swelling, called the bulb of percussion. Below the bulb there are often ripples or waves, which centre on the bulb and radiate downwards across the ventral surface. These are caused by the shock wave from the blow travelling through the flint, and sometimes terminate in a hinge fracture (see below) at the distal end. Another feature commonly seen on the ventral face of flakes are bulbar scars; these are small flakes that sometimes 'pop' off the bulb of percussion when the platform is struck, leaving a scar on the bulb. In their most exaggerated form they can remove the bulb of percussion entirely, and will therefore have their own bulbs on both their dorsal and ventral sides. These flakes are called 'Janus flakes'.

On the dorsal side of the flake one or more negative flake scars will be defined by the ridges (also called arrises) at the intersection of the scars. The

Human Use of Flint

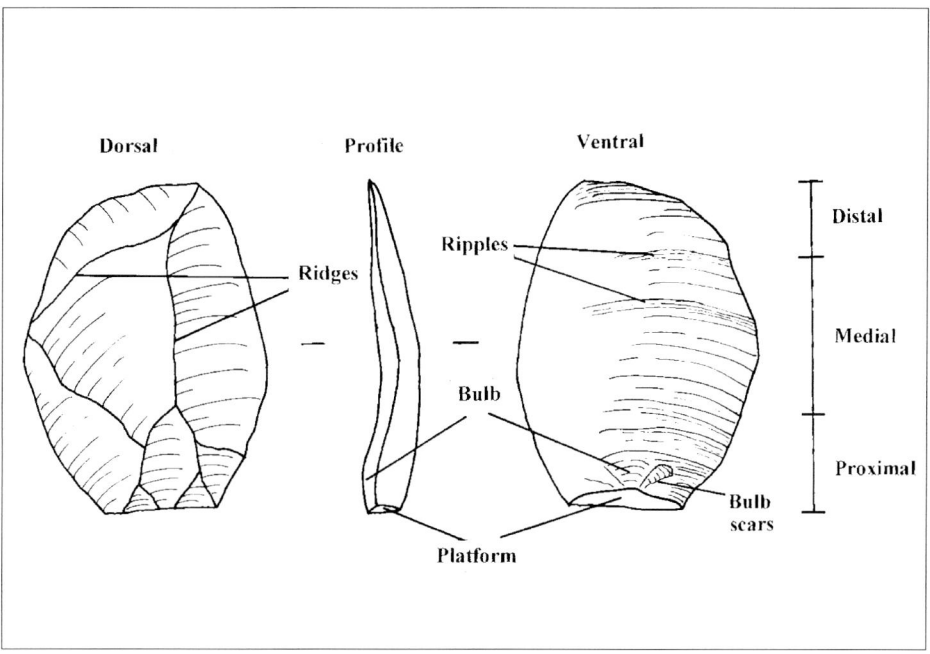

12 The basic attributes of a flake

negative scars might all be orientated in broadly the same direction (indicating that the previous flakes had been removed from the same platform), or they may be from a different direction or even multi-directional. If this flake was one of the first few to be removed from a core, then it may have its dorsal surface partly or entirely covered in cortex. These are referred to as primary flakes, with flakes having a small amount of cortex being known as secondary flakes, and flakes with no cortex called tertiary flakes.

Where the core platform has been prepared prior to the removal of a flake, this can leave easily distinguished features on the flake when it is removed from the core. The ventral edge of the butt will be relatively straight with no projecting overhangs, and there will be a series of small flake scars and abrasion scars along this edge (*13*) extending a few millimetres down the ventral surface, sometimes having a stepped appearance. This technique allows the hammer blow to be placed quite precisely, and generally close to the edge of the platform, which means that the butt is normally narrow. If the platform is struck incorrectly, the knapper has little control over the type of flake that is removed, and this can lead to imperfect flakes with truncated distal ends being produced, referred to as step, hinge and overshoot terminations.

A hinge fracture (*10b*), which can be recognised by the rounded 'hinge' at the distal end of the flake, can occur when the fracture runs into a flaw within

Prehistoric Flintwork

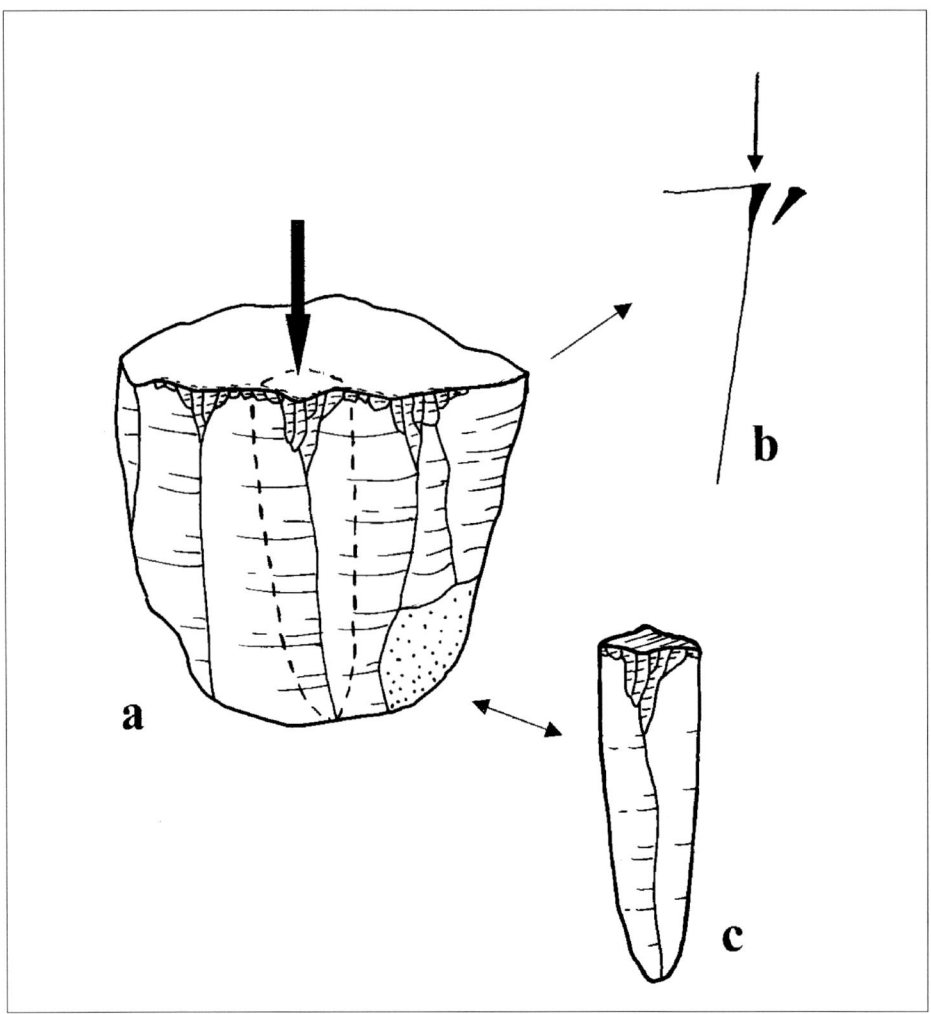

13 Platform preparation: a) Core with abraded edge of platform, showing small flake/chip scars and outline of blade to be removed; b) Removal of overhang (cornice) on edge of platform by abrasion; c) Blade removed showing remnant of abrasion scars on the dorsal side at the proximal end

the flint or a previous step fracture. It can also sometimes occur when there is a combination of insufficient force in the striking blow, and a striking angle that is close to 90°. A step fracture can occur when the striking angle is too acute and results in the outward pressure being greater than the downward pressure (*10c*), and can be recognised by the right-angled break at the distal end of the flake. Once a step fracture has been created, the only ways to overcome it are to either remove a large flake, or to rotate the core and strike a flake from a new platform to remove it.

The third type of imperfect termination is an 'overshoot' (*10d*), possibly as a result of too much downward pressure being applied when striking the platform. In prehistoric flintworking these types of termination are frequently found where the raw material is of poor quality, or the knapper is either unskilled or did not take much care with his flaking process. However sometimes an overshoot can be the intention, perhaps to rejuvenate the core by removing all or part of an opposing platform. Detection of these types of flake derived from excavation or fieldwalking can provide much useful information about the flintworking processes that were being employed.

The ideal type of termination is called a 'feather termination' (*10a*), and is where the fracture has travelled through the flint without prematurely terminating, to remove a perfect flake. Although flakes with feather terminations are technically the ideal type, this does not mean to say that hinge, step and overshoot flakes were always discarded and never used for making tools. In later periods of prehistory these 'imperfect' flakes were frequently turned into tools. They tend to be thicker and have a squat shape, which makes them ideal as the basis for scraping tools. Many of these flakes shattered or were snapped during the flaking process, and the resulting stubby breaks can easily be turned into a scraping edge. The term 'flake' is a generic term used for all pieces that are removed from a core, but flakes are subdivided into a number of sub-types (*14*).

Flake	Any piece struck from a core or nodule that does not fall into one of the following categories. Fig. *14* shows a group of typical flakes, demonstrating the range of sizes and shapes in which they can be found. The significance of the size and shape of a flake in determining the period from which they may have come is explained later.
Blade	A flake whose length is more than twice its width, and which has parallel edges and ridges on the dorsal side. Although many pieces may have the appearance of being a blade, only true blades that fully meet the above criteria should be recorded as such, because the blade is a specific diagnostic piece. It is possible to create proxy blades accidentally that meet the dimensional criteria but do not have the parallel edges and ridges, which show that blades are being consistently produced from the same core. Fig. *14* shows some typical blades on which you can see the features mentioned above. Also note that one of the blades (number 7) has been struck from a two-platform core: the negative scars run from platforms at the top and bottom of the piece.
Bladelets	These are small blades whose width is less than 12mm. These again are diagnostic pieces, as they were specifically made in the Mesolithic period to be turned into a particular type of implement. Some sample bladelets are shown in Fig. 14. These can also be made accidentally in later periods.

Prehistoric Flintwork

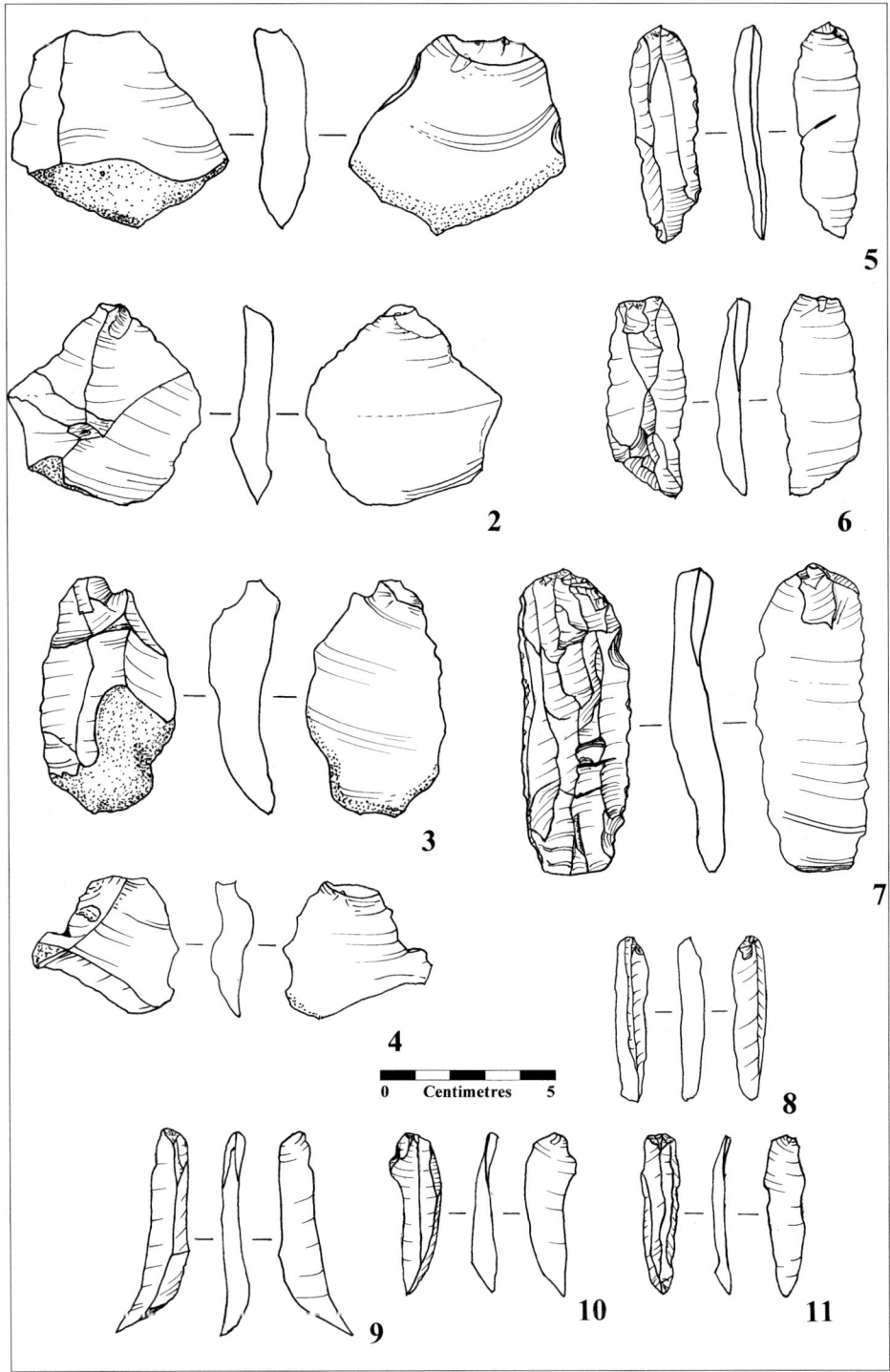

14 Examples of struck flakes (1-4), blades (5-7) and bladelets (8-11); showing dorsal side, profile and ventral side. Note that blade 7 has been removed from a core that had two opposing platforms

Human Use of Flint

HAMMERS AND FLAKES

Prehistoric people used hammers of different materials (*colour plate 6*), and different techniques to remove flakes from a core, depending upon the sort of flake they wanted to remove, and the tool that was being made. Flakes could be detached from a nodule or core by directly striking the platform with a hammer, a technique which is referred to as direct percussion; using the hammer to strike a punch, which has been placed on the platform, and thus remove a flake, which is called indirect percussion; or by the removal of a flake by the application of gradual pressure without striking it, referred to as pressure flaking.

Hard hammers

A hard hammer is normally a small nodule of flint or other hard stone such as granite, sandstone or quartzite. In some parts of the country, suitable hard stones are not available, in which case the hardest type of stone available would have been used instead. The hammerstone would need to fit comfortably into the knapper's hand, and should be of a rounded or oval shape. A hammerstone with flat surfaces is likely to shatter or break, and flint hammerstones will lose small flakes and occasionally larger pieces whilst being used. Hammerstones can be quite easily identified on archaeological sites as they will fit easily into your hand, and one or two prominent points on the stone will have an area of abrasion and numerous small flake scars. Quite often cores of a suitable size were reused as hammerstones after they had outlived their original purpose.

A hard hammer will tend to leave a broad butt on the flake and produce a large bulb of percussion, together with slight crushing of the platform area. Incipient cones of percussion will often be visible on butts at the point of impact (where the bulb meets the butt). In addition the use of a hard hammer, combined with the force that is generally used for the blow, will produce larger and very visible ripples on the ventral face of the flake, and there will be a tendency to produce premature terminations, such as hinge and step fractures. The hard hammer-struck flake shown in Fig. *15* shows the broad butt and large bulb of percussion, typical of such flakes. Where a softer stone has been used as a hammerstone, it is more likely to leave distinguishing features on the flakes closer to those of a soft hammer (see below). Most metal hammers, such as those used for making gunflints and for knapping building flint in more recent times will have produced features similar to those produced by hard hammers. However, soft metal hammers, such as those made from bronze, will produce soft-hammer type flakes.

Soft hammers

Soft hammers were made from bone, antler (*colour plate 6*) or wood, together with some softer stones. Because most of these are made from organic materials, they rarely survive in the archaeological record, so knowledge of soft hammers comes mainly from ethnographic observations and experimental archaeology.

A range of different-sized soft hammers may have been used depending upon the task being undertaken. A soft hammer will produce flakes with a diffuse bulb of percussion, and a pronounced lip at the interface between the butt and the bulb (*15*). Because the force of the blow with a soft hammer is generally less than with a hard hammer, the ripples on the ventral face will be more discreet and sometimes simply not visible. There will also be fewer hinge and step fractures with a soft hammer, and the flakes will tend to be longer with feather terminations.

The presence of a lip is not always a definite indication of the use of a soft hammer. If a broad hard hammer has come into contact with a large section of the platform, the pressure can move outwards as well as down, and thus form a lip; this will also produce a broad butt to the flake whereas a soft hammer would normally have produced a thin butt. The presence of cortex on the platform can also soften the blow of a hard hammer, and whilst this may not cause a lip, it may well produce a diffuse bulb of percussion that looks as if it was caused by a soft hammer. However, it is more likely that a hard hammer would have been used to remove the outer cortical flakes from a core.

Punches were usually used to produce blades and bladelets, as it is an ideal method by which consistently long thin flakes can be removed from a core. The use of a punch has all sorts of practical problems, and we cannot be sure how our prehistoric ancestors overcame them. The main problem would have been how to secure the core in place so that the knapper could concentrate on holding the punch and hammer. It may be possible for the knapper to hold the core between his feet or knees (*16*), but perhaps a second person was required to assist, or the core was secured in place by some other means. The use of a punch can leave some distinctive features on the blade or bladelet. The butt will tend to be thin, as the punch will normally have been placed quite close to the edge of the platform, and the flake will have a distinctive and quite prominent, although small, bulb of percussion. The punches used for indirect percussion were made from antler or bone, together with copper alloy in later periods of prehistory.

Pressure flaking
Pressure flaking is the removal of a flake by the application of gradual pressure. This was normally carried out by placing the tip of an antler tine or sharpened piece of bone onto the platform, and applying pressure by pushing down and in on the pressure point (*17*). The applied pressure needs to be predominantly in the direction that the flake is being removed with an added slight downward pressure (*18d*); this produces a longer flake, as too much downward pressure would produce a short flake. Whittaker (1994) has described pressure flaking

Human Use of Flint

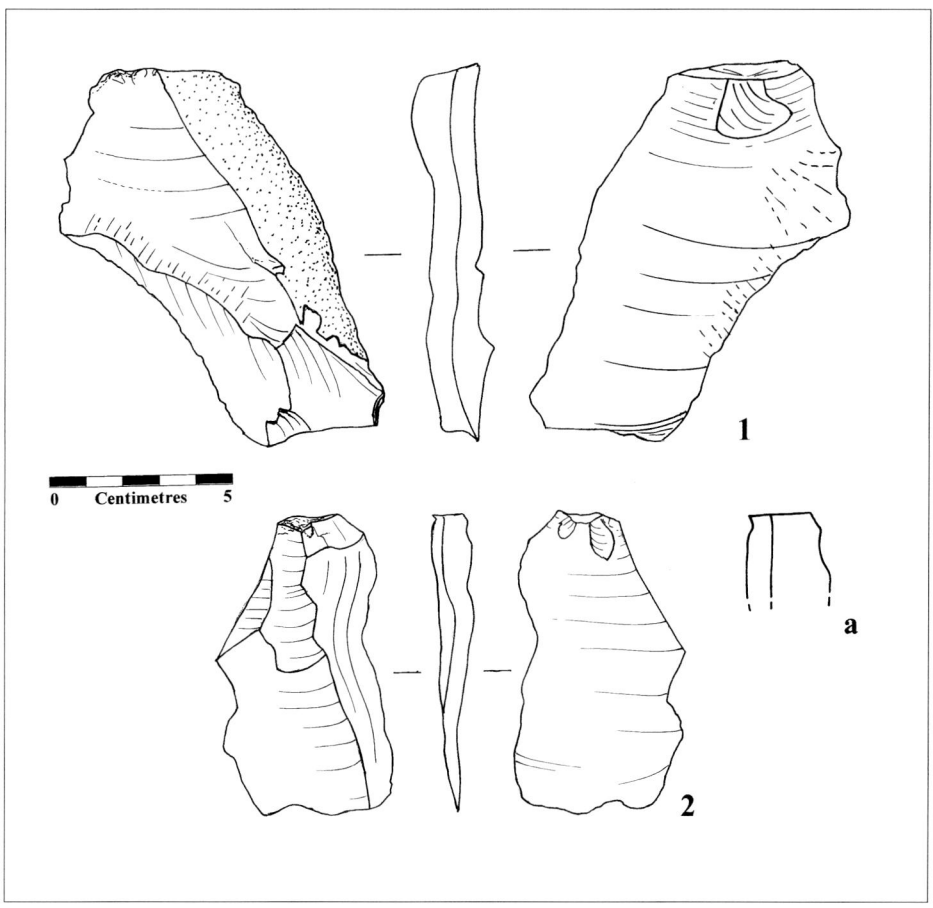

15 Flakes: 1) a typical hard hammer-struck flake; 2) a soft hammer-struck flake. (a) shows an enlarged view of the distinctive lip produced by a soft hammer blow

in detail, and although his methods are predominantly concerned with the production of North American implements, the basics are valid for British prehistoric flintworking as well.

Although in earlier prehistory bone or antler pressure flakers were used, it is possible that in the early Bronze Age copper or bronze flaking tools were being used to produce pressure-flaked items such as the barbed-and-tanged arrowhead. Occasionally copper alloy tools are found on Bronze Age sites, and although commonly described as awls, would have been suitable as pressure flakers.

Although it is possible to say that pressure flakes are generally thinner, smaller and weigh less than percussion flakes, there is no acknowledged definition by which pressure flakes can be easily separated from percussion flakes (Andrefsky 1998).

Prehistoric Flintwork

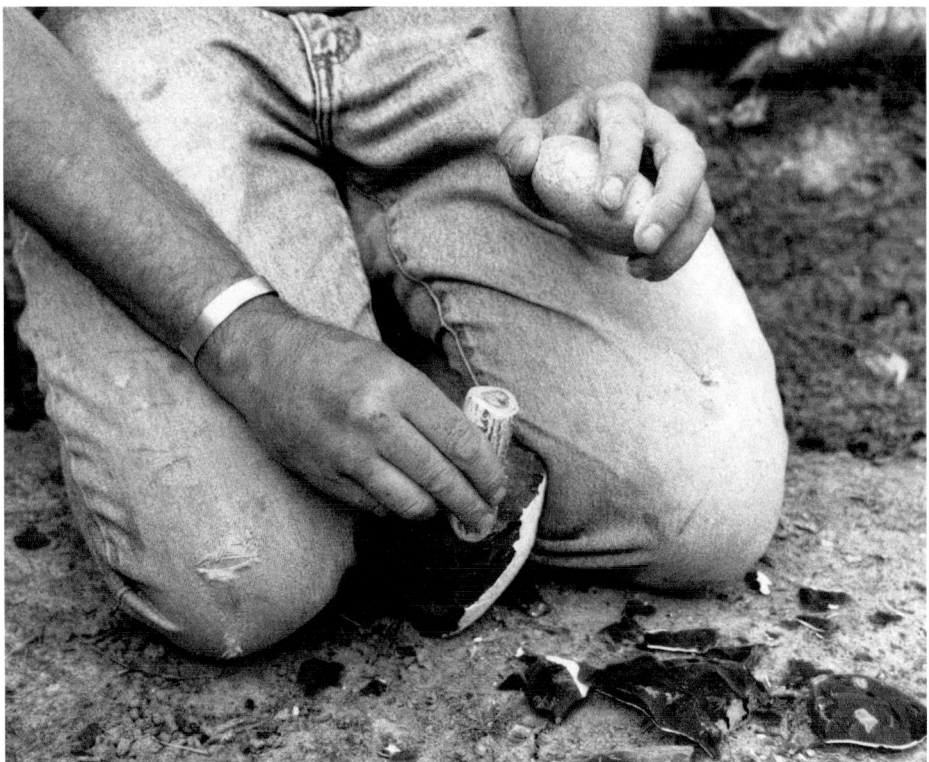

16 A punch being used to remove blades from a core that is held in place between the knees. C. Goodey

DEBITAGE

Debitage is the term used to describe all pieces of waste material that are produced during the manufacture of flint or stone tools and implements. The various forms of debitage have been defined by a number of specialists (e.g. Ballin 2000). The main types that are present in all periods of prehistory are described below, whilst other specialised types, which may occur in one or two periods only, are described in the relevant period sections. Cores, flakes, blades and bladelets are also forms of debitage.

Fragments	Fragments are essentially broken pieces of flakes, blades and bladelets, where the platform, bulb or ridges can still be seen, but the remnant is incomplete and cannot be identified as a particular piece. It is normally possible to differentiate a bladelet from the other types due to its smaller size and specific shape, so these can be classified separately. However, flake and blade fragments are difficult to differentiate and so are normally classified together. The breakage may have occurred during

manufacture or use, or alternatively in antiquity perhaps by being trampled or damaged whilst lying on the ground surface. The break could also have occurred more recently, perhaps by plough damage. Recent breaks can frequently be identified as the broken edge will be fresh, and may expose the different internal colour of the flint. Core fragments are also recognised as a separate category. These are generally pieces that do not have a recognisable platform, which came from a core that was broken during or after knapping.

Chips — Chips are small flakes that are removed as by-products of flaking, platform preparation or retouching of implements. They are normally less than 10mm in size, and should have all the attributes of a flake i.e. a platform, bulb of percussion and so on, although these will be very small. In the past chips were frequently not recognised or recovered during excavations, and it is only more recently with dry and wet sieving being employed on archaeological sites that these small pieces tend to be found. When they are recovered they can number many

17 An example of pressure flaking. An antler tine is used to apply gradual pressure to the edge of a flint blade to remove an invasive flake. *C. Goodey*

	hundreds or thousands, and are a good indication that flintworking was taking place at the site.
Shattered Pieces	This is a general category that flint specialists use to categorise all the pieces of flintwork that they can be reasonably certain were the result of flintworking, but do not display one or more of the main recognition features. For example it may be possible to see on a piece that it has a ridge and part of a negative flake scar, but has obviously been broken or smashed during manufacture or later. The flint specialist will normally be able to differentiate between those that are humanly struck pieces and those that have been produced by nature or the plough!
Axe or biface thinning flakes	The flakes removed from a nodule during the manufacture of an axe or biface can be quite distinctive. Although many such flakes will look like, and cannot be separated from, most other flakes, a great number will have some distinctive features that can help us to establish that production of axes or bifaces was taking place. These flakes will frequently have a curved profile following the shape of the axe roughout, whilst also having negative flake scars on the dorsal side running from different directions reflecting the removal of flakes from all around the edge of the roughout (58).

DISTINGUISHING WORKED FLINT FROM NATURAL FLINT FLAKES

One of the biggest challenges when first starting out is separating the humanly-struck flint from the natural flint; to the untrained eye it all looks the same. There have been many people who have turned up for a day's fieldwalking on the South Downs to be rather taken aback when faced with what appear to be fields that comprise more flint than soil. I can remember one archaeologist coming to work in Sussex from a part of the country where flint was so rare that almost every bit was humanly struck, and being so confused by the sheer quantity of flint that he collected every piece, worked or unworked. Needless to say, over 90 per cent was later discarded.

The recognition of worked flint is not just down to identifying the distinctive features described earlier in this chapter, it is also helpful to have an understanding and feel for some of the features that result from natural processes and other human activities. There is no substitute for handling many pieces of flintwork and trying to identify yourself those that are and are not humanly struck. Any number of books and diagrams will help, but do not provide all the information you need to be able to competently identify worked flint. Nature and other human activity will throw many surprises your way, and to the untrained eye can produce very convincing 'humanly' struck pieces.

Let us first look at some of the pieces created by natural processes such as weathering and chemical action (called thermal flakes). *Colour plate* 7 shows a number of types of flint pieces commonly picked up by people thinking that they are humanly struck. Top right is a piece with what appears to be numerous small flake scars across its surface. This is the result of what is commonly called frost fracturing – essentially the flint whilst lying on the ground surface has reacted to repeated hot and cold events (such as freezing and thawing), which result in small generally circular flakes being forced off its surface, probably as a result of contraction. These can sometimes look quite convincing, but the 'bulb of percussion' is in the centre of the flake and does not connect to any of its edges; there is also no platform, and frequently no negative scars. Top left shows a convincing core, with numerous small negative bladelet-like scars. However if you look closely, some of the negative scars start below the 'platform' and do not connect to it, showing that they have not resulted from a strike on the platform. This piece is called a 'starch fracture' and is the result of impurities within the flint creating a line of weakness, which under stress has resulted in pieces of flint breaking off the nodule leaving these imitation negative scars. Natural flaws and inclusions in the flint can also result in small flake-like scars and breakages when the flint has been subjected to stress. Sometimes pieces of flint that look like flakes or blades are produced through these chemical and weathering actions, but a close look will ensure that they can be discarded as natural. Some things to be wary of are ridges and 'negative scars' on both the dorsal and ventral sides of the pieces – this would be impossible on a humanly struck flake. Also 'negative scars' on an unbroken piece, but with no platform or bulb of percussion present, are a sure sign that the piece is natural.

Convincing flakes can also be produced by mechanical action. Modern agricultural activities result in the smashing of flint nodules in the ploughsoil by ploughs and other agricultural machines. When a plough strikes a flint nodule it can produce a flake which at first sight looks humanly struck. It can have a very prominent bulb of percussion, but a closer look will determine that there is no associated striking platform, and the bulb of percussion simply shows the point where the plough struck the nodule breaking off this flake. The flake will also look very fresh, with no patination on its newly exposed surface.

Another form of mechanical action results from wave damage or from being rolled in a river. The former occurs most frequently to beach pebble and gravel flint, which has been smashed against other nodules on the beach, whilst the latter occurs when the nodule has been in a fast flowing river. Again there will be a prominent bulb of percussion, but no associated striking platform. On small beach pebbles this can be problematic, as the initial flakes of a humanly struck beach pebble could look very similar, so you also need to look at other evidence such as secondary working, its location (if found on a beach then it is almost certainly a result of wave action) and subsequent damage.

This all may sound very daunting, but the best way to learn is to see and handle as much flintwork as you can, and over time you will gain the ability and confidence to identify humanly-worked flint. Sometimes not even the most experienced flint specialists can be absolutely certain whether a particular flake was humanly struck or broken off by mechanical action.

RETOUCH AND MANUFACTURING

When a flint flake has been removed from its core it can have extremely sharp edges, to the extent that it could be immediately used as a tool for cutting without any further modification. However, to be able to use flakes for some tasks, some form of modification to the flake, especially to its working edges, might be necessary. The modification of a flake to create an implement is called retouching.

Retouching is essentially the removal of small flakes from the edge or face of the piece of flint, and can take a number of different forms. When retouch is initiated from the ventral face of a blank it is called 'normal' or 'direct', and when originated from the dorsal side it is called 'inverse'. Retouch is not only used to create the working edge of an implement, but is sometimes used to modify the edge of a flake to make it easier to hold or haft in a handle. Where the retouch removes flakes from one face of a tool it is called unifacial, whilst bifacial describes the removal of flakes from both faces. Retouch along one or more edges of a piece is called edge retouch. Retouch can be performed with a hard or soft hammer, but some retouch can only be produced by using pressure flaking. The production of bifaces and axes requires bifacial flaking of a roughout, normally with a soft hammer, and will be described later on.

The major types of retouch are:

Abrupt retouch
Abrupt retouch is used to blunt an edge. The retouch is performed using either a soft or hard hammer, to strike the face (normally the ventral face) of the flake adjacent to the edge being modified. This face acts as the striking platform, and is struck by a series of blows at regular intervals along the edge, which creates a steep angle of retouch, generally just less than 90° (*18a*). The retouch flake scars tend to be continuous, and frequently overlap.

The blunting of the edge creates an ideal tool for scraping and other non-cutting type actions. It can also be used to modify two alternate edges of an implement, perhaps to create a point. The other use of abrupt retouch is to modify the edge of an implement to enable it to be held comfortably in the hand (as otherwise the edge would be very sharp to hold) or to enable it to be hafted into a handle. For this purpose the abrupt retouch might simply blunt the edge, or could be used to shape two opposing edges so that it creates a tang, which can then be fitted into a bone or wooden handle. This demonstrates that not all modifications of a piece of flint should be interpreted as creating a working edge.

Semi-abrupt retouch
This form of retouch is similar to abrupt retouch, but the angle of the retouched edge is much less acute, generally around 45° (*18b*). This produces a blunted edge, but normally on a much thinner flake, and was usually used for producing finer scrapers, and some other implement types.

Invasive retouch
Invasive retouch is normally used to create a cutting edge, and requires the use of either a soft hammer, or, more normally, pressure flaking. It is a very flat form of retouch, producing long narrow flakes generally at an angle of 10° or less, which extend across the surface of a piece and follow the shape of the flint (*18c*). Invasive retouch is most commonly seen in the production of knives, arrowheads and other cutting implements.

Pressure flaking differs from the direct percussion of hard and soft hammer retouch in that it involves the application of increasing pressure rather than directly striking the flint and has been described at the beginning of the chapter. Pressure flaking allows much greater control over the length, width and shape of the flake that is removed, allowing the manufacture of fine high quality implements.

One common mistake made when first working with flint is to interpret all edge damage on a piece of worked flint as retouch. With so much flint being collected from ploughed fields, and having been damaged by agricultural activities, this is an easy mistake to make. There are two main ways to separate damaged flakes from retouched flakes. The first is to remember that retouch will normally show as continuous small flake scars along the edge, often overlapping, and rarely with gaps. Damage will be indiscriminate, with occasional unconnected small flake scars, and is unlikely to have the uniformity of a retouched edge. Secondly, damage will frequently be much later than the production of the flake, and therefore will quite often 'cut' through the patination to expose the underlying colour of the flint. Retouch will normally be contemporary with the production of the flake and the retouch flake scars will therefore have the same patination as the flake. However, there are situations where retouch is added, for example in the later Bronze Age, to an earlier (Neolithic) flake, and may therefore cut through the patination. Here the regularity of the retouch would be the deciding factor in whether this was true retouching, or simply later damage.

Prehistoric Flintwork

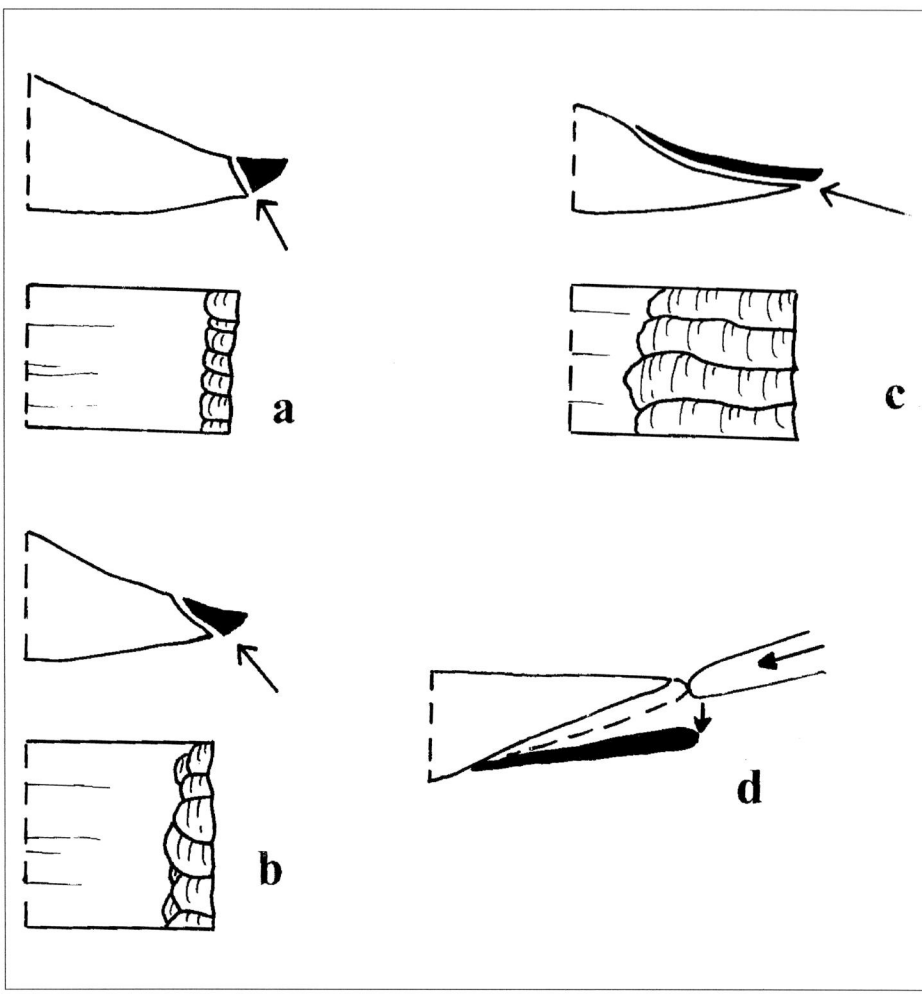

18 Retouching: a) Abrupt retouch; b) semi-abrupt retouch; c) invasive retouch; d) pressure flaking – the arrows show the 'in and down' direction of pressure needed to remove the retouching flake

HEAT TREATMENT

In some parts of the world flint was heated prior to being worked, as this improved its flaking quality. Experimentation has shown that heat-treated flint allowed better control over the length of the blades being produced, whilst reducing the frequency of step and hinge terminations (Kooyman 2000). The heating of flint removes some of its moisture content, and can also change its colour and texture.

There is little evidence for the use of heat-treated flint in British prehistory. However, it is possible that heat-treated flintwork may not be being recognised. Some recent heat-treating experiments produced flint that was easier to work than in its untreated original state. However, the colour and texture of the heat-treated flint appeared little different from other untreated flint available locally.

3

COMMON TOOL TYPES

In the following chapters, the different types of implements and tools are considered period by period. However, there are some types that occur in all or most periods of prehistory with variations in shape, size and sub-types. In this chapter, we will look at a number of these recurring tool types, with general observations on their manufacture, use and recognition. In the following period chapters, where these types occur the descriptions will concentrate more on the period variations, recognition features and aspects of the tool relevant to that period.

SCRAPERS

Scrapers are probably the most common type of implement in almost all periods of prehistory (*19*). Frequently, more scrapers are found on a site than any other tool type and they can be found in large numbers. Scrapers can vary significantly in quality, some having carefully retouched scraping edges, whilst others have short lengths of edge retouched or heavily abraded through use. The size of scrapers is as much dependent upon raw material availability as the scraping task for which it is to be used.

Scrapers were probably used for working soft materials such as hide, but may also have been used for woodworking. Experimental work has shown that they can be utilised for a wide variety of scraping tasks on both soft and hard materials. Some larger scrapers may have been hafted into wooden, bone or antler handles for use, however it is more likely that the majority were used as simple hand tools.

There are many different sub-types of scrapers (*colour plate 8*) some of which are discussed below, whilst others that are peculiar to one period are discussed in the relevant chapter. It is sometimes difficult to assign scrapers into clear-cut categories. At Hurst Fen, Clark (1960) divided the scrapers into the following five categories, which are occasionally still used by some lithic specialists:

    Class A   End scrapers
    Class B   Double-ended scrapers

Prehistoric Flintwork

    Class C   Disc scrapers
    Class D   Side scrapers
    Class E   On broken flakes

However, Clark's scheme was very site specific and did not cater for the great variety of types that actually exist, therefore the following major scraper sub-divisions are those most frequently used today.

End scrapers
End scrapers are normally the most common type of scraper found, and therefore the most varied in size and form. They can be produced on either flakes or blades, and frequently have some cortex remaining on the dorsal side of the blank. This is probably because the thicker flakes produced by the primary working of a core (which tended to retain cortex) were more suitable for making into an end scraper than the thinner secondary flakes. But the presence of cortex can sometimes be because the scrapers were expedient tools that were quickly produced from the most suitable piece of flint available, or due to the size of the raw material.

End scrapers were produced by retouch at the distal end, or less frequently at the proximal end. The retouch can be semi-abrupt or abrupt, or more rarely invasive, although this can vary from period to period. Although the distal end is normally convex shaped, it can also be straight or irregular. The retouch can also extend partially down one or both lateral edges. End scrapers made on large rounded flakes with abrupt or semi-abrupt retouch around the convex distal end, and extending partway along each lateral edge, are sometimes called 'horseshoe' scrapers.

Some end scrapers that were made on longer flakes and blades have a narrow pointed distal end, which was retouched to form a scraping edge: these are sometimes called 'nosed scrapers'. Nosed scrapers can look like blunted or broken piercers, but they can be distinguished as the 'point' of the nosed scraper will have been blunted by the retouch, whilst the retouch on a piercer forms a point, or the broken end will have no retouch at its tip.

Double-ended scrapers
These have retouched convex ends at both the distal and proximal extremities of the flake. The retouch rarely extended along the lateral edges, but was restricted to the two ends.

Side scrapers
These are also manufactured on both flakes and blades, but this varies by period. The semi-abrupt or abrupt retouch extends along one lateral edge of the piece. The edge is normally slightly convex in shape, but could also be straight. Sometimes a side scraper can be retouched along both lateral edges. Cortex is often present on side scrapers, sometimes on the opposite lateral

edge to the retouch, where it presumably made the scraper more comfortable to hold whilst it was being used. Abrupt blunting retouch on the opposite lateral edge may have been added for the same reason. The frequency of side scrapers varies by period, in some periods they are very common, whilst in others they can be rare.

Side-and-end scrapers
Combined side-and-end scrapers are normally manufactured on broad flakes and blades. They have a retouched convex distal end, with the retouch extending along one of the lateral edges or occasionally along both lateral edges. Sometimes the retouch is continuous, but there can also be a gap between the retouched distal end and the retouch on the lateral edge. The lateral edge is also normally convex, but could be straight.

Discoidal scrapers were a variant of the side-and-end scraper. They were manufactured on short rounded flakes, which had abrupt or semi-abrupt retouch around the convex distal end that extended around both convex lateral edges. The retouch normally stopped near the butt end of the flake, and therefore did not extend all the way around its circumference. The overall shape of the finished scraper was of an almost round disc, and for that reason, it was unlikely that these scrapers were hafted.

Hollow scrapers
Hollow or concave scrapers were more scarce than side-and-end scrapers. They were normally manufactured on flakes, and have a broad concave area of abrupt or semi-abrupt retouch along one lateral edge of the flake, or occasionally at the distal end. Hollow scrapers should not be confused with notched pieces, which have a much smaller area of retouch forming a distinct notch. Nor should they be confused with natural damage, which can sometimes be mistaken for retouch. The main variant of the hollow scraper was the Bronze Age 'horned scraper'.

BURINS

A burin is a flake or blade that has been modified by the removal of a narrow splinter (spall) from a break, an unmodified surface or a prepared surface (*19*). They are sometimes referred to as gravers after their supposed function as engraving tools, but were also probably used to make and prepare bone and antler tools using the groove and splinter technique. They are frequently found on sites dating from the Upper Palaeolithic to the early Neolithic period.

There are a number of different types of burins, many of which are not immediately apparent to the untrained eye. Occasionally they can be combined on the same flake with other tool types, normally end scrapers. The flake or blade on which the burin is made is frequently broken whether by design or

Prehistoric Flintwork

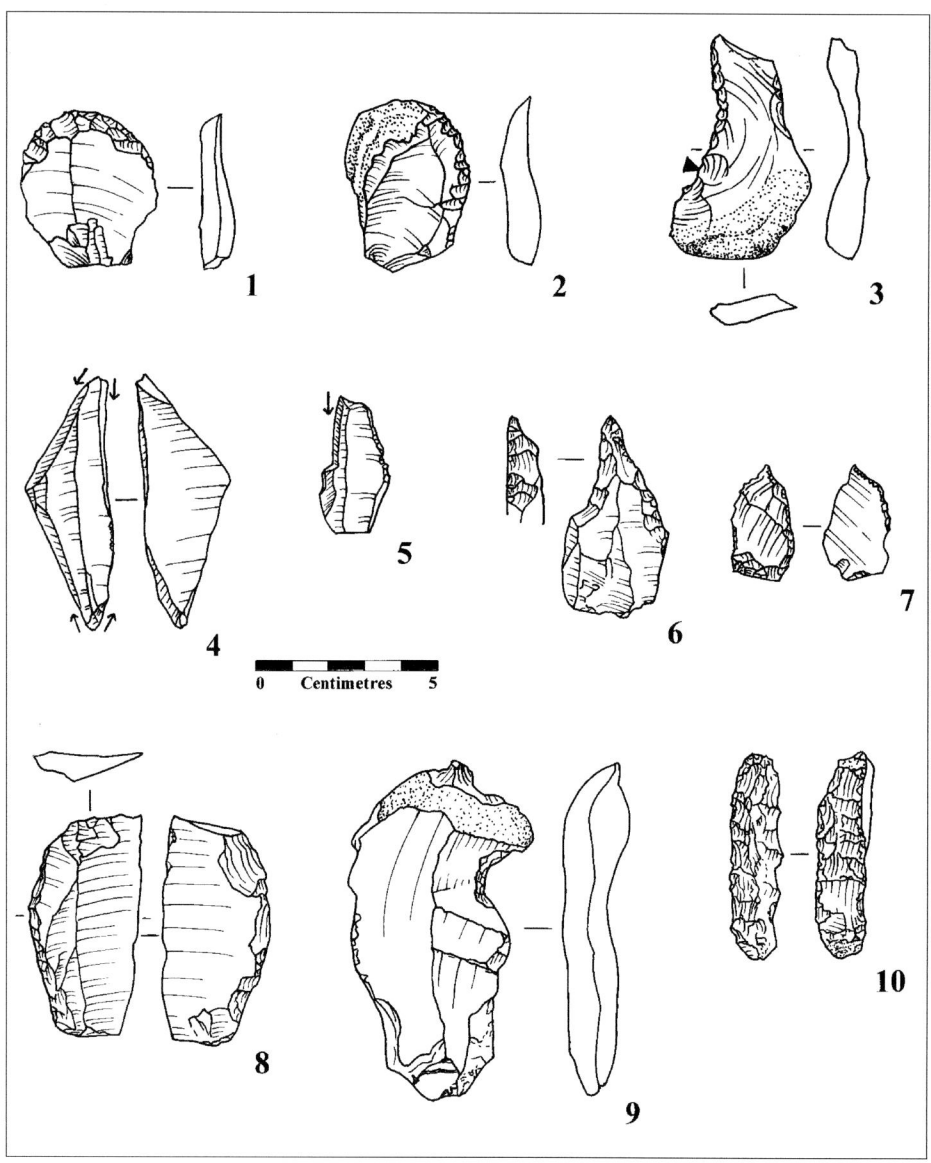

19 Common tool types: 1) End scraper; 2) Side scraper; 3) Hollow scraper; 4) Dihedral burin; 5) Truncation burin; 6) Piercer; 7) Awl; 8) Backed knife; 9) Notched piece; 10) Fabricator

accidentally. The burin is then manufactured on the broken edge. The burin spall is removed from the distal end, proximal end or lateral edge of the blank by either percussion or pressure. Sometimes the burin spall is removed from an unmodified natural surface or break, but normally the break or surface will have been prepared or crested beforehand to provide a platform for the removal blow.

There are three main types of burin. Firstly the truncation burin, where the burin spall has been removed from a retouched truncation at one or both ends of the flake or blade. These truncations can be convex, concave or oblique. The most frequent variety of a truncation burin is a single-angle removal. There are also double-angle removals from the same prepared break, and more rarely alternate-angle removals, where the point of departure for the removals is a break or natural surface at both the distal and proximal end of the piece.

The second type of burin that is encountered is the dihedral burin, where the spall is removed from a previous burin facet, which is normally unretouched, or from a break or unmodified natural surface. The third and simplest form of burin was the break burin, which was formed by the removal of a burin spall from the edge of a broken blade or flake.

The by-product resulting from the manufacture of a burin is the burin spall (*28*). If the spall was struck from an unprepared surface, then it will have all of the characteristics of a normal small bladelet or flake with a triangular section. If struck from a prepared truncation, the spall will have a remnant of the prepared surface on its butt, whilst a spall removed from the prepared lateral edge of a flake or blade appears to be retouched along its length.

PIERCERS AND AWLS

These two tools are frequently grouped together without differentiation, however there are differences between the two types, and they should be separated into the individual types as they probably performed different functions.

Both can be made on flakes or blades, with part of the blank, normally at the distal end, shaped by retouch into a point (*19*). Both tools can be easily used in the hand, and there is no conclusive evidence that they were hafted, although it is possible that some were. In the case of an awl, the point is abruptly retouched along one edge or two alternate edges, so that when it is rotated through 360° to pierce a hole, both edges perform a cutting role. Awls frequently have a thin cross section, and it is difficult to see how they could have been used to pierce any tough materials.

The piercer, or borer as it is sometimes called, has abrupt retouch on the two lateral edges converging to form the point, which normally gives it a thicker triangular cross section. The piercer was probably used in a twisting motion backwards and forwards to create a hole, and could have been used on tougher materials than the awl. Piercers can vary considerably in size, with some being made on very large flakes. The points can also vary, with some being short, whilst others can be as long as the remaining body of the flake. The French term *bec* (meaning beak) is sometimes used to describe a piercer.

KNIVES

Knives were normally made on longer flakes and broad blades, and were made in a variety of different forms that are described in the relevant period chapters below. Some forms of knife were finely made, and may have been produced for specific tasks. However it should be remembered that most flakes and blades had naturally sharp edges, and could have been utilised for most simple cutting tasks without any further modification. The two most common types of knife were simple unretouched knives and invasively-retouched knives.

Simple knives had an unretouched straight cutting edge, so that the unmodified and naturally sharp edge of the flake or blade could be utilised. The opposing thicker lateral edge was normally abruptly retouched to blunt it. This would either facilitate holding the knife, or enable it to be hafted into a wooden handle. Knives that were retouched on the opposing lateral edge are called 'backed knives' or 'blunted-back knives' (*19*). Occasionally, the opposing lateral edge was not retouched, but was left as an unmodified thicker edge, which sometimes had a remnant of cortex. These pieces are sometimes referred to as 'cutting flakes/blades' rather than knives.

The invasively-retouched knife tends to be slightly thicker, with the cutting edge modified by invasive retouch (often bifacial) along all or part of its straight edge. The opposing lateral edge was normally blunted with abrupt retouch (backed), but could also be left unmodified. The sharpening of the cutting edge by invasive retouch resulted in a more durable knife, which could be re-sharpened by further invasive retouching when the cutting edge became blunted.

NOTCHED PIECES

Notched pieces are found in most periods of prehistory but are never a common tool type. They appear to be an expedient type of tool, and can be found on flakes and blades of all types, sizes and shapes (*19*). On occasions, even broken or smaller fragments of flakes have notches added to their lateral edges. The notches were formed by a small number of abrupt or semi-abrupt retouch blows, normally struck from the ventral side of the piece, which had removed small flakes thus creating a deep curved incision into the lateral edge of the flake. The notch was frequently located towards the distal end of the flake, and occasionally was actually on the distal end. A notch would rarely have been more than 10mm wide and between 2 to 7mm deep, and should not be confused with hollow scrapers where the concave retouched area will take up most of the lateral edge. Occasionally pieces with two notches can be found. It is very easy to confuse notched pieces with flakes that have been damaged accidentally. A plough striking the edge of a flake can easily create an apparent notch.

AXES AND OTHER CORE TOOLS

Axes varied considerably from one period to another, from simple handaxes in the Palaeolithic through to the finely ground axes of the Neolithic period. Also included in this category are adzes, picks and other forms of heavy tool that were manufactured in different periods. These are all discussed in detail in the relevant chapters, but there are a few general comments that can be made. The basic attributes of the three main varieties of 'core' tool are (after Field 1989):

Axe: Tendency to straight profile and lenticular (biconvex) cross section
Adze: Tendency to curved profile and sub-triangular cross section
Pick: Tendency to oval or quadrangular cross section and pointed working edge

The main difference between an axe and an adze is that the cutting edge of the axe blade would be parallel to the handle and it would be used in a cutting/chopping action, perhaps for felling trees. An adze would have its cutting blade at a right angle to the handle and would be used in a chopping or gauging action, more suitable for multi-purpose woodworking tasks.

Axes and adzes could be made from either large flakes or nodules, whilst picks tended to be made only from nodules. Having selected a suitable nodule or flake of raw material, the initial flaking was carried out, normally with a hard hammer, probably removing flakes from one face of the blank first, and then from the opposite face, ensuring that the overall shape of the intended axe was maintained throughout. This initial flaking would remove most of the cortex from the blank, and shape it into the approximate outline of the axe. This is called a roughout (*57*). Apart from the initial flakes that would have cortex on the dorsal side, the negative scars on the preparation flakes would be multi-directional, reflecting the removal of flakes from that surface from both edges of the blank.

A study of discarded roughouts shows that there were a number of reasons for abandonment. A misdirected blow whilst removing flakes could break the roughout, or alternatively remove too large a flake thus making the continuation of flaking impractical. Flaws were often encountered in the flint nodules, even with good quality flint, and could lead to the roughout being discarded.

The next stage in the manufacture process was to shape the roughout into the final shape of the axe; the 'preform' (*57*). All of the remaining cortex was removed, any high ridges were reduced in size and the cutting edge was carefully retouched with shallow flake removals to form a straight and sharp edge. The finishing flakes during this shaping process were normally removed with a soft hammer, and so have thin curving profiles, narrow butts, a diffuse bulb and small lip associated with soft-hammer production, together with multi-directional negative scars on the dorsal side. Discarded preforms are sometimes found, having been broken during the final stages of production, or abandoned due to flaws or simply because they cannot be shaped into the required form.

The final finishing of the axe normally required a little more work. Sometimes a number of small flakes were removed to sharpen the cutting edge. Alternatively a tranchet sharpening-flake could be removed with a blow from one lateral edge, which removed a transverse flake across the blade of the axe and by doing so produced a sharp cutting edge (*40*). In the Neolithic period however, the axe was often ground over all or part of its cutting edge and surface to produce the classic ground or polished axe typical of this period.

FABRICATORS

Fabricators occur throughout prehistory, and were made on elongated thick flakes, blades or a fragment of a nodule or core (*19*). They can have an oval, circular, rectangular or diamond cross section, sometimes with one flat side, and are generally rod-shaped. They are normally flaked over their surface, in much the same way as an axe preform, and have one or both rounded ends that are abraded and worn from use. The other end and the edges of the piece may also have some wear, possibly from the tool having been hafted into a handle. Fabricators are thought to have been used for retouching other flint tools, or for grinding, or may have also been used as part of a fire lighting kit. Whatever their use, in some periods they appear to have been elaborately made, and seem to have been carefully curated items.

4

THE PALAEOLITHIC PERIOD

The Palaeolithic period or Old Stone Age covers a vast period of time, stretching from before 600,000 years ago in Britain, through to the beginning of the Holocene some 10,000 years ago. Traditionally the period has been split into three parts: the Lower, Middle and Upper Palaeolithic, each having distinctive flintworking technologies and tool types. During this time Britain was affected by major changes in climate, which fluctuated between cold stages (glacials) and warmer stages (interglacials). During the height of glacials, ice sheets covered much of Britain, extending as far south as the line of the river Thames during the Anglian cold stage. Even those parts of Britain not covered by the ice sheet would have been severely affected and it is unlikely that there was much human activity in Britain during these glacial maximums. However, during relatively warm periods within the glacials themselves (interstadials), some species such as mammoth, horse, woolly rhino, reindeer and arctic fox were present and humans appear to have been able to occupy Britain alongside these animals. Still, the main periods of occupation in the British Isles were restricted to the warm interglacial stages. During these times temperatures increased to modern levels, the ice sheets retreated northwards, and numerous temperate climate mammal species (bovids, wild pig, rhino, hippo, red deer and roe deer) moved in to take advantage of the fertile grasslands and regenerating woodland. Early humans would have followed these animals northwards, and it is from these warmer stages or during occasional shorter warmer phases that most of our evidence for human activity comes. However, Lower Palaeolithic finds are more common from warm periods 500-300,000 years ago than later interglacials and no occupation appears to have occurred in the penultimate interglacial *c*.100,000 BP. This could be due to the breaching of the land bridge between Britain and the continent at 400,000 BP and progressively extended periods of isolation in later interglacials due to sea level rise.

Because of the extensive remodelling of the landscape during the glacial phases, there are very few sites dating from the Lower Palaeolithic that have *in situ* archaeology, with one or two notable exceptions such as Boxgrove (*colour plate 9*). Most of our evidence for human activity during this period comes

57

from redeposited material found in river gravel and other glacial deposits, and has generally been discovered during quarrying activity (Wymer 1999). Almost all evidence for Lower Palaeolithic activity is found in the southern part of Britain, with almost none further north than the Midlands. Whether this is due to a real lack of activity, or simply due to later glaciations removing all evidence, is not clear.

The Middle Palaeolithic is now considered to cover the period from 245,000 BP to the first emergence of modern humans at around 40,000 BP and coincides with the appearance of more complex forms of flintworking technology and the presence of Neanderthals in Britain. The Ipswichian interglacial (100,000 BP) produced a number of sites that have all produced warm climate mammal species. However, there is no evidence of any stone tools at these sites, suggesting that there was no human occupation at this time. From the last glacial stage (the Devensian), hand axes have been found in conjunction with mammoth remains, which suggests that there was some occupation during the warmer parts of this cold phase.

The Upper Palaeolithic covers the period from 40,000 BP up to the beginning of the Mesolithic around 10,000 BP. This coincides with the latter part of the Mousterian period in France, which sees the emergence of modern humans and major changes in flintworking technology. Although there are a few sites in Britain that have produced Upper Palaeolithic flintwork dating from the earlier part of this period, there seems to have been a hiatus in occupation that coincided with the final cold stage, around 18,000 BP, and it was probably only around 13,000 BP that Britain began to be recolonised.

Apart from a few fragments of bone and teeth, and a single wooden spear, the only remains surviving that confirm human activity during the Palaeolithic are the stone tools and debitage. There is much debate on many aspects of Palaeolithic stone tools and this book is not the place to recount or discuss the relationship between the stone tools and different hominid species. A typology dividing the stone tools of the Palaeolithic into four divisions or 'modes' is generally used as the basis for categorising Palaeolithic flintwork (Barton 1997, Wymer 1999). The fourfold typology is ordered in a relative sense based on a presumption that there is a technological progression over time. However, it also allows for there to be overlaps in time between the different phases, whether locally or otherwise, and is flexible enough to permit some variation within each division.

Lower Palaeolithic flintwork from redeposited contexts is generally heavily patinated, and this can be a major recognition feature when it occurs in mixed assemblages with later material. Because much of the flintwork will have been transported to where it is found in the river gravels or glacial action, the pieces are likely to be very abraded. This can often be mistaken as crude retouch, but is recognised by being present on all edges and ridges, and because it is rarely very regular.

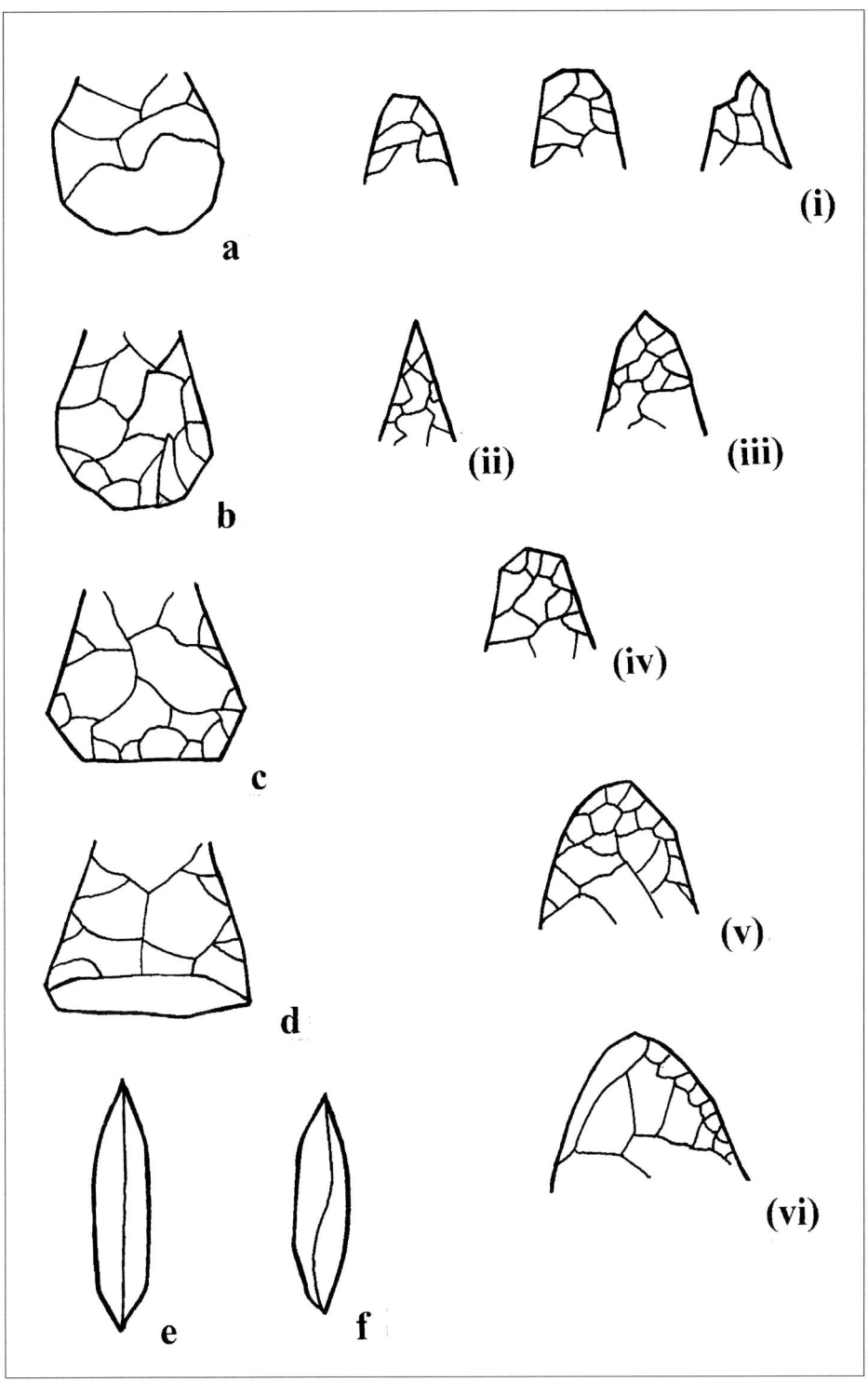

20 Lower Palaeolithic handaxe typology: Attributes of the butt (a to d), point (i to iv) and edge (e and f, v and vi) – see text for full description. *After Wymer*

Prehistoric Flintwork

The major distinctive type of tool used in the Lower Palaeolithic was the handaxe. Handaxes have been classified (Wymer 1999) into a typology of thirteen different forms listed from A to N. The first three types belong to Mode 1 technology, whilst the remaining ten are Mode 2. The shape of a handaxe may have been functional in that it was designed for a specific task, or more likely it was as a result of the size and shape of the available raw material.

Handaxes have been further categorised by the attributes of the butt, point and edges as follows (20):

Butts	(a)	Over 50 per cent cortex or natural fracture on butt
	(b)	Trimmed butt
	(c)	Trimmed butt with chamfered corners
	(d)	Flat based butt
Points	(i)	Rounded, lingulate or irregular point
	(ii)	Acute point
	(iii)	Ogee point
	(iv)	Basal point
Edges	(e)	Straight-sided
	(f)	Twisted edge (usually reversed 'S')
	(v)	Without tranchet edge
	(vi)	With tranchet edge

MODE 1 TECHNOLOGY

This technology comprised simple flake pebble tools and flakes, and was derived from the oldest (Oldowan) stone tools. The earliest tools were simple but the economic effectiveness of simple core-working traditions is borne out by their continued use throughout the Palaeolithic. The flakes were removed from a core with a hard hammer, and had large bulbs of percussion and broad platforms, and tended to be quite thick. The flakes were normally removed from a core haphazardly from one face. Occasionally they were removed more systematically by striking alternate flakes from each face, using the previous removal as a platform for the next blow. Most flakes have some cortex still present on the dorsal side.

Some of the flakes were used as tools for cutting, simply employing the unmodified sharp edges. Others were semi-abruptly or abruptly retouched to form a steep scraping edge. The scraping edges were normally convex and at the distal end of the flake, but could also be along one of the lateral edges of the flake. Occasionally flakes were modified by a single blow applied a short way into the piece that removed a single small flake, which left a notch on the edge of the blank; these are called 'Clactonian notches'.

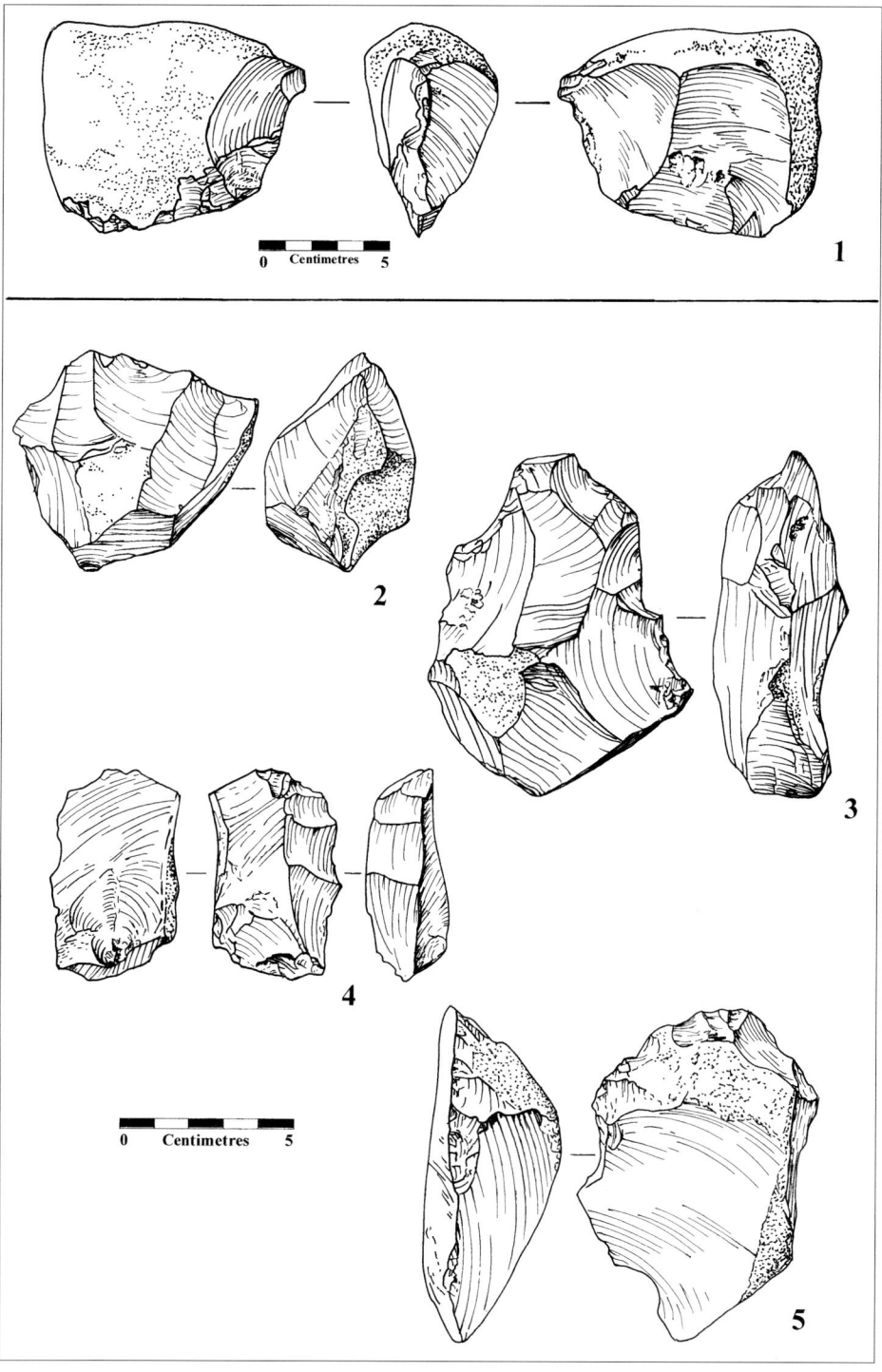

21 Lower Palaeolithic Mode 1 flintwork: 1) Chopper-core (A); 2) Biconical core (B); 3) Proto-handaxe (C); 4-5) Retouched flakes. Various sites. *After Wymer*

The cores were normally pebbles or smaller rounded nodules, with no attempt at platform preparation, or curation of the core. It is possible that some of the cores were utilised as tools, with the acute edge formed by the alternate flake removals being used as a chopper. However, there is some debate as to whether they were actually used as choppers, or were simply cores (Ashton *et al.* 1992). These cores are sometimes referred to as 'chopper-cores'. There are no true handaxes in Mode 1 assemblages, but in both Europe and Africa non-classic biface forms may be found alongside Mode 1 industries. The Mode 1 'non-classic biface forms' are (*21*):

Type A	Chopper-core
Type B	Biconical core
Type C	Proto-handaxe

In Britain Mode 1 assemblages are generally referred to as Clactonian, after the Essex coastal town of Clacton-on-Sea where some of the first material of this type was found in Britain. They are generally confined to the Lower Palaeolithic.

MODE 2 TECHNOLOGY

The Mode 2 technology comprised predominantly handaxes, together with retouched flakes (*22*). The handaxes were elaborate bifacial tools, which were made in a variety of different forms (Wymer 1999):

Type D	Stone-struck crude handaxe
Type E	Small handaxes: less than 10cm length and usually of irregular shape
Type F	Pointed handaxe
Type G	Sub-cordate handaxe
Type H	Cleaver
Type J	Cordate (heart-shaped) handaxe
Type K	Ovate handaxe
Type L	Segmental 'chopping' tool
Type M	Ficron handaxe
Type N	Flat-butted cordate handaxe – *bout coupé* or Coygan type

Handaxes were made predominantly from nodules of flint and other stone, but occasionally large flakes were used as a blank for smaller handaxes (*23*). The flakes were removed from the nodule or large flake in a very systematic and skilful way, requiring the knapper to be thinking one or two steps ahead throughout the creation of the tool. A sequence of steps was required to make the handaxe, starting with flakes being removed with a hard hammer to initially

The Palaeolithic Period

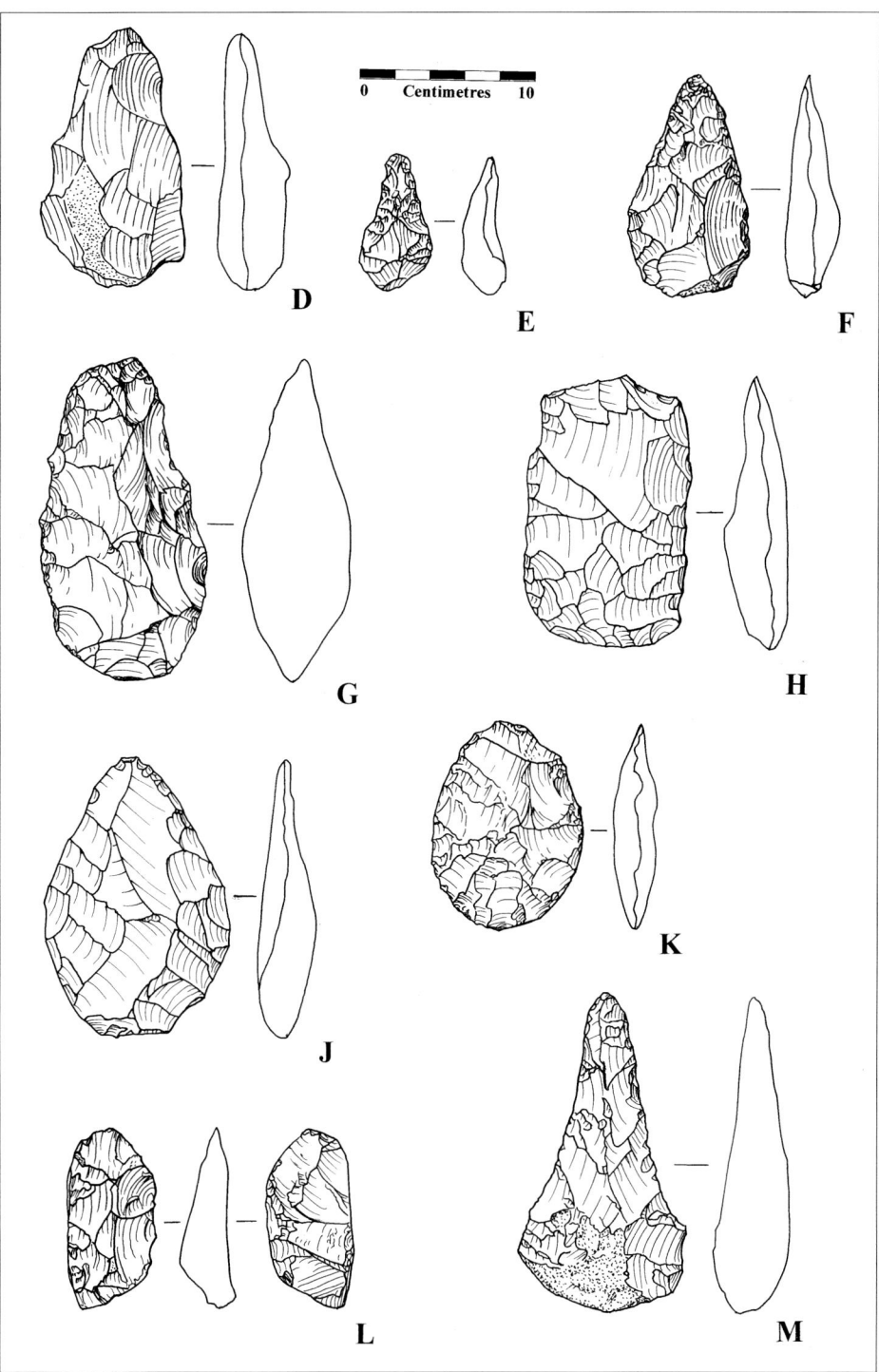

22 Lower Palaeolithic Mode 2 handaxes: D) Crude stone-struck; E) Small; F) Pointed; G) Sub-cordate; H) Cleaver; J) Cordate; K) Ovate; L) Segmental 'chopping' tool; M) Ficron. Various sites. *After Wymer, Timms and Wenban-Smith*

shape the nodule (roughout). This initial shaping was carried out by working around the circumference of the nodule removing flakes alternatively from each face, using the scar of a previous removal on one face as the platform for a removal from the opposite face. Along the way, numerous problems would arise due to the quality of the raw material or misjudged blows, but these could generally be overcome by the knapper's skill (Lord 1993).

Having achieved the roughout shape, further flaking was then carried out to thin down the size of the handaxe and achieve its final shape. These 'thinning' flakes would have been removed in the same manner as the initial flakes, but using a soft hammer (antler or bone), and requiring the frequent preparation of the striking platform. The platform edge would have been prepared by being abraded with a coarse stone to ensure that it could be struck accurately with the hammer. The final shaping of the handaxe was frequently achieved by the removal of the last few smaller soft hammer-struck flakes from along the intended cutting edge. However, a number of handaxes, especially those of ovate or cordate shape, were sharpened by the removal of a 'tranchet flake'. The tranchet sharpening-flake was struck from the lateral edge of the handaxe, near the intended cutting edge, which removed a transverse flake across the blade of the axe and by doing so produced a sharp cutting edge. The tranchet flake produced by this process is a distinctive piece. During the excavations at Boxgrove, the knapping debris resulting from the manufacture of a handaxe was found (*colour plate 10*) *in situ*. Subsequent refitting of the flakes resulted in the reconstruction of the nodule from which the handaxe was made, (apart from the missing handaxe itself) thus establishing the entire knapping process. Also at Boxgrove is conclusive evidence for the use of soft hammers, with antler hammers found with small fragments of flint embedded in them.

As the name suggests, handaxes were used in the hand, and there is no evidence for them having been hafted. It is believed that they were used as all-purpose butchery tools, but they could have been used for a range of other tasks as well. Ovates and cordiforms were probably used in a delicate manner like a knife not an axe. Some forms may have been suited to other tasks. The Mode 2 handaxes are collectively called Acheulian after the type-site of St Acheul in Northern France where they were first described. They are normally found in the Lower Palaeolithic, but are also occasionally found in Middle Palaeolithic assemblages.

Other tools associated with Mode 2 assemblages included retouched flakes and scrapers (*23*). The scrapers were often manufactured on thicker flakes and were retouched normally along one lateral edge or at the distal end. There was no regular form to the scrapers, with suitable flakes apparently being selected as required. Other flakes may have been utilised for various cutting and boring tasks, or for working wood and bone. A number of flakes from Hoxne were analysed for microwear, and found to have been used for

The Palaeolithic Period

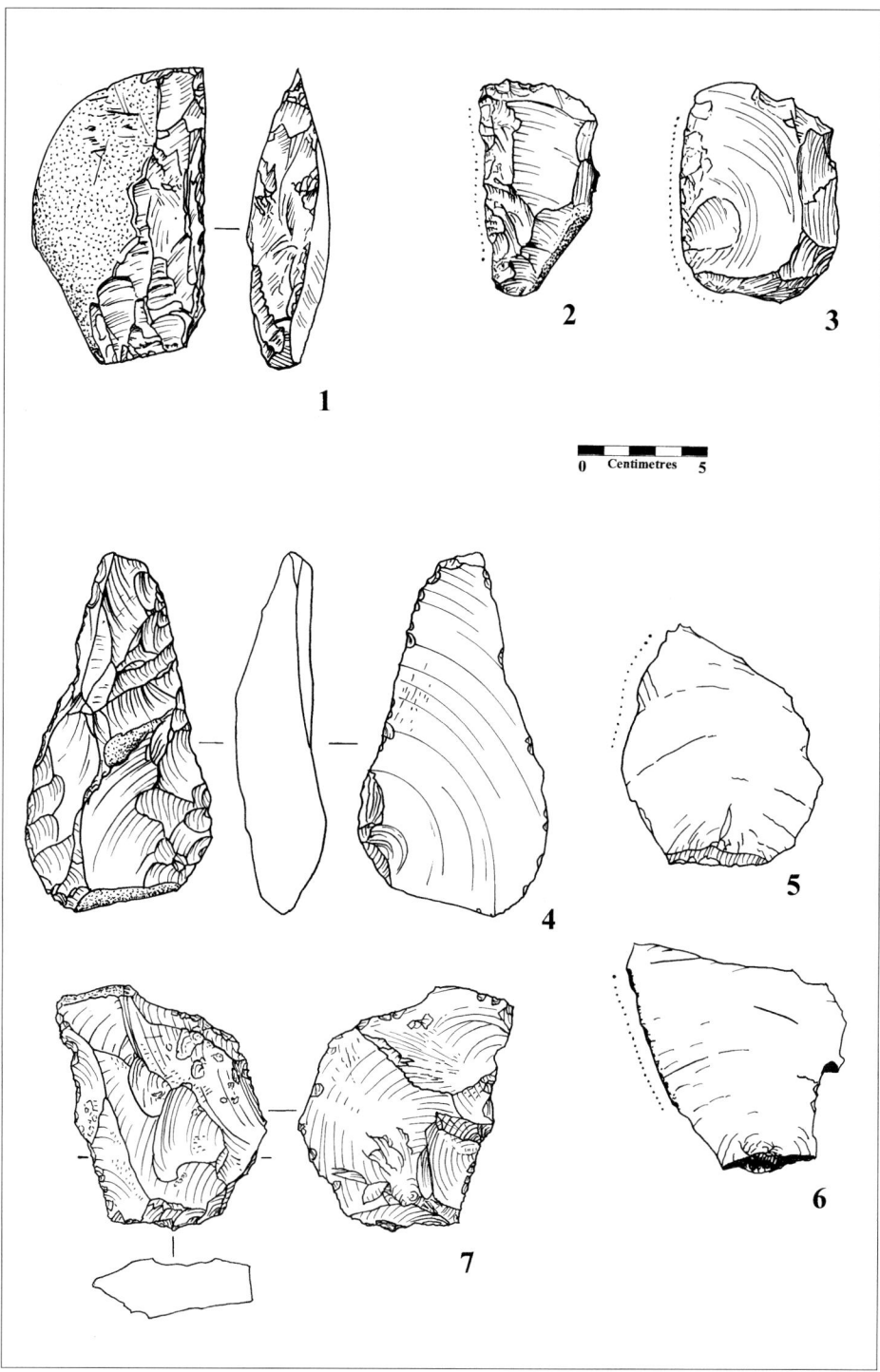

23 Lower Palaeolithic Mode 2 implements: 1-3) Scrapers; 4) Unifacial pointed handaxe on a flake; 5-6) Utilised flakes from Hoxne; 7) Flaked flake. Various sites. *After Wymer, Wenban-Smith, Keeley and Ashton et al.*

Prehistoric Flintwork

a number of different tasks (Keeley 1980). These flakes were utilised either without modification of the working edge (*23*), or occasionally with some areas of minimal retouch.

Flaked flakes are also frequently found in Lower and Middle Palaeolithic assemblages (*23*). They have been defined as 'a flake that has had one or more smaller flakes removed from one of its edges' (Ashton *et al.* 1991). It is not clear why flakes were removed from existing larger flakes, and in some cases scrapers, but the technique may have been used as a simple method to produce tools.

CLACTONIAN AND ACHEULIAN INDUSTRIES

It was thought until recently that the Clactonian industry was earlier than the apparently more developed Acheulian handaxes (*colour plate 11*), and therefore these two different modes represented two culturally different groups. However, more recent work at a number of sites has shown that the two industries may have been contemporary. There are a number of theories that have been put forward to solve this dilemma. Firstly, the two technologies represent two contemporary archaic human groups with different knapping skills, perhaps living in two distinctly different habitats (Ashton *et al.* 1994). Secondly, the two different technologies may have been carried out by the same people, but as a response to different requirements, perhaps handaxes for one task, and flake tools for another. Finally, the two industries may simply result from differences in available raw material (Wenban-Smith 1998). On a number of sites where a Clactonian technology was being used, the raw material is not of a good quality, and may not have been suitable for making Mode 2 handaxes.

MODE 3 TECHNOLOGY

This technology is defined by the presence of Levallois flakes, retouched flakes and some handaxes, including *bout coupé* forms. The various tool forms found in Mode 3 assemblages have been classified in some detail by Bordes and others (e.g. Bordes 1961) based on the more extensive discoveries in France.

Levallois cores and flakes
The Levallois technique was used to produce flakes of a predetermined shape and size. Evidence for the technique can be found in both Mode 3 and Mode 2 assemblages, although it is most commonly found in Mode 3 assemblages dating to the Middle Palaeolithic. The technique involves the creation of an oval tortoise-shaped core from which flakes, or blade-like flakes, have been removed with a hard hammer (*24*). One face (the upper) of the core was flaked continuously around its circumference so that the entire surface was covered with the negative scars running from the edge into

The Palaeolithic Period

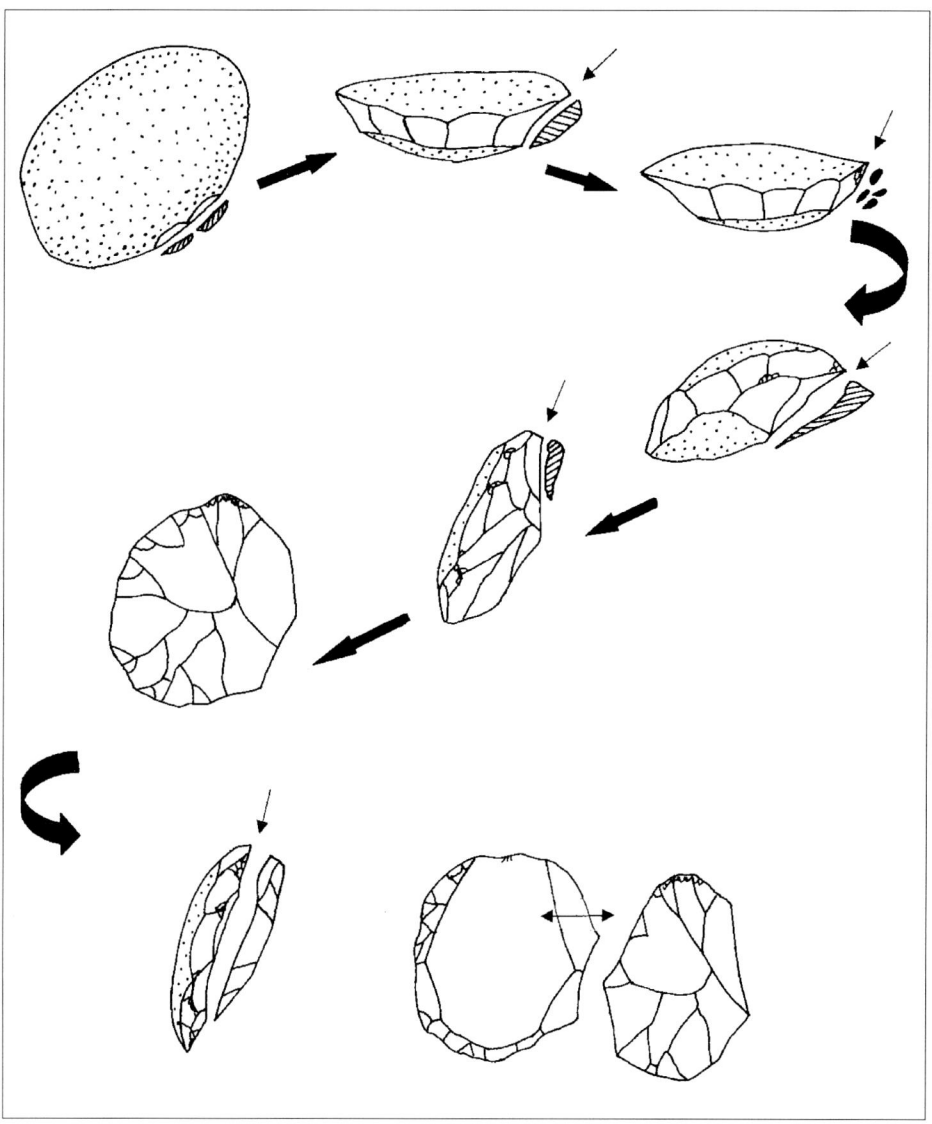

24 Levallois technology. The sequence of core reduction showing the preparation of the core, through to the final removal of the Levallois flake. *After Lhomme* et al.

the centre. The other (lower) face was only flaked around its perimeter, and frequently had an area of cortex remaining in the centre. The core was then prepared at one end to create a platform, which was then struck with a hard hammer to remove the predetermined flake from the upper face. It was often then possible to remove additional flakes from the same surface of the core, but normally the core was discarded after the first flake had been removed. A Levallois core therefore has a number of characteristic features that can be used for recognition (Van Peer 1992):

1. The core will have two convex faces opposite to one another
2. The build up is asymmetric: one of the faces is thicker than the other
3. The former face is flaked (not always continuously) around its perimeter, and has cortex remaining in the centre
4. In one area of this face, there is a greater number of flake scars
5. The other face shows a large negative flake scar and multiple traces of flakes detached before this last flake

The flakes that were removed by this technique were then modified into a range of different tools and retain certain recognition features:

1. A considerable number of flake scars on the dorsal surface
2. A transversal as well as longitudinal dorsal convexity
3. A more or less symmetrical build up along the axis of flaking, and
4. A facetted butt

Points
A similar technique was used to produce triangular flakes that were used to make points (*25*). To obtain a triangular flake, initial flakes were removed from either end of the core leaving a basal triangular scar. After preparation of the platform the final triangular flake was removed with a hard hammer, its predetermined shape defined by the ridges left by the earlier removals.

In an unmodified form these triangular flakes are known as 'Levallois points'. Some points were semi-abruptly or invasively retouched along both lateral edges converging to form a point at the distal end of the flake. These are called 'Mousterian points'. Both types of point were probably hafted onto the end of a wooden shaft to form a spear.

Side scrapers
Side scrapers are the dominant type of scraper found in Mode 3 assemblages, and were manufactured on the lateral edges of flakes or pebbles (*25*). Side scrapers, manufactured on flakes, tended to use longer flakes, Levallois flakes or flake fragments. One straight or slightly convex lateral edge was modified with semi-abrupt retouch to form the scraping edge, whilst the opposite edge was left

The Palaeolithic Period

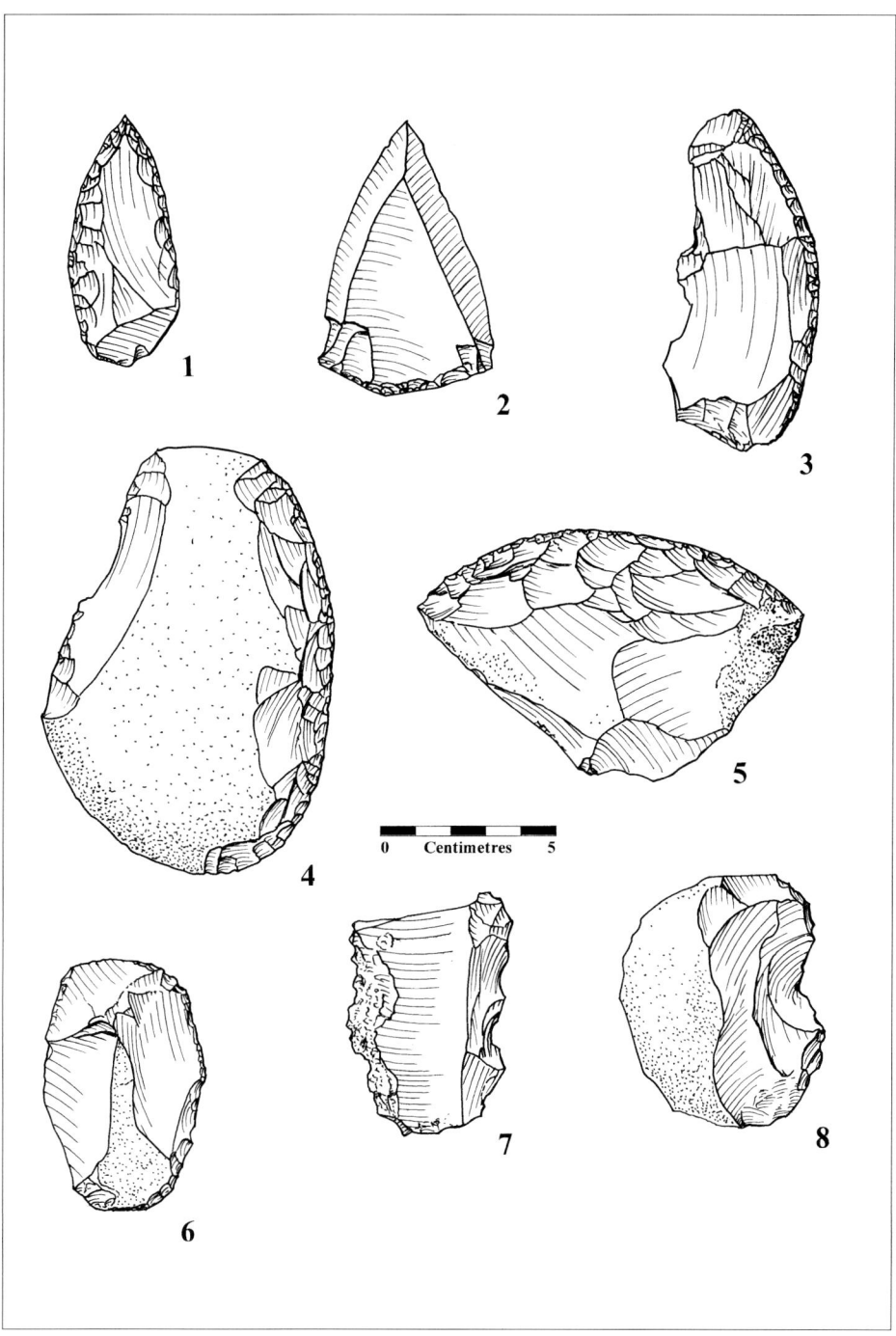

25 Middle Palaeolithic Mode 3 implements: 1) Mousterian point; 2) Levallois point; 3-4) Convex side scrapers; 5) Transverse scraper with *Quina*-type retouch; 6) Backed knife; 7) Denticulate; 8) Clactonian notch. *After Bordes*

unmodified. Small oval pebbles were also used as side scrapers, with one straight or slightly convex longer edge modified with abrupt and semi-abrupt retouch to form the scraping edge. The opposite edge and the rest of the pebble retained a covering of cortex. Other types of scraper were very rare, but included transverse scrapers where the retouch was across the distal end of the flake.

Some scrapers had heavy scalar retouch along a convex edge, where the negative scars from the retouch overlapped to form a scaled scraping edge. These are called *Quina*-type scrapers. The distinctive negative flake scars that result from *Quina* retouch generally have a fan shape and a hinged distal edge (Inizan *et al.*).

Backed knives
Backed knives were made on flakes. One straight or slightly convex unmodified lateral edge of the flake was used as the cutting edge. The opposite edge was blunted by being abruptly retouched, or retained its cortex to facilitate handling (25).

Denticulates
Denticulates were flakes or flake fragments that had one lateral edge modified by a series of denticulations (notches), frequently extending along only part of that edge (*25*). The opposite edge was left with cortex on it, or was abruptly retouched. These pieces were likely to have been used in a saw-like action, and were a reasonably common tool type in some assemblages.

Notches
These tools were manufactured on flakes that had one lateral edge prepared by abrasion or retouch to form a platform, and then a single large flake removed, leaving a large notch (Clactonian notch). The opposite edge frequently retained its cortex (*25*).

Burins
Burins were a rare tool type in Mode 3 assemblages. The burins were on flakes that had been modified by the removal of a spall from a break, an unmodified surface or a prepared surface at one end of the piece.

Flake cleavers
Few flake cleavers have been found in Britain (Robinson 1986). These tools were manufactured on large, thick Levallois flakes where the butt had often been removed. One or both of the lateral edges were modified by retouch, which had occasionally removed flakes from both faces of the blank (i.e. bifacially), but this never extended across the whole surface. The cleaver edge was normally located at the opposite end to the butt, and was formed by the removal of a tranchet flake from one lateral edge (*26*). The tranchet cleaver edge was never retouched.

The Palaeolithic Period

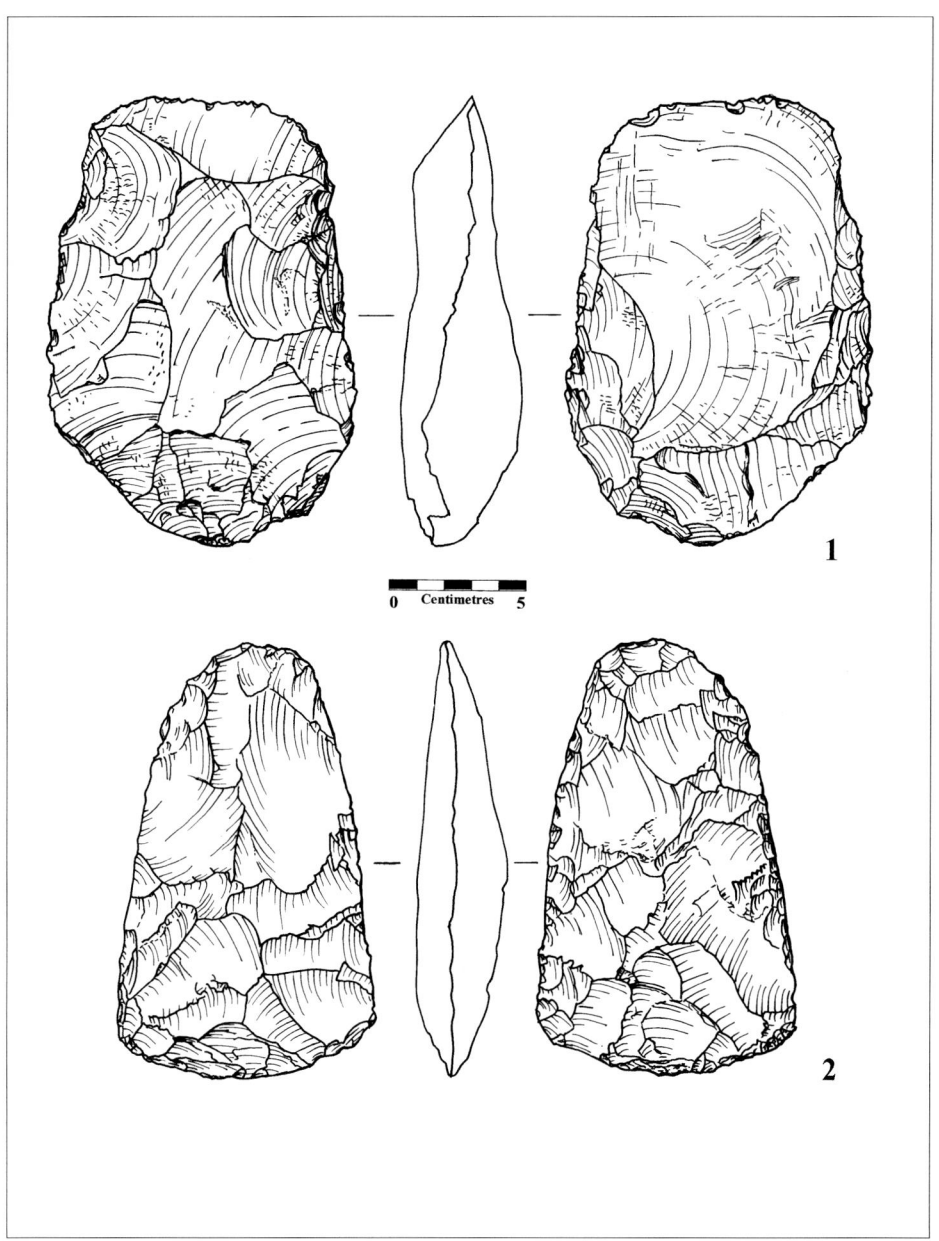

26 Middle Palaeolithic Mode 3 flintwork: 1) Flake cleaver made on a Levallois flake from Baker's Hole; 2) *Bout Coupé* or Coygan handaxe (Type N) from Coygan Cave. *After Robinson and Aldhouse-Green* et al.

Bout coupé handaxes

The *bout coupé* handaxe (Type N) is defined as being 'sub-rectangular in shape, thin, with a rounded tip and a straight/convex base which also acts as a third cutting edge, the base is frequently finished by parallel flaking, and the profile is always straight, never twisted' (Coulson 1986). There has been some questioning of the *bout coupé* handaxe as a typological or cultural marker, mostly due to the lack of a clear definition, and although many have been found in Middle Palaeolithic contexts it cannot be demonstrated conclusively that they only belong to that period. Indeed, it has recently suggested that the term *bout coupé* be replaced by the term 'Coygan-type' handaxe after the clearly defined handaxe of *bout coupé* type (26) recovered from Coygan Cave, Carmarthenshire (Bishop 2002).

MODE 4 TECHNOLOGY

This flintworking technology is associated with the Upper Palaeolithic and appeared in Europe some 40,000 years ago. It is characterised by the production of long narrow blades from carefully prepared cores; the blades were then used as blanks for a whole range of different tools.

Nodules were carefully selected and then initially shaped with a hard hammer to achieve a core of the right shape and size for continued working. Having created a platform, the front of the core was bifacially flaked to create a 'crested' ridge. The crested ridge was then removed with a carefully placed blow on the platform. As the shock wave from the blow tended to follow the ridge created, it guided the removal of the 'crested blade', which then created a pair of parallel ridges running the length of the core face. These ridges then guided the direction of subsequent removals thus creating a series of long thin blades. Cores can have either a single platform or two opposing platforms; the latter are commonly called bipolar cores.

Some of the blades that were produced were curved and had carefully prepared platforms, whilst others were straight with less platform preparation. This could be due to differing techniques required to produce different types of tool, or may reflect different skills and abilities of the knappers. It is not clear whether the blades were removed by direct percussion or with a punch. This may have varied depending upon the requirements of the final product. The careful, efficient working of the flint nodules, together with the preference for long thin blades, suggests that a considerable amount of care was being taken in the curation and exploitation of the raw material.

It was not only blades that were produced during the Upper Palaeolithic. Flakes were also produced in large numbers, especially during the initial shaping of nodules. Although blades were used as the basis for most of the tools, flakes were also used as blanks for tools. Over 90 different types of tool were produced during the Upper Palaeolithic. The Upper Palaeolithic can

The Palaeolithic Period

be split into two phases, earlier and later, divided by a glacial when there was apparently no human activity in Britain. Readers are referred to other sources (e.g. Barton 1997) for a detailed summary.

THE EARLIER UPPER PALAEOLITHIC

The earlier phase has been divided into three sub-divisions. The first is characterised by Jermanovice leaf points, whilst the other two have affinities with the continental Aurignacian and Gravettian industries.

Leaf-shaped points
One of the most distinctive tools of the earlier Upper Palaeolithic was the leaf-shaped point (*27*). These were made on long blades, normally between 100–150mm long, and were triangular in cross section with a point at the distal end. They were invasively retouched over one or both faces of the blade, and the extent of the retouch varies from piece to piece. Most were invasively worked over the ventral face with the dorsal face having less invasive retouch. Frequently the dorsal face retouch was confined to the edge or at the point.

Jermanovice leaf points were bifacial and unifacial leaf-shaped points made from long blades. They had a triangular cross section and were pointed at one end. The blade points were retouched unifacially on the ventral surface, with the retouch frequently limited to the extremities of the blade. Occasionally the blades were straightened by partial surface chipping, probably to enable them to be hafted into wooden handles as spear points. At Beedings in Sussex a group of Jermanovice points was found, some of which had impact breaks, and were apparently being recycled into other tools such as scrapers and burins (Jacobi 1986).

Tanged points
Font-Robert tanged points occurred in Gravettian assemblages (27). They were manufactured on blades with invasive retouch either over much of the dorsal surface, or just confined to the edges. At one end a point was formed, whilst at the other end the retouch was used to narrow the blank to form a tang, which was frequently almost as long as the blade.

Backed pieces
These Gravette points may have developed from the backed knives of the Mousterian. They were small narrow blades or bladelets with abrupt retouch along one lateral edge, whilst the opposite edge was normally left unmodified (*27*). It is not clear whether these tools were hafted or held in the hand.

Scrapers

End scrapers were a common tool type, and had a number of standardised forms that could be formed on both blades and flakes (27). One end of a blade (normally the distal end) was carefully retouched by removing small blade-like chips to form a scraping edge, which was frequently a perfect semi-circle. Some scrapers were made on thick flakes with a steep convex scraping edge, and are called 'carinate scrapers', whilst others had a narrow convex projection at the scraping end and are called 'nosed scrapers'. 'Straight scrapers' were made on longer flakes and blades, and had abrupt retouch along one straight lateral edge.

Burins

Burins were a very common tool type, and are found in a variety of recurring forms (27). The simplest form of burin was the break burin, which was formed by the removal of a burin spall from the edge of a broken blade. A truncation burin was made by the removal of the burin spall from a retouched truncation at one end of the flake or blade. These truncations can be convex, concave or oblique. The most frequent variety of truncation burin is a single- angle removal, however there are also double-angle removals from the same prepared break. Another major type of burin that is encountered is the dihedral burin, where the spall is removed from a previous burin facet, which is normally unretouched, or from a break or unmodified natural surface. Busked burins have the burin spall terminating in a previously retouched notch on the side of the blank.

Piercers

Piercers were made on small flakes that had been abruptly retouched around part of the edge to form a point (27). Sometimes advantage was taken of a natural edge with the opposing edge modified by retouch, whilst others had both edges abruptly retouched so that they converged to form the point.

Combination tools

Sometimes two different types of tool were combined together on a single blade (27). Various combinations are known, including piercer/burins and scraper/burins. There are also combinations of two tools of the same type, such as two scrapers or two burins. All are generally referred to as combination tools.

THE LATER UPPER PALAEOLITHIC

This final phase of the Palaeolithic, which started around 12,500 BP has been divided into two parts, the Late Upper Palaeolithic (Creswellian), and the Final Upper Palaeolithic. The Creswellian flintwork assemblages have mostly been

The Palaeolithic Period

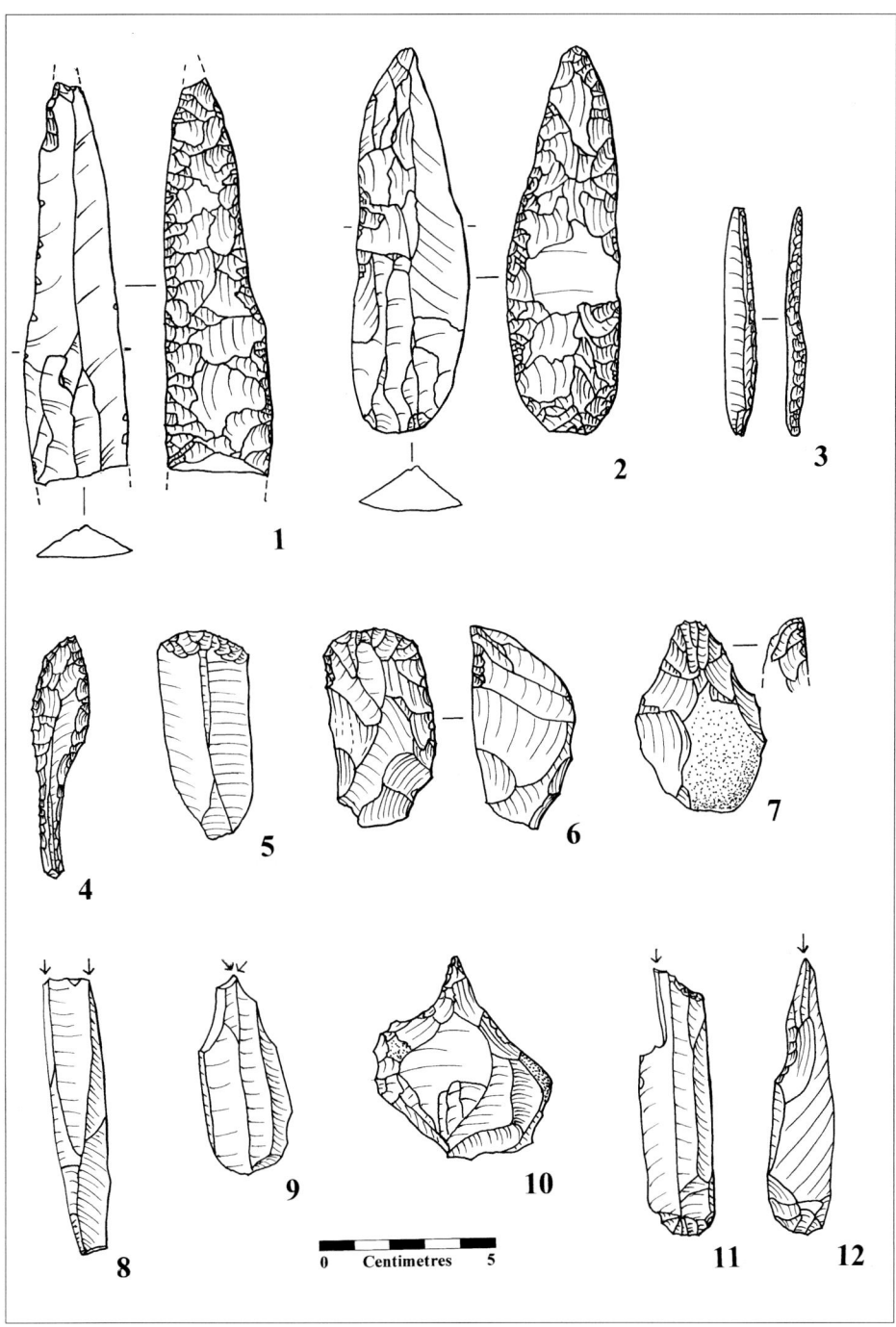

27 Earlier Upper Palaeolithic flintwork: 1-2) Leaf-shaped points; 3) Backed piece; 4) Font-Robert tanged point; 5) End scraper; 6) Carinate scraper; 7) Nosed scraper; 8-9) Dihdral burins; 10) Piercer; 11) Combination tool (truncation burin and end scraper); 12) Combination tool (busked burin and end scraper). *After Campbell and Timms*

found in cave sites such as Anston Cave, Gough's Cave and Kent's Cavern. The continental parallel for the Creswellian is called the Magdelanian. The following types (28) are associated with Creswellian assemblages (Jacobi 1997):

Cores and blades
Good quality flint was selected, even though this may have meant having to transport the raw material some distance from its source. It is possible that the cores were broken down into blades at, or close to, their source; and then transported or exchanged in blade form. The absence of evidence for the initial stages of core reduction at many of the Creswellian sites appears to confirm this (Barton 1997).

The blades appear to have been removed from asymmetrical cores with a single flaking direction. A second opposing platform may have been utilised to correct flaking errors. Core platforms were abraded, and the blade butts were frequently facetted. The blades frequently had a longitudinal curved profile.

Some blade cores may have been prepared using the *en éperon* technique (28). This is characterised by small convergent removals that isolate a spur (*éperon*) on the edge of the platform (Barton 1990). This allows greater precision when using a punch or detaching a blade with a direct blow, and if the spur is positioned above a dorsal ridge, this acts as a guide for the removal.

Trapezoidal backed blades
These blades had a trapezoid shape that was defined by a pair of divergent and rectilinear truncations oblique to the longitudinal axis. The shorter lateral edge between these truncations was either wholly or partially backed. When the backing was partial it may have formed a shoulder at its contact with the unmodified portion. These forms are called 'Cheddar points', and were more likely to have been used as knives than as weapon points. Another variation was the 'Creswellian point', which had an oblique truncation at one end of the blade with the retouch continuing along the shorter lateral edge.

End scrapers
Scrapers were made on blades that had been retouched at one end to form a small convex scraping area. The lateral edges of the blade were also frequently modified with semi-abrupt or scalar retouch.

Burins
Most burins were made on prepared truncations on blades. A number of trapezoidal backed blades had burin-like removals originating from the oblique truncations. It is not clear whether these were the result of impact damage or the creation of a specific tool.

The Palaeolithic Period

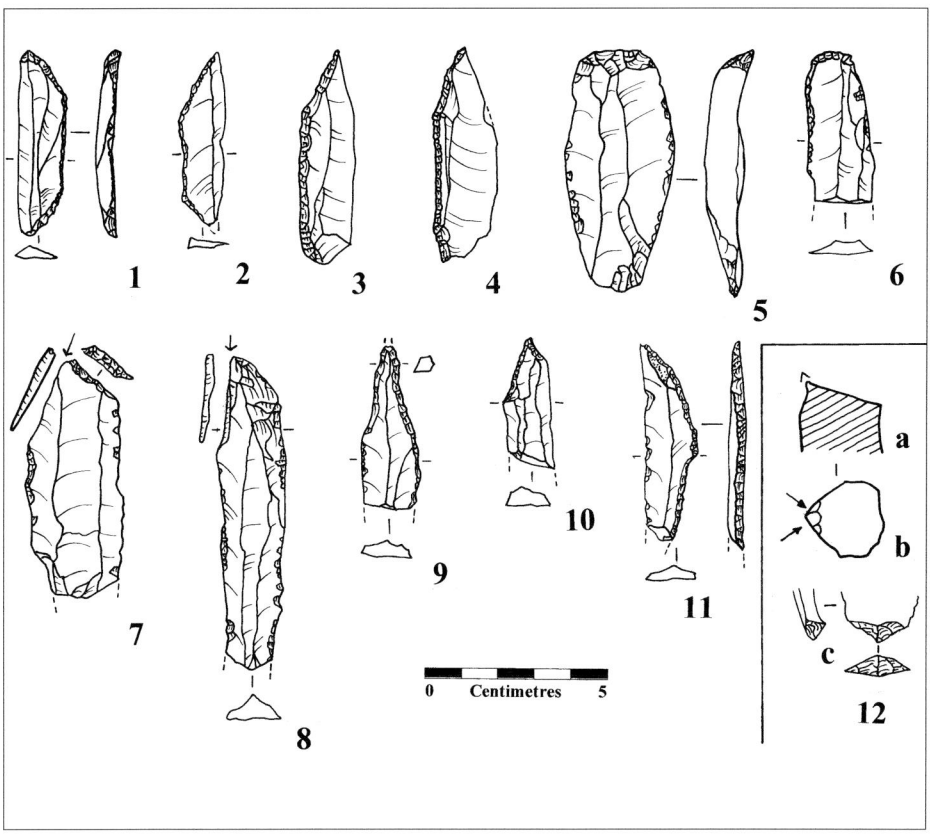

28 Later Upper Palaeolithic flintwork: 1-2) Cheddar points; 3-4) Creswellian points; 5-6) Scrapers; 7-8) Burins (also showing spalls); 9-10) Piercers; 11) Shouldered-backed blade. From Kent's Cavern, Mother Grundy's Parlour, Anston Cave, Gough's Cave and Langwith Cave. *After Campbell.* 12)Illustration of the *en éperon* technique a) side view of core; b) top view of core; c) butt end of blade. *After Barton*

Piercers/Becs

Piercers were frequently made on broken backed blades, and were also combined with scrapers on blades. The retouch was normally on both edges of the same face of the piece, as they converged to form a point.

Other backed blades

There were numerous forms of retouched blades that occurred in assemblages of this date. These forms include partially-backed, truncated-backed, convex-backed blades, and shouldered-backed tools (Campbell 1971).

THE FINAL UPPER PALAEOLITHIC

The second part of the later Upper Palaeolithic is generally referred to as the

Final Upper Palaeolithic, and is represented by over 120 find spots and sites in Britain. The debitage included blades, bladelets and flakes, removed with soft and hard hammers, and cores, which appear to have been reduced in the same way as those in Creswellian assemblages. Cresting was frequently used to prepare the cores for blade production. Core tablets were also a by-product of the knapping process. Core tablets are produced when an exhausted platform was removed from a core with a sharp blow at right angles to its side, thus creating a new platform. Core tablets were also often removed to rejuvenate a damaged platform or to correct faulty flaking angles. The most extensively excavated Final Upper Palaeolithic site is at Hengistbury Head in Dorset, where all stages of the knapping process, together with many finished tools (*29*) were found (Barton 1992).

End scrapers
These were made on both flakes and blades, and were mostly simple end scrapers with a convex distal end modified by semi-abrupt retouch. A small number of scrapers had additional retouch along one or both lateral edges. Occasionally scrapers were combined with other tools (e.g. burins) to make composite/combination tools. Double-end scrapers were also produced in very small numbers.

Tanged and shouldered points
Tanged points were manufactured on blades with direct abrupt retouch used to form a tang at the proximal end and a point at the distal end. The retouch was applied to both lateral edges of the proximal end to thin the blade and thus form the tang. As a result the tang could be central to the main axis of the point, or offset to one side. In the latter case the retouch forms a distinct shoulder at the point where the tang joins the main body of the point. At the distal end the point was frequently formed by abrupt retouch along one lateral edge, which then converged with the opposing natural edge. Occasionally only the part of one lateral edge close to the point was retouched. 'Shouldered points' were also formed on blades. Direct abrupt retouch was used at the proximal end of the blade to form a distinct shoulder on one lateral edge. Occasionally there was additional retouch on the opposite lateral edge near the base. The distal end of the blade was made into a point by an oblique truncation from above the shoulder. Both tanged and shouldered points were probably hafted as arrow points, and fragments of points or tangs resulting from impact breaks are frequently found in assemblages.

Burins
Both dihedral and truncation burins are present in roughly equal proportions in Final Upper Palaeolithic assemblages. Dihedral burins were mostly made on breaks, with others made on natural surfaces. Truncation burins were made on

oblique, concave or straight/convex truncations. A small proportion of both types have multiple burins on the same blank.

Piercers/Becs
These were made on flakes and blades, and occasionally burin spalls, with abrupt retouch on the lateral edges converging to form a point. They were also united with other tool types into combination tools. A *Zinken* was a type of piercer that was made on a thick blank with abrupt retouch forming the point, which was offset from the main axis of the blank.

Curve-backed blades
This tool form was manufactured on a blade or bladelet, and had one lateral edge abruptly retouched to form a convex shape. The opposite lateral edge was normally unretouched and straight. Some pieces had a gap in the retouch at the mid-point along the lateral edge creating an angle between the two areas of retouched edge, and these are called angled-backed blades.

Curve-backed points were curve-backed blades which had both lateral edges at the point end retouched to converge into the point. The retouch on the opposite edge rarely extended very far from the point. The retouch at the point could also be bifacial. Another form of point was a Penknife point, a distinctive piece from the Final Upper Palaeolithic with affinities to similar pieces in some German Upper Palaeolithic assemblages. These had abrupt retouch forming an arc from the unretouched opposite edge at the base of the point to create a small tang (*29*).

Straight-backed blades
These have direct abrupt retouch along one lateral edge of a blade or bladelet forming a straight-backed edge. The profile of the blank tends to be flat and not curved. In some cases, normally where the blank had a naturally abrupt edge, only part of the lateral edge was retouched. Use-damage is frequently present on the opposite unretouched edge, suggesting that these pieces were utilised as knives, although it is not clear whether they were hafted.

Bruised blades
These are usually stout blades of thick or triangular cross section, which can frequently be 120mm or more in length (*29*). They typically have invasive scalar retouch and battering-damage (bruising) along their edges. The blades are mostly soft hammer-struck, and the bulbs are generally heavily abraded. The function of these pieces is uncertain, although experimentation has shown that the edge-damage can be caused by chopping materials such as hardwood, bone and antler, or they were perhaps used for shaping soft stone hammers (Barton 1998).

Prehistoric Flintwork

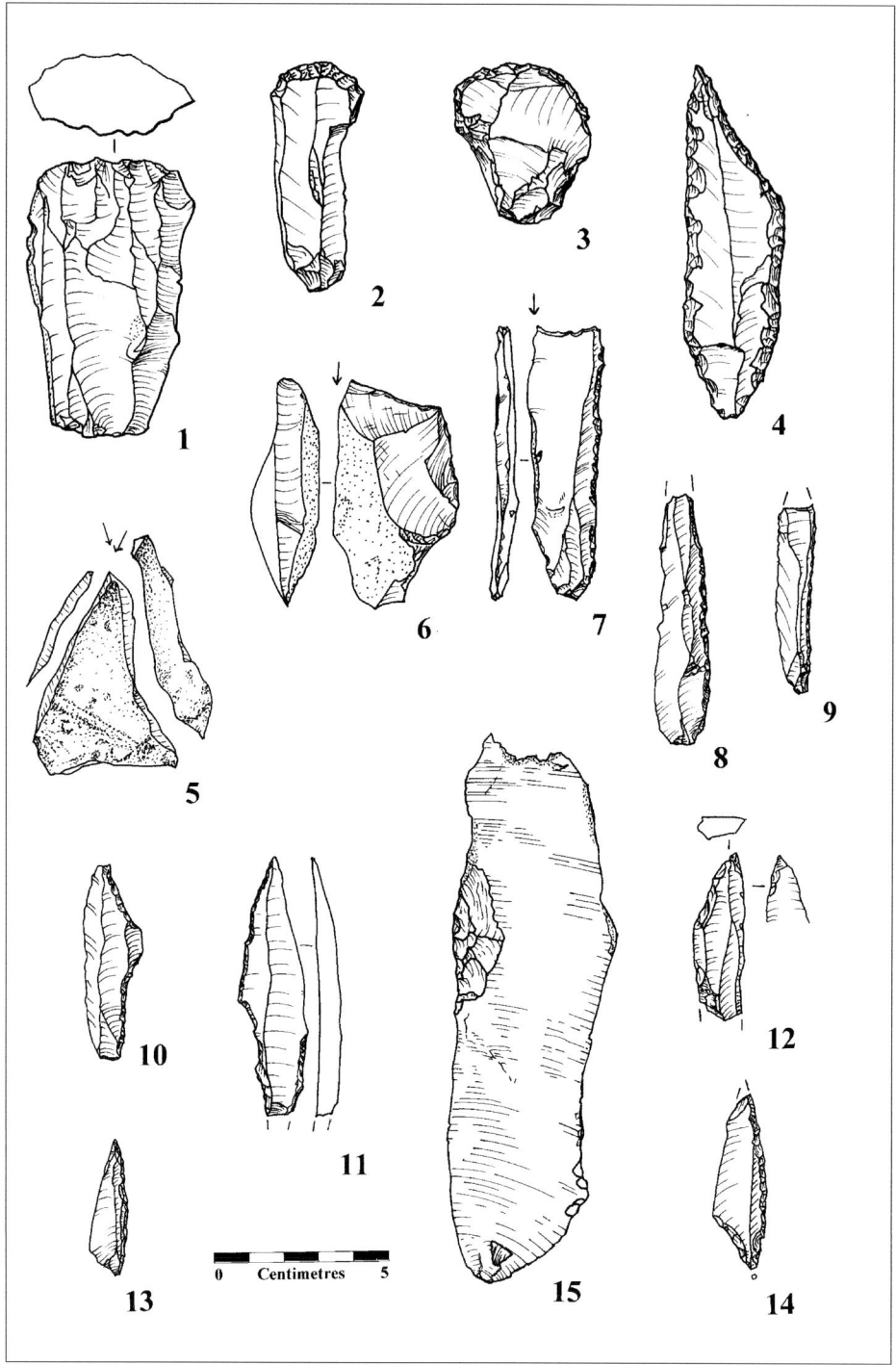

29 Final Upper Palaeolithic flintwork: 1) Blade core; 2-3) End scrapers; 4) Piercer/Bec; 5) Dihedral burin and spalls; 6-7) Truncation burins; 8-9) Straight-backed blades; 10) Shouldered point; 11) Tanged point; 12) Curve-backed point; 13) Backed point; 14) Penknife point; 15) Bruised blade. From Hengistbury Head except nos. 14-15. *After Barton*

Other tools that are occasionally found in small numbers on Final Upper Palaeolithic sites include notched pieces and denticulates normally made on flakes, and truncated blades. Although microliths are found in some Northern European Upper Palaeolithic assemblages, there are very few associations of microliths in Final Upper Palaeolithic assemblages in Britain.

5

THE MESOLITHIC PERIOD

The post-glacial period started around 10,000 BP, initially with an open environment, but by around 9,700 BP temperate conditions had returned to southern Britain, with an expansion in woodland (including the colonisation of juniper, birch, pine and hazel) and woodland animals such as elk, roe deer, pig and beaver. This heralds the start of the Mesolithic period, which is dominated by woodland-based hunter-gatherer activity. Traditionally the Mesolithic period has been divided into two parts; the earlier Mesolithic covering the period from 10,000 BP through to *c*.8,500 BP, and the later Mesolithic from *c*.8,500 BP to the start of the Neolithic around 5,400 BP. Britain became separated from mainland Europe as a result of rising sea levels around 8,000 BP.

The flintwork assemblages found dating from the Mesolithic reflect a hunter-gatherer background, with tool kits predominantly based on hunting equipment. There are two flint implements that are particularly characteristic of the Mesolithic period. First, and most important, is the microlith, which was used in arrows and other composite tools, and broadly defines the whole of the Mesolithic flintworking technology. The microlith will be discussed at some length below. The second implement is the tranchet adze, an important tool that was probably used for carpentry.

Microliths were made from bladelets, and this requirement for bladelets established the basis for most of the Mesolithic flintworking process, except at those sites where microliths are absent or rare. The end product (in this case the microlith) defined the whole process, from the selection of the flint raw material through to the manufacture of the implement. To make microliths, the requirement was not to produce an occasional bladelet from a core that otherwise produced ordinary flakes, but to be able to produce bladelet after bladelet from the same core, all of a consistent size and shape.

To produce bladelets, good quality flint was preferred, but where not available poorer quality flint was used, together with other types of stone where no flint was available. Having selected a nodule of flint, great care was taken throughout the knapping process. The first step was to remove most or all of the cortex from the nodule, which was probably normally done with a hard hammer. Next a striking platform was created by removing a flake from the nodule to provide a suitable platform surface; this was probably also done with a hard hammer.

Much attention was given to the maintenance of the core and its platform(s) throughout the knapping process, including the preparation of the platform edge to remove overhangs, and the rejuvenation of the core when a platform was exhausted. Blades and bladelets were removed from the core with great precision using a soft hammer or perhaps with a punch, although there is little evidence for this. Sometimes cresting was used to assist in the first blade/bladelet removal from a platform, although this was not always necessary. The resulting piece of debitage is called a crested blade, and is very distinctive (*31*). Having removed the crested blade, subsequent removals could follow the ridges left by its removal.

The Mesolithic blades and bladelets are very distinctive as they have all the attributes of soft hammer/punch produced pieces, i.e. small butts, diffuse bulbs of percussion and a lip, together with the distinctive abrasion scars on the dorsal sides of their butts that come from the preparation of the platforms prior to their removal from the core. The blades and bladelets rarely have cortex present on the dorsal side, although a minority in every assemblage will. This confirms that the cores were being initially worked by removing flakes, normally with a hard hammer (or the hardest hammer available) to remove the cortex, before being used for blade/bladelet production. Amongst the bladelets found in some assemblages are small numbers of plunging bladelets, together with hinge and step fractures, demonstrating that while considerable care was being exercised throughout the flaking process, errors and miss-hits were still possible, although this is sometimes the result of a less than perfect raw material.

The process of removing bladelets from a core meant that the platform soon became exhausted, and no further bladelets could be sensibly removed from it. When this occurred, the process appears to have been to turn the core through 180°, to create a new platform at the opposite end and to continue to remove bladelets from this new platform. When this second platform was also exhausted, one of the old exhausted platforms was removed with a sharp blow at 90° from its side, thus creating a new platform, and allowing the removal of bladelets to continue. The piece, including the exhausted platform, removed from the core is a very distinctive piece of debitage, called a core tablet, and is found predominantly in the Mesolithic period (*31*). Mesolithic core tablets would be difficult to tell apart from those used in the Upper Palaeolithic or early Neolithic periods, however the bladelet removals on the Mesolithic cores would leave smaller negative scars, which it may be possible to use to identify them. Core tablets were also often removed to rejuvenate a damaged platform or to correct faulty flaking angles.

Although a single platform was commonly used initially, as described above, there is also some evidence for two opposing platforms being used concurrently

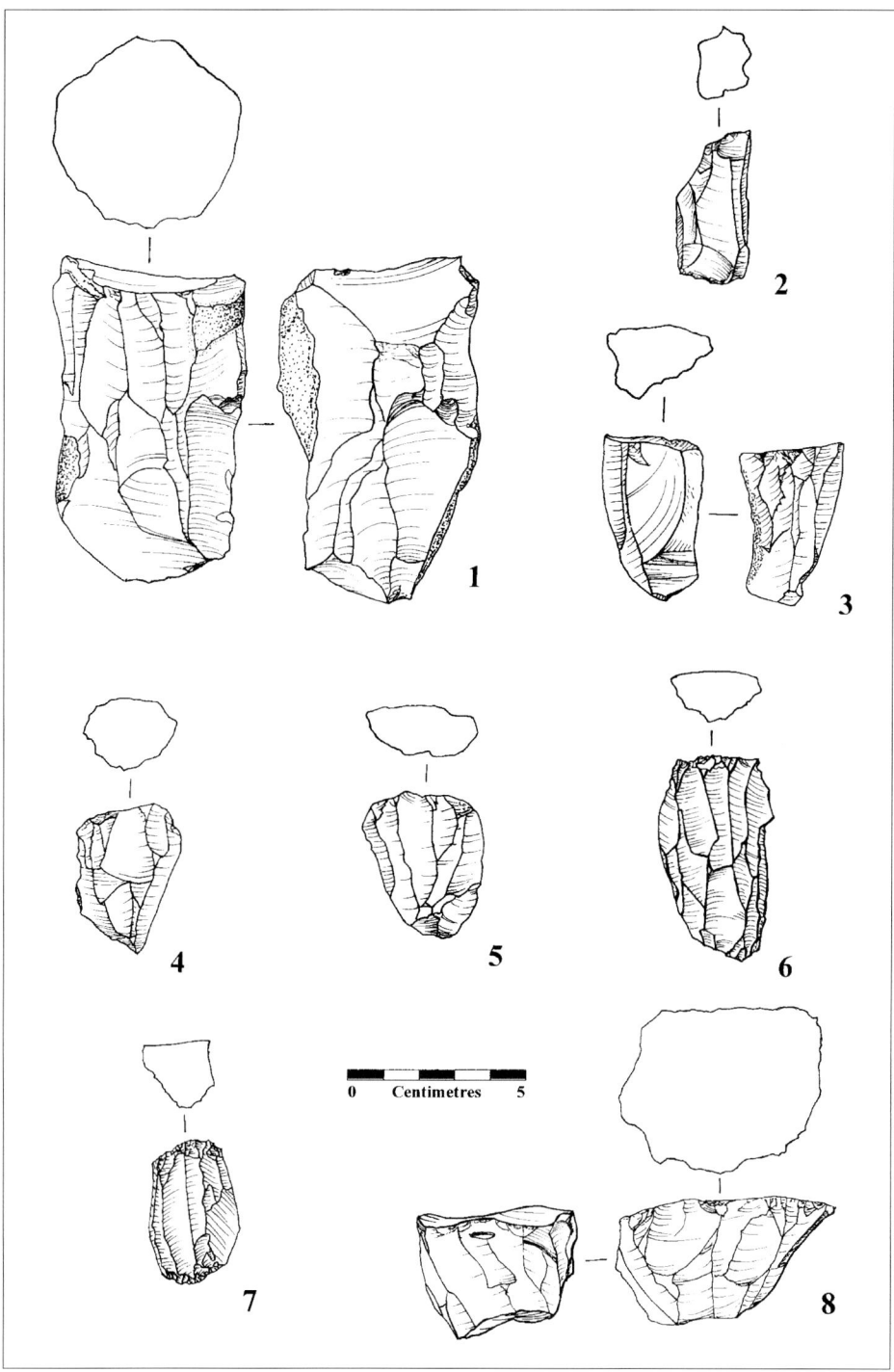

30 Mesolithic bladelet cores: 1) Large blade and bladelet core with two opposing platforms; 2-5) Single-platform bladelet cores; 6-7) Bladelet cores with two opposing platforms (bipolar); 8) Single-platform bladelet and flake core. From Streat Lane and Hengistbury Head. *After Butler and Barton*

with alternate bladelets being removed from each in turn. This latter method would have had the advantage of keeping the core cylindrical throughout, but when a platform became exhausted a core tablet would have been removed to allow the removal of bladelets to continue.

Mesolithic bladelet cores therefore had abraded platforms, although when discarded the final platform would normally have had incipient cones and overhangs left from the last one or two removals. They had either one, or two opposing, platforms and were generally cylindrical or pyramidal (previously called coned) in shape. In the early Mesolithic period cores tend to be larger than those found on later Mesolithic sites, which can be quite small. But size can also be as a result of the small size of the original raw material nodule selected, as well as the very careful working of the core, and the flintknapper's ability to obtain the maximum number of bladelets. Cores were probably curated, that is they were carried around by the knapper who then removed bladelets from the core as and when needed. During the early Mesolithic period it was quite common for thick flakes to be used as cores; a truncation on the flake was used as a platform from which bladelets were then removed. Examples of Mesolithic bladelet cores are shown in Fig. 30.

As well as the core tablet, there were many other examples of core rejuvenation that were used during the Mesolithic period. Numerous flakes, which remove part or all of a platform, were probably produced as a result of the creation of a new platform on both flake and blade/bladelet cores. Sometimes an opposing platform was partly or completely removed from a bladelet core by a plunging blade or flake that purposefully overshot (*11*). Another type of rejuvenation flake is called the *flanc de nucléus*, (*31*) and removed all or part of the flaking face of the core, thus allowing flaking to recommence from the same platform. Sometimes, however, similar pieces can be removed by accidentally striking the core platform too far back from its edge.

It should not be thought that only blades and bladelets were produced during the Mesolithic period. Flakes were also produced in great numbers, as a by-product of initial core reduction, as waste produced during the manufacture of tranchet adzes and other core tools, and for use as implements. Flakes will normally equal or outnumber the blades and bladelets on a Mesolithic site, and where microliths are absent, and core tools predominate, flakes will make up the majority of the debitage. Flakes may have been removed with either a hard or soft hammer, and a large proportion of both types will display the distinctive evidence of platform abrasion on the dorsal side of the butt. Research has shown that the hard hammer flakes tend to be larger, and are more likely to have cortex on the dorsal side, whereas soft hammer flakes are smaller and less likely to have cortex. This is an obvious result of the flaking process outlined above where hard hammers were used initially, and then soft hammers used for the more careful secondary working. Flake cores also tend to be small and well worked, normally with one or two platforms

The Mesolithic Period

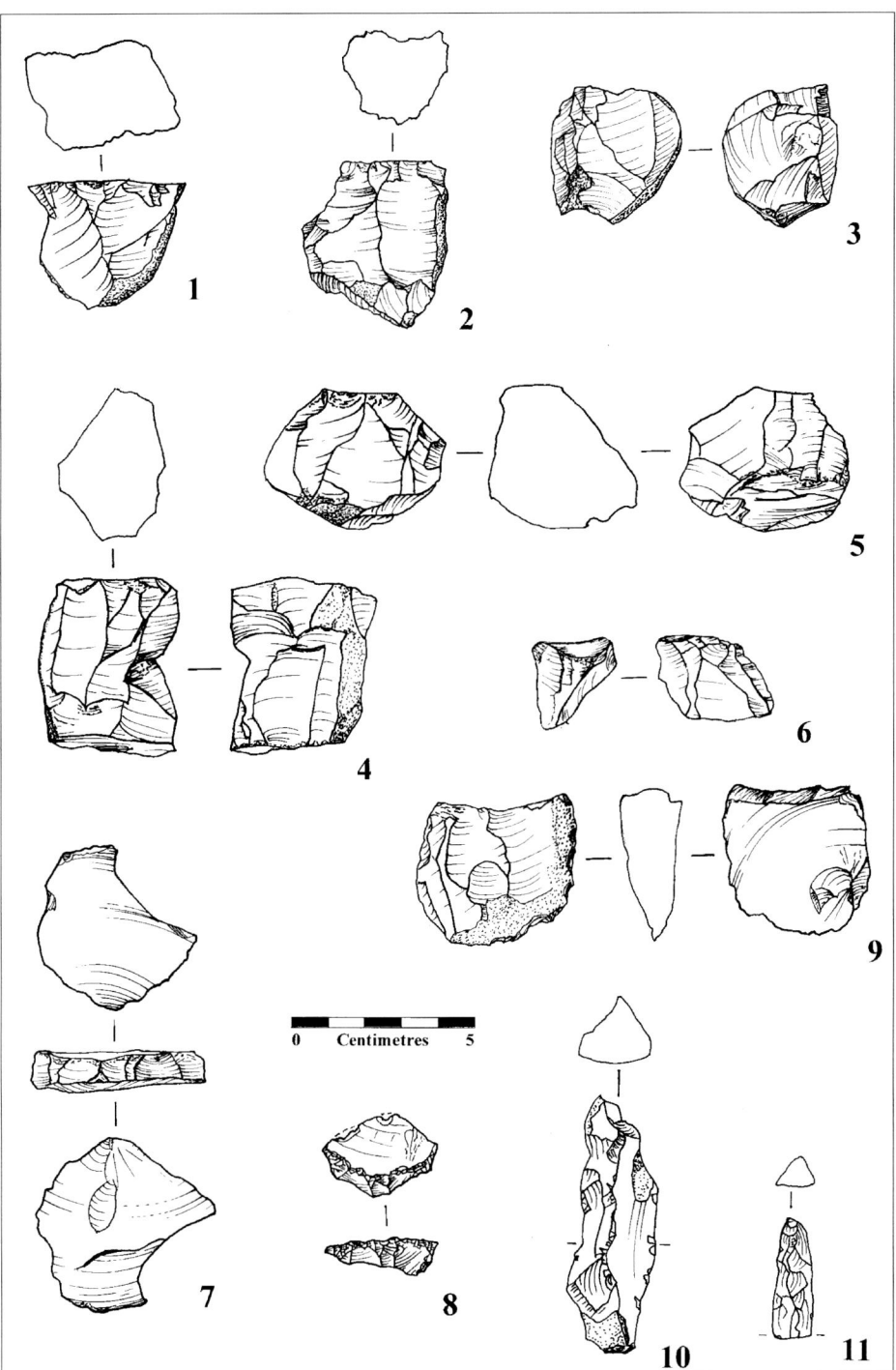

31 Mesolithic flake cores and core debitage: 1-2) Single-platform flake cores; 3) Worked-out two-platform flake core; 4) Two-platform flake core; 5) Multi-platform flake; 6-8) Core tablets; 9) *Flanc de nucléus*; 10-11) Crested blades. From Streat Lane, Pyecombe and Hengistbury Head. *After Butler and Barton*

(*31*) but without the uniformity of the bladelet cores, although many flake cores were subsequently used as blade or bladelet cores. Sometimes after they had been exhausted cores could be reused as hammerstones.

In summary, the debitage from a typical Mesolithic site will include a mixture of flake and blade/bladelet cores with prepared platforms, generally of good-quality flint. The bladelet cores have one or two opposed (bipolar) prepared platforms, are well worked-out, and are normally cylindrical or pyramidal in shape. Core tablets, crested blades and other core rejuvenation flakes will be present in varying proportions. The flakes will be predominantly soft hammer-struck, but hard hammer flakes are also present and a large proportion of the flakes may have evidence of platform preparation. Blades and bladelets will be present in some numbers, and will have been removed with a soft hammer or punch and have evidence of platform preparation.

MICROLITHS

Microliths are one of the major implement types encountered during the Mesolithic period, frequently outnumbering other implements. They were probably multi-functional in that they were used in a number of different composite tools and hunting weapons. They were used most frequently in the manufacture of composite arrows, as the tip or point to a wooden shaft, and also as barbs along the sides of the arrow shaft (*32*). Some examples of microliths arranged in this way have been found both on the continent and here in Britain. One example found in peat at Seamer Carr in North Yorkshire comprised up to 16 microliths possibly arranged along a single (decayed) wooden shaft (David 1998). There are also some examples of microliths found embedded in animal bones. Other possible uses of microliths have been proposed, including reaping tools, harpoons, drill bits, and in threshing or grating blocks (Clarke 1976), or simple cutting tools (Healy *et al.* 1992). The quantity of microliths found on Mesolithic sites, and the variety of shapes and sizes, suggests that they were used in very large numbers, both in hunting and gathering activities.

Most microliths are manufactured from bladelets using the microburin technique (Inizan *et al.* 1992; Neeley *et al.* 1994). This involves the breaking down of the bladelet into a number of smaller pieces, which are then individually turned into microliths. The first stage is the creation, by retouch, of a small notch on the edge of a bladelet supported on a stone anvil. The bladelet is then broken obliquely at the notch (*33*) to remove the proximal end. This creates two pieces, firstly the piece that will be turned into the microlith by retouching one or more edges to create one of the forms detailed below, and secondly a waste piece called a microburin. The microburin has the original butt and bulb of the proximal end of the bladelet, together with part of the notch and the intersecting break facet (*34*).

The Mesolithic Period

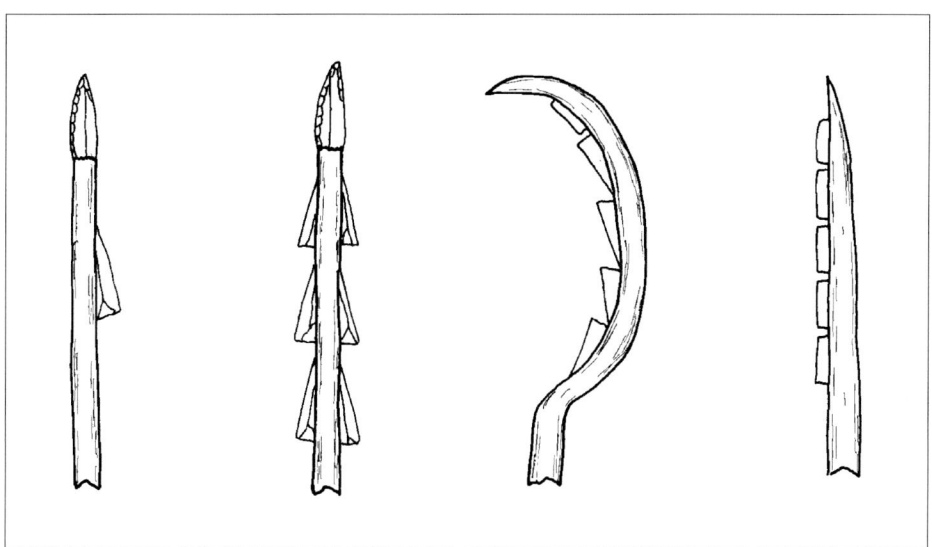

32 Examples of hafted microliths. After Clarke (1976)

   Not all microliths were produced using the microburin technique, and experimentation has shown that even when the technique is employed it does not always result in a recognisable microburin (Finlay 2000). The numerous snapped bladelets and proximal bladelet ends without notches found on Mesolithic sites could be the by-products of a microlith production technique that involved the simple snapping of bladelets into smaller pieces which were then modified by retouching into microliths, or may simply be knapping failures. A second microlith might have been made from the same bladelet, perhaps by using the microburin technique to remove the proximal end, but then either snapping the blade to obtain suitable pieces, or by using the microburin technique at the distal end to remove the tip. Distal end microburins are much more rare than the proximal end variety. Another form of microburin is the Krukowski microburin (*34*), although this may have resulted from an accidental break whilst retouching a microlith; breaking off the tip; leaving a microburin type facet at the break; or as a by-product from the repointing of a microlith.

  Some research has been undertaken on microliths using microwear analysis, but the results have been inconclusive. However, experimentation has identified breaks on microliths that were thought to have resulted from impact against a hard object, such as bone or the ground (Barton and Bergman 1982), as would be the case if they were being used in projectiles (*34*).

  The first classification of microlith forms was proposed by Clark in (1934a), who divided microliths into eight groups dependent upon their shape and the extent and location of retouch (*35*). More recently modifications have been proposed to this classification scheme (e.g. Jacobi 1978 and Palmer

Prehistoric Flintwork

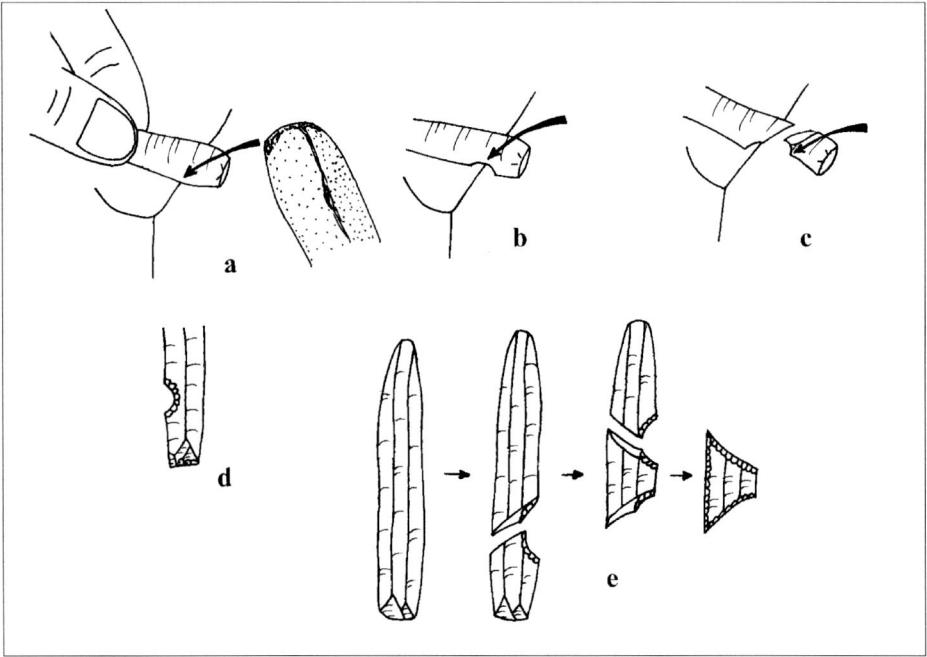

33 Microlith production using the microburin technique. Using an anvil (a) a small notch is created (b and d), and the proximal end of the bladelet is then broken off producing a microburin (c). Part (e) shows the transition from the original bladelet, discarding first the proximal microburin, and then a distal microburin, leaving the mesial section which is retouched to form the microlith. After Piel-Desruisseaux

1977), however Clark's model is still used by some lithic specialists as the basis for classifying microliths, although some of the terminology has changed.

CLASSIFICATION OF MICROLITH FORMS (After Clark 1934a, with modifications)

Group A: Obliquely-blunted forms
Group A comprises pieces that are obliquely blunted down part of one edge, sometimes with a minimal amount of retouch on the opposite edge near the point. Obliquely-blunted points occur throughout the Mesolithic period, although they reduce in size from around some 40mm in length in the early Mesolithic to about 20mm in length in the later Mesolithic. Clark grouped them into two varieties; those that form an angle with either the left or right edge blunted (*35*, 1 and 2), and those that form an arc with either the left or right edge blunted (*35*, 3 and 4).

The Mesolithic Period

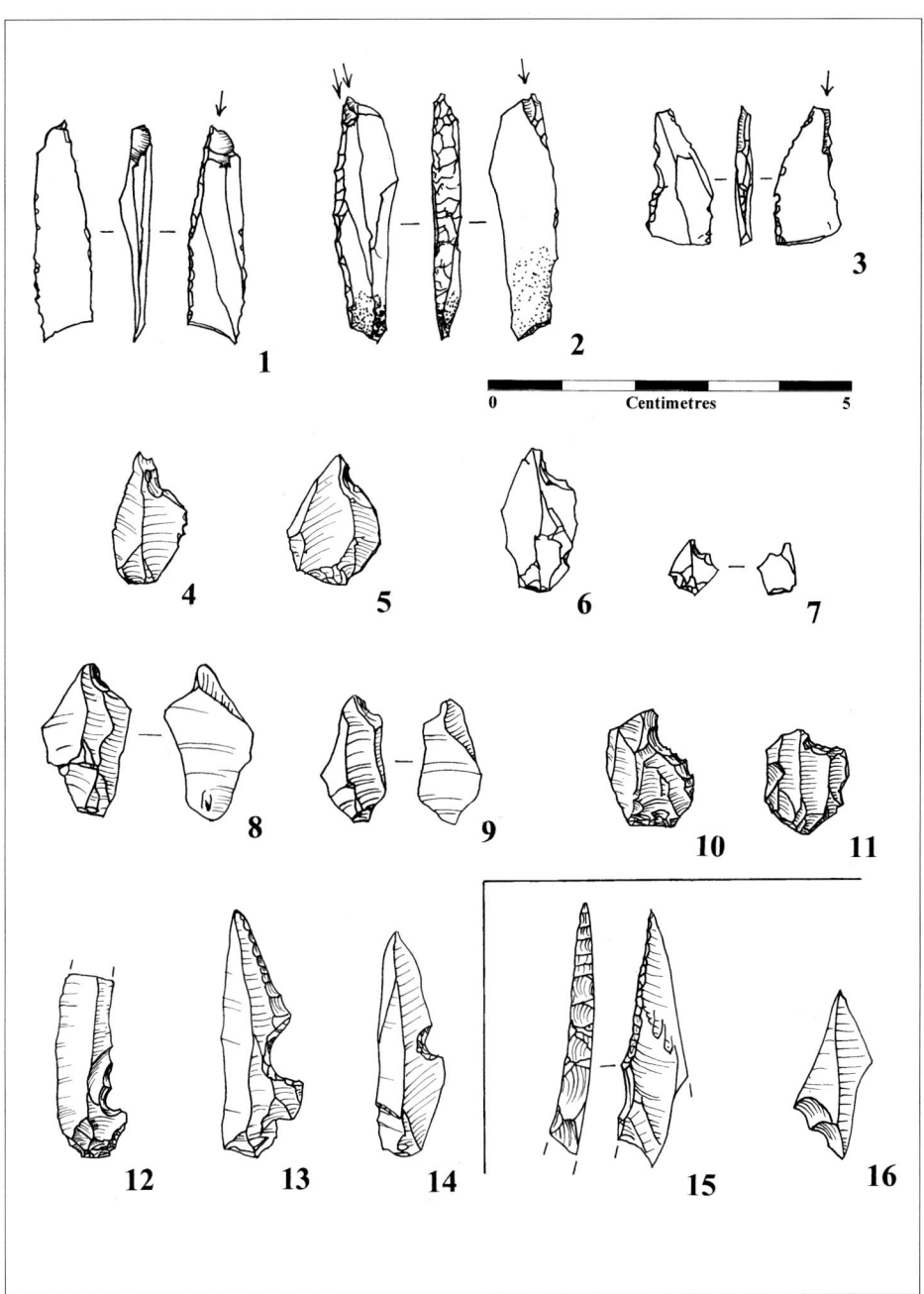

34 Microlith debitage: 1-3) Microliths with impact fractures; 4-9) Microburins; 10-11) Microburin miss-hits; 12-14) unfinished microliths; 15-16) Krukowski microburins (enlarged). From Hengistbury Head and Star Carr. *After Barton and Clark*

Group B: Backed forms

This group comprises pieces that are backed or blunted down one or both edges, with sometimes the blunting only extending partially down one edge. Clark divided these into two groups; firstly straight-backed types, where the retouch extends down the whole of one edge (*35*, 5), and secondly pieces that are partially-backed down one edge, and occasionally backed down the whole of the opposite edge (*35*, 6). Lanceolate (lance-point shape) forms have two curved retouched edges terminating in a point and are an early Mesolithic form. Rod forms have two retouched straight parallel edges, and tend to date to the later Mesolithic.

Group C: Blunted down one edge and across the base

This group comprises pieces that are blunted down one edge, and also either obliquely (*35*, 7 and 8) or transversely retouched (*35*, 9 and 10) across the base. Sometimes referred to as bi-truncated microliths.

Group D: Geometric forms

This group is the largest group with some seven different types of geometric forms. These types of microlith appear during the transition from the early to later Mesolithic and continue on throughout the later Mesolithic. The borderline between some of these categories is hazy; for example crescents often discretely merge into lozenges. The seven types are: Isosceles (*35*, 11) and Scalene triangles, which occasionally have retouch on the opposite edge (*35*, 12 and 13); Crescents with the arc blunted (*35*, 14): or with the straight edge blunted (*35*, 15); Lozenge forms (*35*, 16); Lanceolate forms (*35*, 17); Sub-triangular forms, where one end terminates in the unretouched tip of the original bladelet (*35*, 18); Trapezoids (*35*, 19); and Rhomboids or Rhombic points (*35*, 20).

Group E: Points with inverse retouch at the base

This group has retouch blunting the opposite side of the piece at the base, forming either a straight base or a pointed base (*35*, 21).

Group F: Hollow-based points

This group includes the classic Horsham point, and is divided into four different categories dependant upon whether the piece is symmetrical or asymmetrical, and the direction of the retouch at the base. They are 1a: Symmetrical and retouched from the dorsal side (*35*, 22); 1b: Asymmetrical and retouched from the dorsal side (*35*, 23); 2a: Symmetrical and retouched from the ventral side (*35*, 24), and 2b: Asymmetrical and retouched from the ventral side (*35*, 25).

The Mesolithic Period

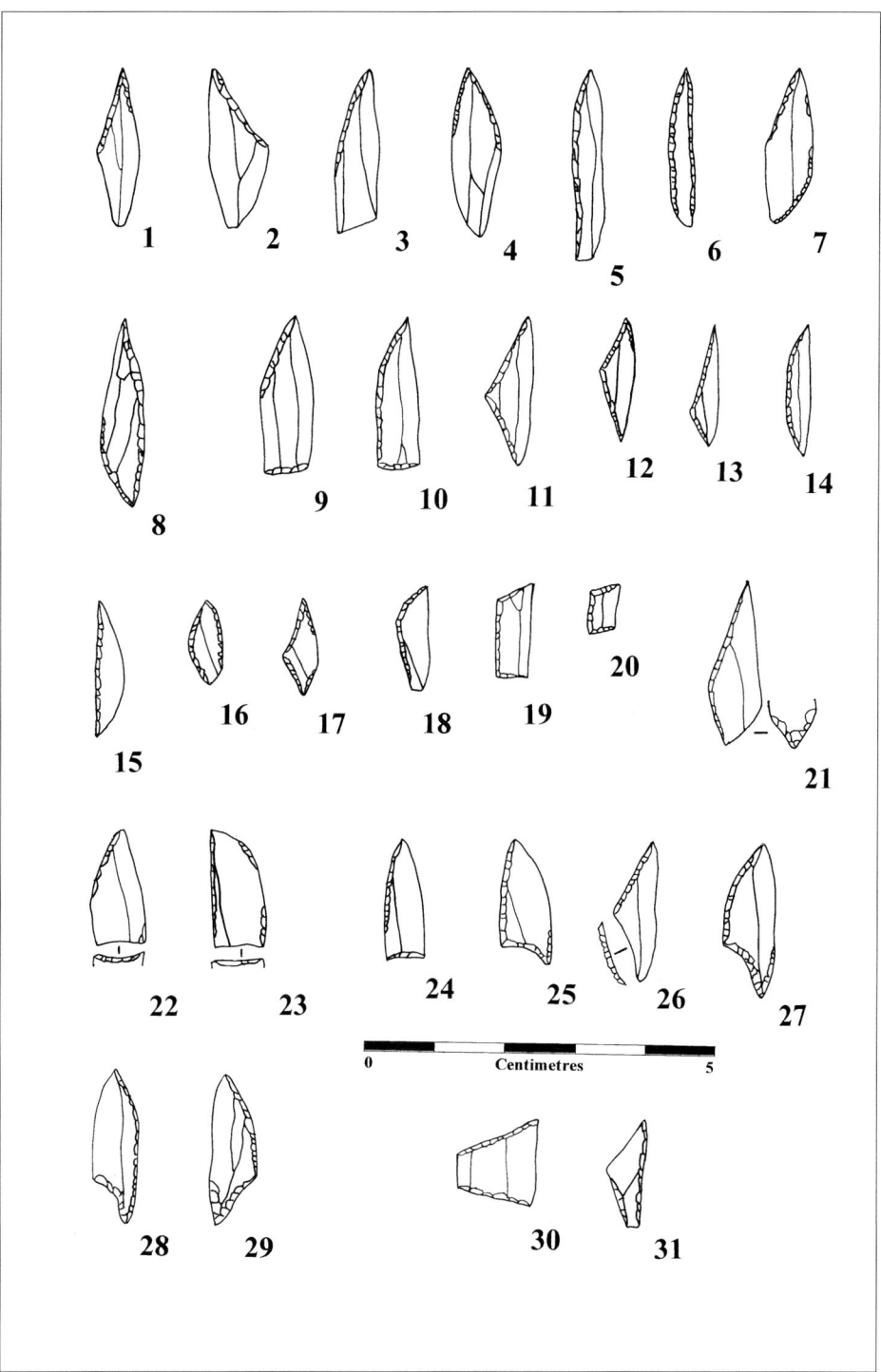

35 Clark's microlith classification scheme. 1-4) Type A; 5-6) Type B; 7-10) Type C; 11-20) Type D; 21) Type E; 22-25) Type F; 26-29) Type G; 30-31) Type H. See text for descriptions. *After Clark*

Prehistoric Flintwork

Group G: Shouldered or tanged points
These forms differ from the Upper Palaeolithic tanged points in that they are much smaller, and are made using the microlith notch technique to create an offset tang. Clark divided them into two groups; those with the tang formed by a notch retouched from dorsal side (*35*, 26-29), and those with the tang formed by a notch retouched from ventral side They date from the earlier Mesolithic, and may have parallels with some continental cultures.

Group H: Trapeze-shaped microliths
Also referred to as micro-tranchet microliths. They can be classified as narrow based, with either straight or curved edges, or broad based with either straight or curved edges (*35*, 30 and 31). These should not be confused with *petit tranchet* arrowheads, which are a Neolithic arrowhead form.

AN ALTERNATIVE MICROLITH CLASSIFICATION

Roger Jacobi developed a typology of microliths for the Wealden Mesolithic flint assemblages, which divided up 13 classes of microlith and bladelets into four groups (Jacobi 1978). These are: a) Broad-blade microliths b) Narrow-blade microliths c) Hollow-based bladelets; and d) Inversely retouched bladelets (*36*). This is a simpler classification, which provides greater flexibility in microlith typology, moving away from some of Clark's more hypothetical forms.

Group a:
1a and b	Obliquely truncated (b: with additional retouch on leading-edge)
$1a^c$ and $1b^c$	Partially backed (b^c: with additional retouch on leading edge)
2a	Isosceles triangle
$2a^s$	Large scalene triangle
2b	Bi-truncated trapezoidal blade/bladelet
3a	Bi-truncated rhombic blade/bladelet
3b	Obliquely truncated with retouch to symmetrical pointed base
3c and 3d	Lanceolate
4	Convex-backed

Group b:
5a and 5b	Straight-backed bladelets (b: with additional retouch on leading edge)
5c and 5d	Asymmetrical and symmetrical micro-tranchet
5e	Straight-backed bladelet with retouch on leading edge and squared base

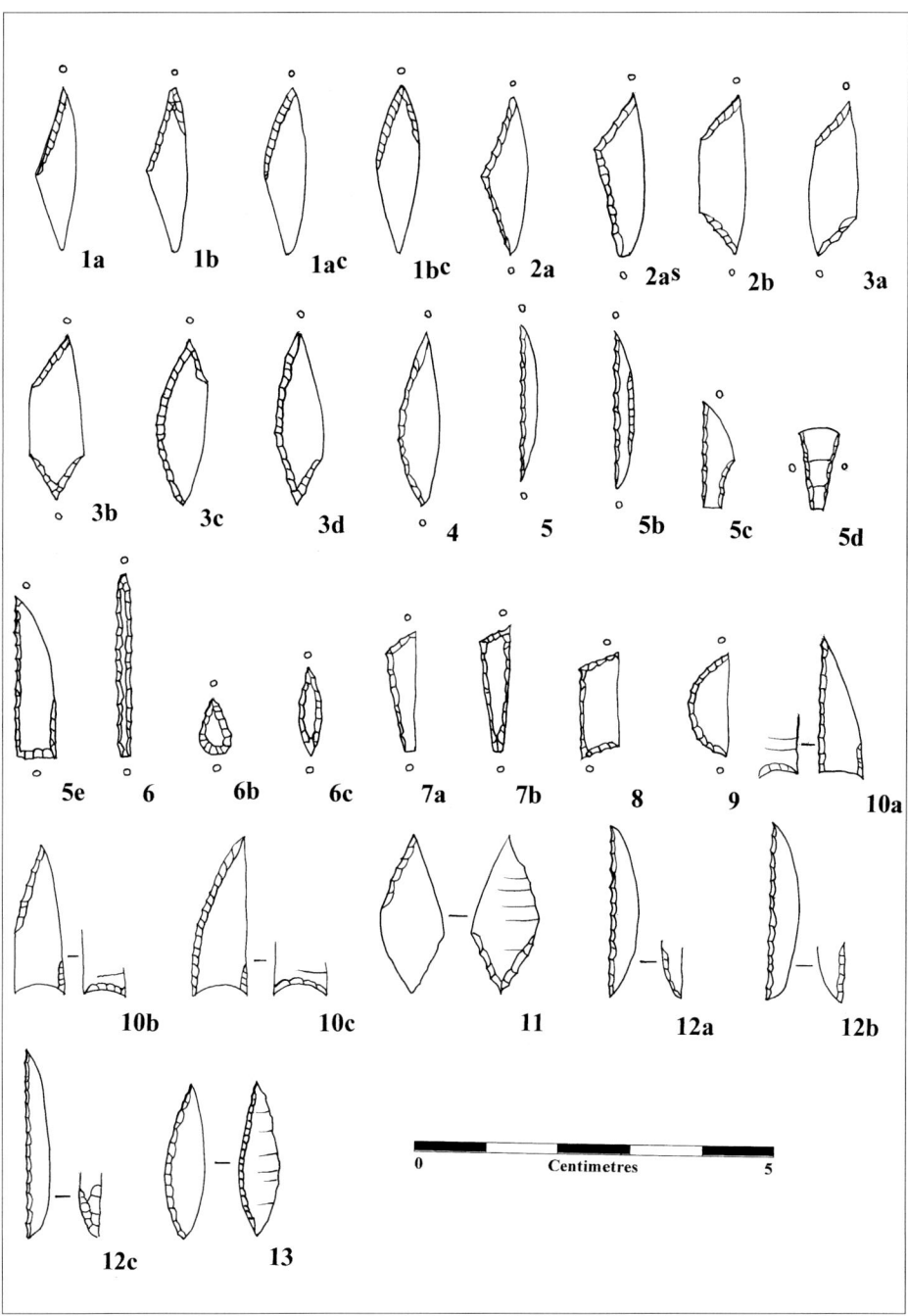

36 Jacobi's microlith classification scheme. See text for descriptions. *After Jacobi*

6a	Rod
6b	Pear-shaped microlith
6c	Boat-shaped microlith
7a and 7b	Small scalene triangles (scalene micro-triangle)
8	Four-sided microlith (micro-rhomboid)
9	Lunate microlith

Group c:

10a	Asymmetrical point with concave basal modification (Horsham point)
10b	Obliquely-truncated with concave basal modification
10c	Symmetrical point with concave basal modification

Group d:

11	Obliquely-blunted with inverse retouch to symmetrical pointed base
12a	Straight-backed with inverse retouch on the leading edge
12b	Straight-backed with inverse retouch on the same lateral edge
12c	Straight-backed with inverse retouch on both lateral edges
13	Convex-backed blade with inverse retouch along the leading edge

MICROLITHS AS A DATING AID

Due to the variety of different microlith forms, and armed with the knowledge that there are variations in the types of microlith that make up assemblages of different dates, it is possible to use microliths as a rough dating tool. There are few accurate radiocarbon dates for the Mesolithic period, but those that are secure have confirmed the broad chronological sequence. For the earlier Mesolithic, microliths tend to be larger, and at first sight appear to be simpler shapes. Three major typological groupings of microliths have been identified, and are named after the sites at Star Carr, Deepcar and Horsham (Reynier 1998). The classification of these three groups can be summarised as:

Star Carr type:
Dominated by broad, obliquely-blunted points, with isosceles triangles and trapezoids being the only other microlith forms present in any frequency. Such assemblages are few in number, and mostly restricted to northern England, Wales and Scotland where they are normally situated at higher altitudes.

Deepcar type:
Characterised by obliquely-blunted points and long slender partially-backed points. Isosceles triangles and elongated trapezoids are rare. The partially-backed points outnumber obliquely-backed points, and there are an unusually

1 Flint raw material: tabular flint (left) nodular flint (top right) and beach pebble (centre bottom)

2 Flint seams showing in the chalk cliffs of the South Downs, and a shingle beach near Birling Gap, Sussex

3 Nodules of the distinctive Bullhead flint with a thin orange layer below a greenish-black cortex

4 A prehistoric flintknapper at work: reconstruction at the Roc de Cazelle archaeological park in the Dordogne. Note the other stone and antler hammers at his feet

5 A selection of flint cores; mostly well worked out Mesolithic bladelet cores

6 A modern flintknapper's kit, showing a range of hard and soft hammers, pressure flakers, and a rubbing stone. *C. Goodey*

7 Various natural pieces of flint: Top and bottom right are frost fractured pieces, top left is a starch fracture, whilst the others are natural or thermal flakes

8 A selection of different (mostly later Neolithic) scrapers

9 The Boxgrove excavations. Copyright: Boxgrove Project

10 In situ knapping debris from handaxe manufacture at Boxgrove. Copyright: Boxgrove Project

11 Acheulian handaxe from Barcombe, Sussex

12 A Mesolithic tranchet adze manufactured on flint from a Clay-with-flints outcrop at Pyecombe, Sussex

13 A section through a pit at the Streat Lane Mesolithic site, showing the darker 'tip lines' where waste from cooking had been thrown into the pit

14 A reconstruction of a tent structure at Le Thot, France, resembling the remains of a similar structure found at Streat Lane

15 A reconstruction of a lean-to shelter constructed against a rock face at Tursac, France

16 Replica hafted arrowheads: left to right are leaf-shaped, transverse and barbed-and-tanged

17 Neolithic axe roughout, polished axe and flaked axe (from left to right)

18 A *polissoir* on Fyfield Down near Avebury. The long grooves resulting from the continual polishing or sharpening of axes can clearly be seen on this stone

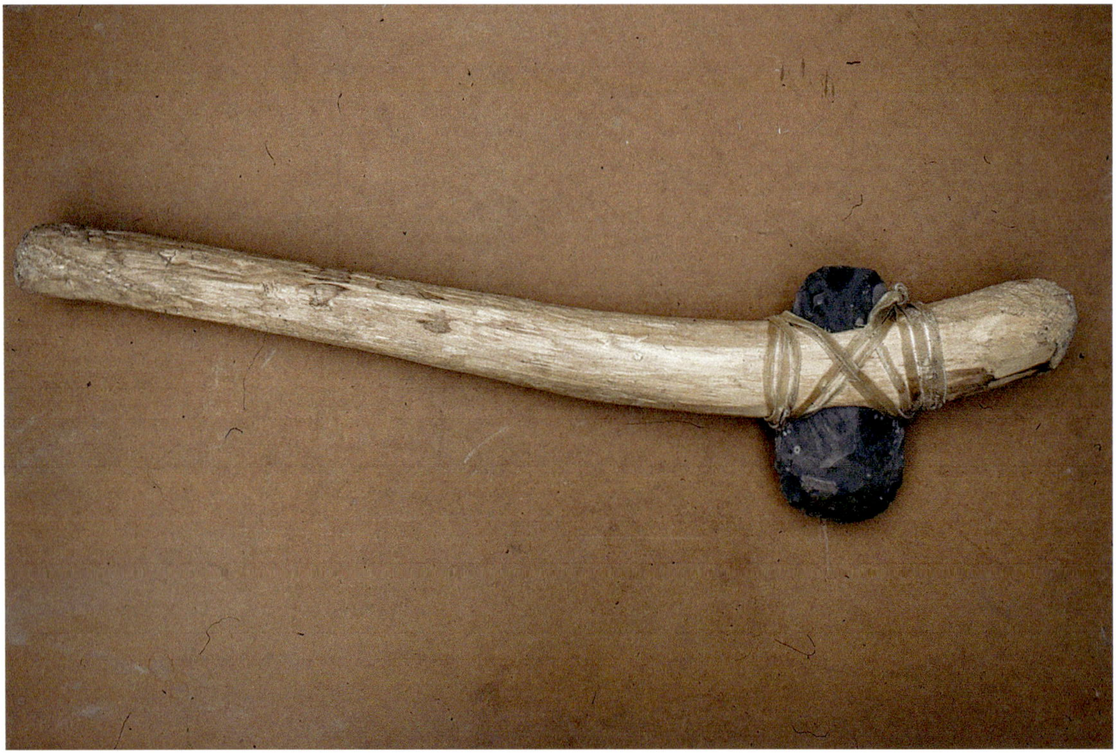

19 A modern example of a flaked axe hafted into a wooden handle

20 A Neolithic flaked axe

21 Above: A gallery radiating out from the bottom of a flint mine shaft at Grimes Graves, Norfolk. Note the seam of flint on the lower right hand side of the photograph. The wooden supports are modern

22 Below: Antler pick, with axe roughout and axe-thinning flakes from the Cissbury flint mines, Sussex

23 Above: The excavation of a Neolithic flint mineshaft by the British Museum at Harrow Hill, Sussex in 1982. *Fred Aldsworth*

24 Right: A flint open-cast quarry excavated at Harrow Hill in 1986 by Robin Holgate

25 An early Bronze Age round barrow

26 Modern replica one-piece sickles, showing how they may have been hafted into a wooden handle

27 The Amesbury Archer: An example of a Beaker burial with 16 barbed-and-tanged arrowheads, together with two flint caches that included flint knives, scrapers, a fabricator and flakes as grave goods. *Copyright: Wessex Archaeology*

28 Crowlink Barrow, Sussex. The flint cairn was used as a source of raw material in the later Bronze Age

29 The continued use of flint as a building material into the Roman period is illustrated here by its employment in the walls of Richborough Castle in Kent

The Mesolithic Period

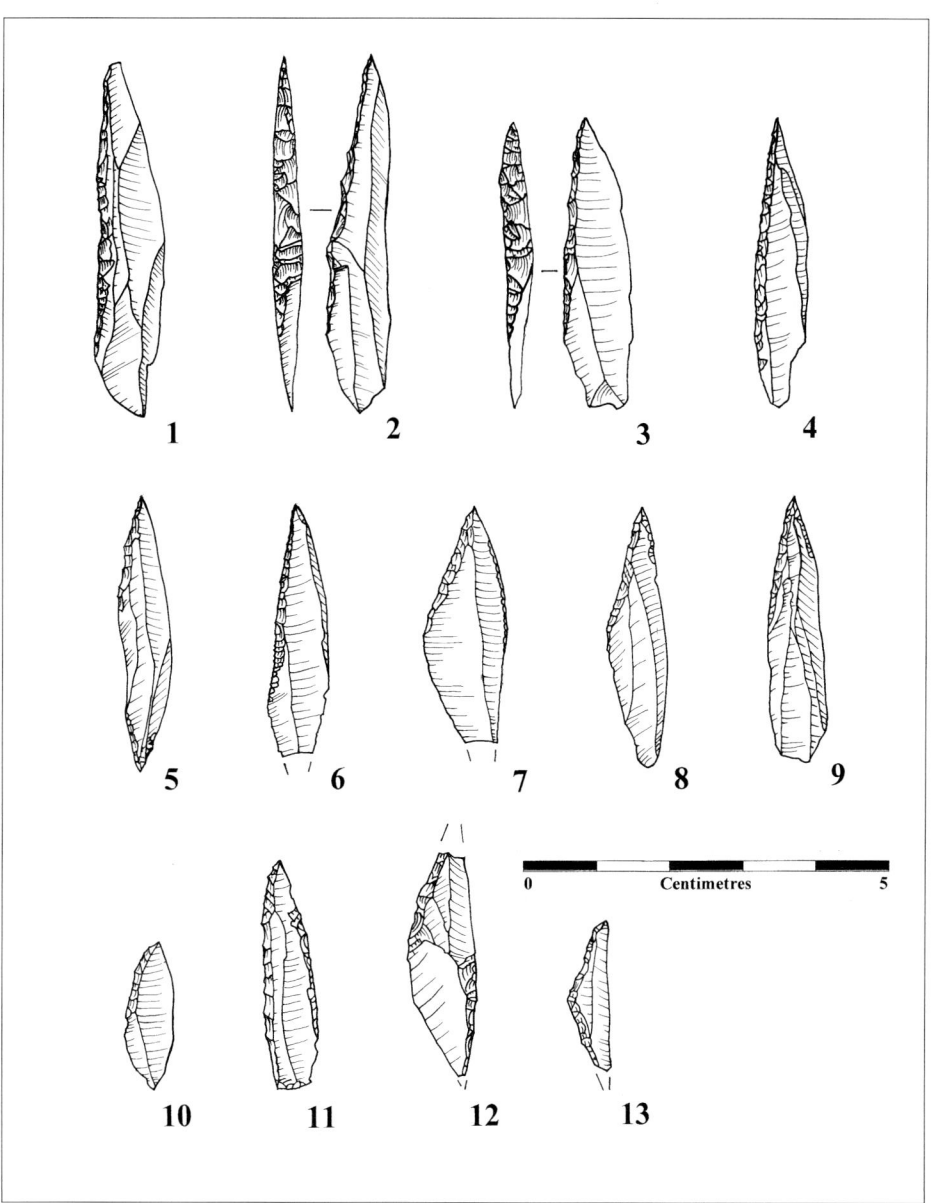

37 Hengistbury Head microliths: 1-10) Obliquely-blunted microliths (2 has bidirectional retouch, 5 has additional basal retouch, and 8 and 9 have additional retouch near the tip); 11) Straight-backed bladelet; 12) Obliquely bi-truncated microlith; 13) Isosceles triangle. *After Barton*

high proportion of points with leading-edge retouch. These assemblages are more numerous than the other types, and are spread fairly evenly across southern England, Wales and the north of England, but are scarce in central England.

Horsham type:
These assemblages have a diverse array of microlith types. Usually dominant are short squat obliquely-blunted points. Partially-backed points are absent or rare. In addition there are various geometric forms such as isosceles triangles and rhomboids.

However, the most distinctive microlith form is the hollow-based point, including the Horsham point. Horsham-type assemblages have an almost exclusive south-east England distribution, mostly corresponding to the Wealden area, but also extend northwards as far as Lincolnshire, and west to Somerset and Devon. The Horsham assemblages are derived from northern France, and are possibly later than Deepcar assemblages. They may continue into the later Mesolithic period, but this is not certain, and could be described as middle Mesolithic.

In the later Mesolithic, some of the earlier microlith forms such as obliquely-blunted points continue to be used, although they are generally much smaller in size. The obliquely-blunted microlith is scarce in uncontaminated later Mesolithic assemblages, so it is likely that this type may be residual on most of the later Mesolithic sites. However, the predominant microlith forms are the various geometric types. The reasons for this change are not entirely clear, although a change in hunting strategy may be responsible. Arrows may have been tipped in a different way, with these smaller less robust points perhaps being more appropriate for close range hunting in a wooded environment (Holgate 2003).

Microliths from a number of different sites are illustrated in figures *37* to *39* to give an idea of the variety and types of microlith found, and these can be compared with the examples in the categorisation above. The three sites have been chosen so that there are examples from the early Mesolithic, a Horsham assemblage, and then the later Mesolithic. Firstly, there are some microliths from the early Mesolithic site at Hengistbury Head in Dorset. The microliths from this site are overwhelmingly obliquely-blunted points, with just a few straight-backed points, obliquely bi-truncated points, and an isosceles triangle (*37*). Second is the site of Kettlebury 103 in Surrey, of the Horsham tradition (Ellaby 1987), which produced obliquely-blunted points, a high proportion of triangles and asymmetrical hollow-based Horsham points (*38*). The third site is a later Mesolithic site at Hermitage Rocks in East Sussex (Jacobi *et al.* 1981), which produced mostly scalene pieces and short lanceolate pieces, with smaller numbers of straight-backed points and four-sided pieces, and a single Horsham point (*39*).

The Mesolithic Period

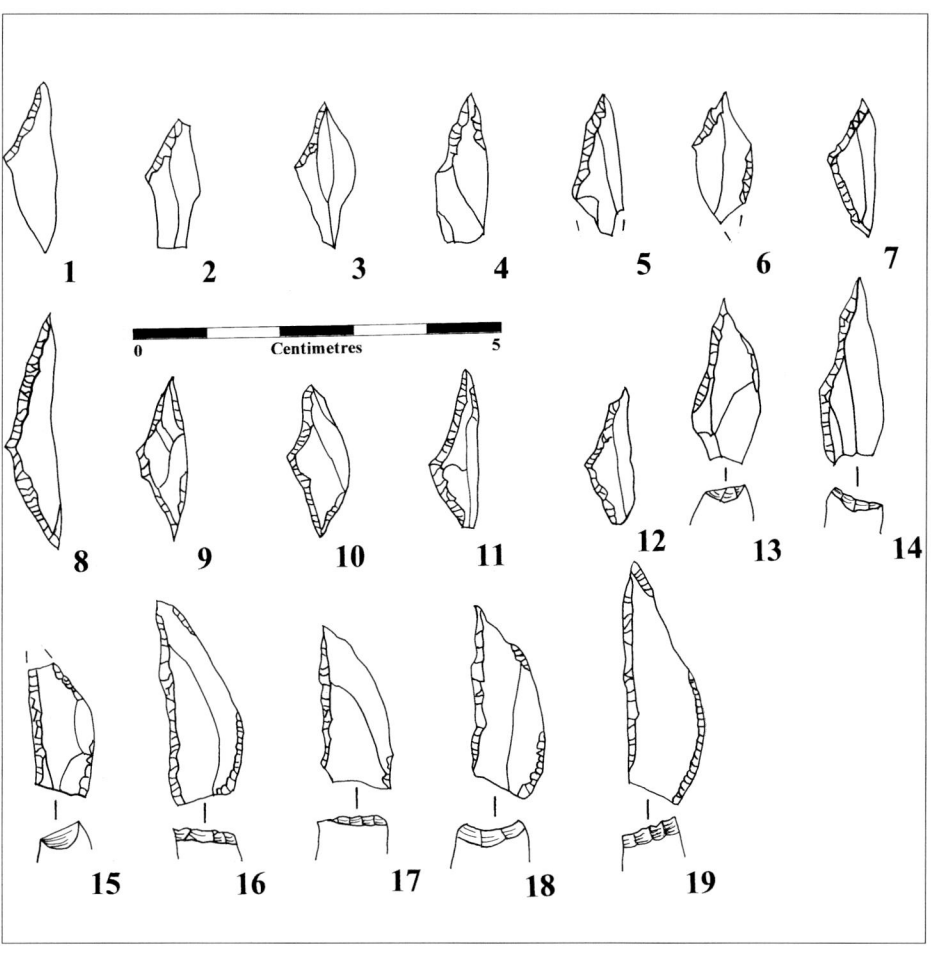

38 Kettlebury 103 Microliths: 1-6) Obliquely backed points; 7-12) Isosceles triangles; 13-19) Horsham points. *After Ellaby*

TRANCHET ADZES

The tranchet adze is a very distinctive core tool that was manufactured during the Mesolithic period, and is frequently mistakenly referred to as an axe. There have been suggestions that tranchet adzes continued to be used in the Neolithic, but there is no definite evidence for this. The tranchet adzes concerned came from surface collections that produced mixed Mesolithic and Neolithic assemblages. In the southeast there is an apparent increase in the use of tranchet adzes during the later Mesolithic, however elsewhere the opposite appears to be true with more tranchet adzes being associated with early Mesolithic assemblages. In the north of Britain, where a variety of raw material sources was used in the different phases of the Mesolithic, it is possible to link tranchet adzes with some degree of certainty to either the earlier or later Mesolithic.

The process by which a tranchet adze was manufactured from a nodule of flint was as follows. Having selected a suitable nodule of raw material, initial flaking was carried out with a hard hammer, probably removing flakes from one face of the nodule first, and then removing flakes from the opposite face (Ashton 1988). This would have removed most of the cortex from the nodule, and shaped the nodule into the approximate outline of the adze; this is called a roughout (*40*). The preparation flakes from this initial flaking have the expected broad butts and pronounced bulb of percussion resulting from the use of a hard hammer. On the dorsal side of the preparation flakes, the negative scars would be multi-directional, reflecting the removal of flakes from that surface from both edges of the nodule.

The next stage of manufacture was to shape the roughout, and to prepare the surface of the adze near to the blade for the removal of the final sharpening flake. On some sites the finishing flakes removed during this shaping process have some of the characteristics associated with soft hammer production: thin profiles, narrow butts and longitudinally curved, but without the diffuse bulb and small lip of typical soft hammer-struck flakes. It is therefore more likely that the finishing flakes were removed with a hard hammer, with blows falling close to the edge of the platform formed by the edge of the nodule (Ashton 1988). However, on other sites these finishing flakes have all of the attributes associated with having been removed with a soft hammer. Once the overall shape of the adze had been achieved (called a preform (*40*)), the final tranchet adze-sharpening flake that gives the adze its name could be removed.

The sharpening flake was struck from the lateral edge of the adze, near the blade, which removed a transverse flake across the blade of the adze and by doing so produced a sharp cutting edge. Occasionally one or two small additional flakes may have been removed to tidy up the blade of the adze. The tranchet adze-sharpening flake is a distinctive piece: having been removed with a hard hammer, a prominent bulb and butt are normally present, together with the relict edge of the preform adze blade on one edge (*40*). As well as having a sharpening flake removed during its manufacture, any breaks or blunting to the cutting edge whilst in use could be simply repaired by the removal of a further sharpening flake.

In southern Britain, tranchet adzes were probably manufactured from flint nodules obtained from the Clay-with-flints outcrops on the chalk Downs (*colour plate 12*) or occasionally from beach deposits. These would have provided suitably sized nodules for working into adzes, which could have been exploited by hunter-gatherer groups during their annual cycle of food and resource procurement (Holgate 2003). Some tranchet adzes may have been made from large flakes. Tranchet adzes would have been hafted, probably into a wooden

The Mesolithic Period

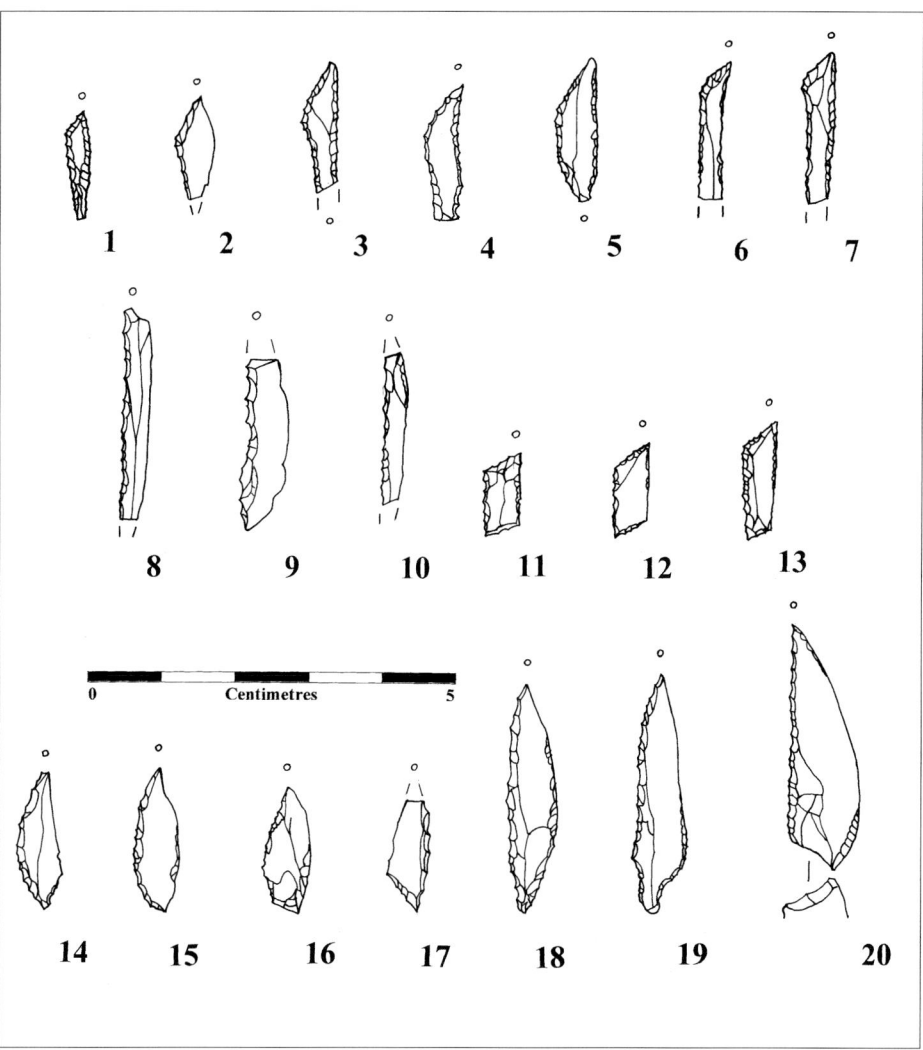

39 Hermitage Rocks microliths: 1-7) Scalene pieces; 8-10) Straight-backed bladelets; 11-13) Four-sided pieces; 14-17) Short lanceolate pieces; 18-19) Elongated lanceolate pieces; 20) Horsham point. *After Jacobi* et al.

handle or antler sleeve, as evidenced by examples from Denmark, although no British examples of handles have yet been found. The abrasion on the butt-end edges of tranchet adzes, where the flint would have rubbed against the handle, and damage or breaks to the cutting edges of discarded adzes gives some indication of their use. It is likely that they were used for various woodworking tasks, such as boat building, and not for cutting down trees.

Tranchet adzes, which can vary in size from in excess of 300mm to less than 70mm, were almost certainly carefully curated (*41*). The distribution of re-sharpening flakes, and the huge variation in the size of finished tranchet adzes shows that when an adze became damaged or blunted, it could simply

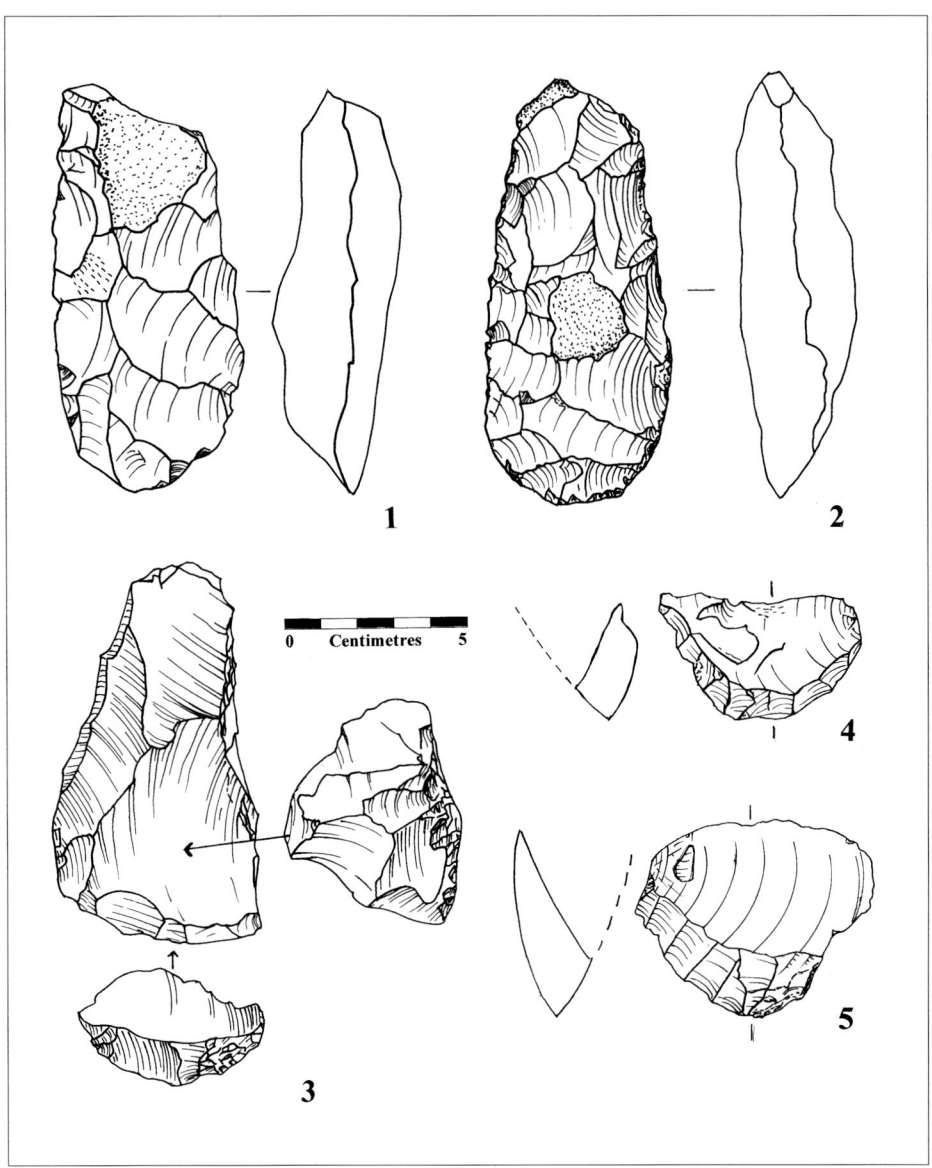

40 Tranchet adze production: 1) Roughout; 2) Preform; 3) Tranchet adze with refitting sharpening flakes; 4-5) Sharpening flakes. From various sites including Pyecombe and Farnham. *After Butler and Clark* et al.

The Mesolithic Period

be re-sharpened (Care 1979). In the Sussex Weald numerous sharpening flakes have been found, together with small tranchet adzes, which have been reduced in size by re-sharpening. Closer to the chalk Downs, and the source of the raw material, the adzes tend to be larger, reflecting less of a need for curation. There are of course exceptions to this, for example the large tranchet adzes found in the river Thames (Field 1989).

NON-TRANCHET ADZES AND AXES

There are examples of other flaked adzes and axes being produced during the Mesolithic, although many have probably been confused with Neolithic flaked axes. They were produced in the same way as a tranchet adze, but without the removal of the final tranchet adze-sharpening flake; instead the tip of the adze or axe is sharpened by having a number of small flakes removed from around its working edge. It is possible that they originated as tranchet adzes, but were later re-sharpened in this different manner.

HASSOCKS ADZES

The Hassocks Adze is found in southern Britain, almost exclusively to the south of the River Thames, and is quite rare. These large core tools were manufactured from large pieces of nodular flint (*42*). The nodule was shaped using a hard hammer to remove most of the cortex and form the nodule into a fairly uniform shape, which left one surface of the tool flat. The flat surface could be a natural surface of the nodule, or could be created by the removal of a large flake, or several smaller flakes. This flat surface was then used as a platform to remove a number of flakes at an acute angle to the working edge. Occasionally the flat surface may have some additional flakes removed at the working edge to improve it. This resulted in a V-shaped profile to the working edge, and the tool was then hafted into a handle, so that the working edge was at a right angle to the handle.

Abrasion of the edges indicates that some Hassocks Adzes were hafted at the butt end, but on others, the body of the tool was additionally flaked to narrow it about two thirds of the way up from its working end. The adze was then fixed to its handle at this 'waisted' point. This made an ideal tool that could have been used for a range of tasks from woodworking through to digging.

PICKS

Picks were another core tool, manufactured from nodules of flint from which most of the cortex had been removed using a hard hammer. They tend to be less symmetrical and more roughly finished than the tranchet adzes, and generally retain some cortex away from the working edge (*42*). The working

Prehistoric Flintwork

end normally tapers to a point, and is sometimes sharpened with a tranchet-type blow at its tip. Picks were usually of a similar size to the tranchet adzes, and may have been hafted or alternatively used in the hand. They were probably used for digging, perhaps during the gathering of plant materials. The name 'Thames Pick' is sometimes seen, and was previously used for any axe, adze or pick found in the River Thames.

SCRAPERS

Mesolithic scrapers were manufactured on both hard and soft hammer-

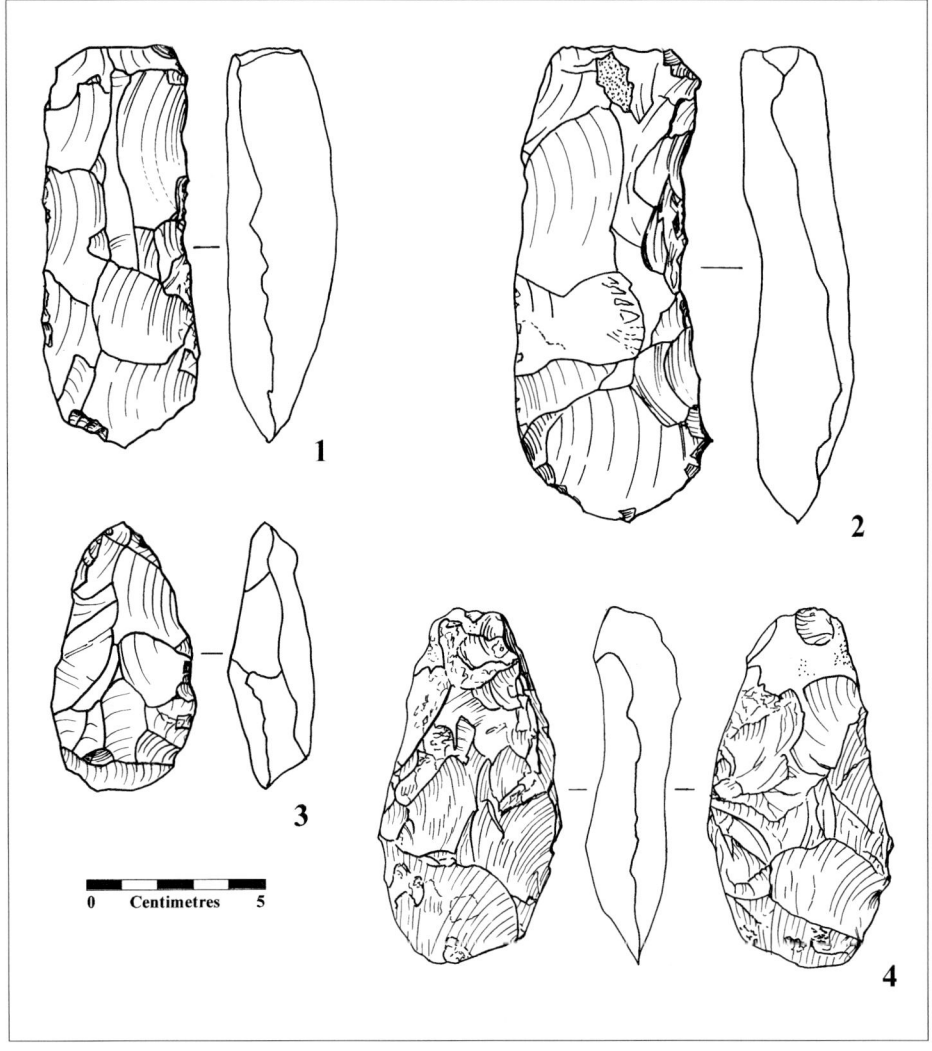

41 Examples of Mesolithic tranchet adzes. From Pyecombe, Sharpesbridge and Thatcham. *After Butler and Wymer*

produced flakes and blades. In both cases the blank will frequently exhibit the basic traits of Mesolithic flintworking, i.e. evidence of a prepared platform on the dorsal side of the butt, together with small butts and diffuse bulbs where the blank is soft hammer-struck. The range of scrapers found in Mesolithic assemblages is remarkably undiagnostic, and sometimes they can be surprisingly crude. There is no evidence for Mesolithic scrapers having been hafted, and it is more likely that due to their small size they were used as simple hand tools. Scrapers are present on almost all early Mesolithic sites, but are frequently absent on later Mesolithic sites. It is not clear whether this is due to the fact that later Mesolithic sites tend to be task related and therefore scrapers may have not been used at all sites, or whether they do become rarer. During the Mesolithic, retouch was frequently applied to other parts of the periphery than the end of the flake, thus producing a wide variety of scraper shapes. Although it is difficult to assign them into clear-cut categories, the following scraper types are normally recognised (*43*).

End scrapers are the most common type of scraper, and therefore the most varied in size and form. Typically Mesolithic end scrapers were produced either on flakes or elongated flakes, and are normally not as large as the horseshoe scrapers produced in the early Neolithic. The retouch can also extend partially down one or both lateral sides. Most end scrapers have some cortex remaining on the dorsal side of the blank. Mesolithic end scrapers are normally convex shaped, but they can also be straight, nosed, or irregular. Double-ended scrapers are also found, with retouch at both the distal and proximal ends of the flake.

Side scrapers are normally manufactured on flakes, but can sometimes be found on blades. The semi-abrupt or abrupt retouch extends along one lateral edge of the piece, which is normally convex in shape, but could be straight. Cortex is often present on the opposite lateral edge to the retouch. Very rarely a side scraper can be retouched along both lateral edges. Side scrapers are not very common on Mesolithic sites. Combined side-and-end scrapers are normally manufactured on broad flakes, and rarely seen on blades. They have a retouched convex distal end, with the retouch extending along one of the lateral edges, and (very rarely) along both lateral sides. Side-and-end scrapers are less common than the other types of scraper. Hollow or concave scrapers are also quite rare in the Mesolithic period. They are normally manufactured on flakes, and have a broad concave area of abrupt or semi-abrupt retouch along one lateral edge of the flake, or towards the distal end of an irregularly shaped flake. There is rarely any other retouch on the flake.

Micro-scrapers are surprisingly common on Mesolithic sites, and are some-times referred to as thumbnail scrapers. Originally thumbnail scrapers were thought to be early Bronze Age, but these small scrapers frequently turn up in well-stratified Mesolithic contexts. They tend to be less well made and not as rounded as the early Bronze Age types on which the retouch frequently extends around the entire circumference. Micro-scrapers were

Prehistoric Flintwork

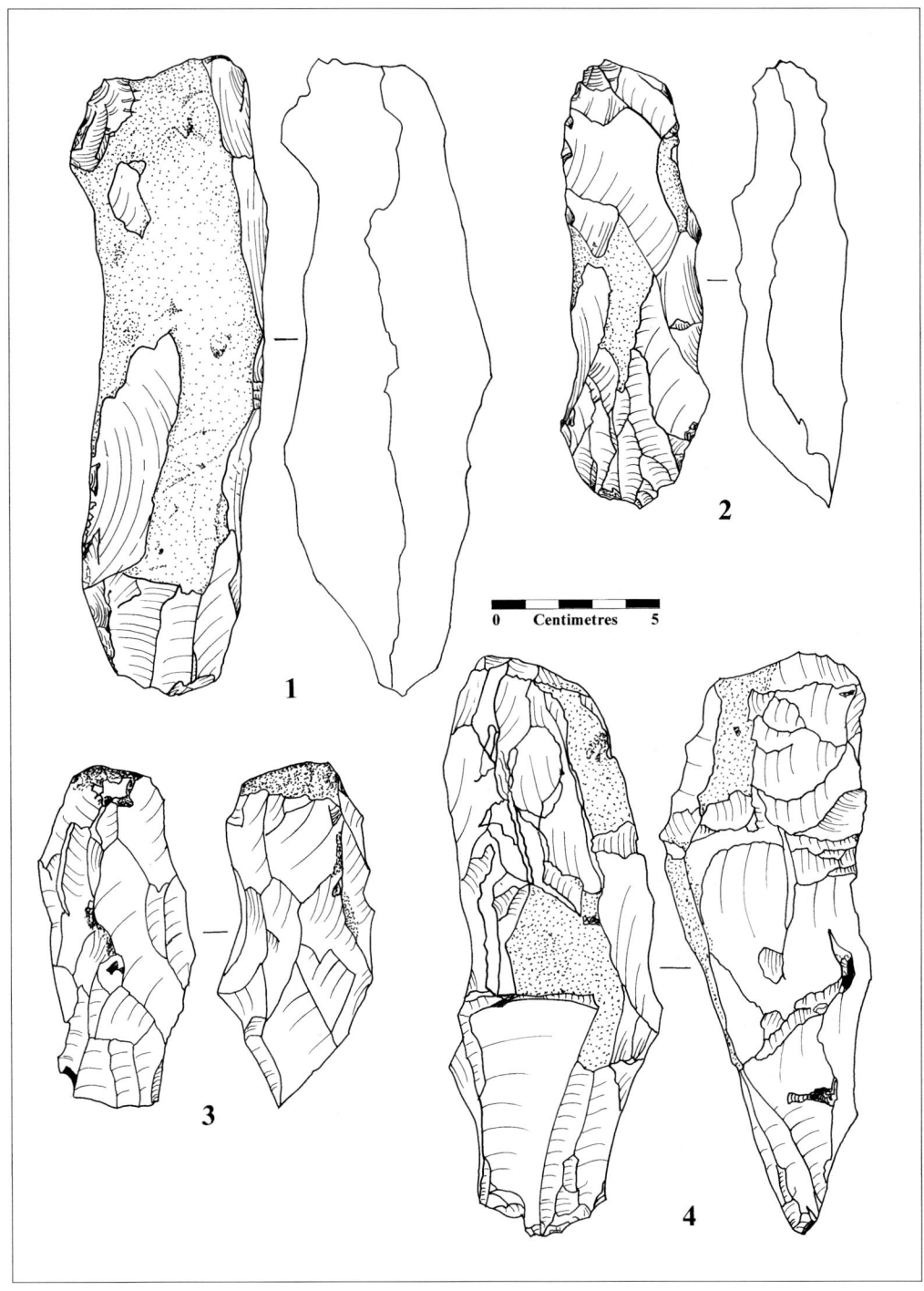

42 Mesolithic picks and adzes from Pyecombe (1 and 2) and Hassocks (3 and 4). *After Butler*

The Mesolithic Period

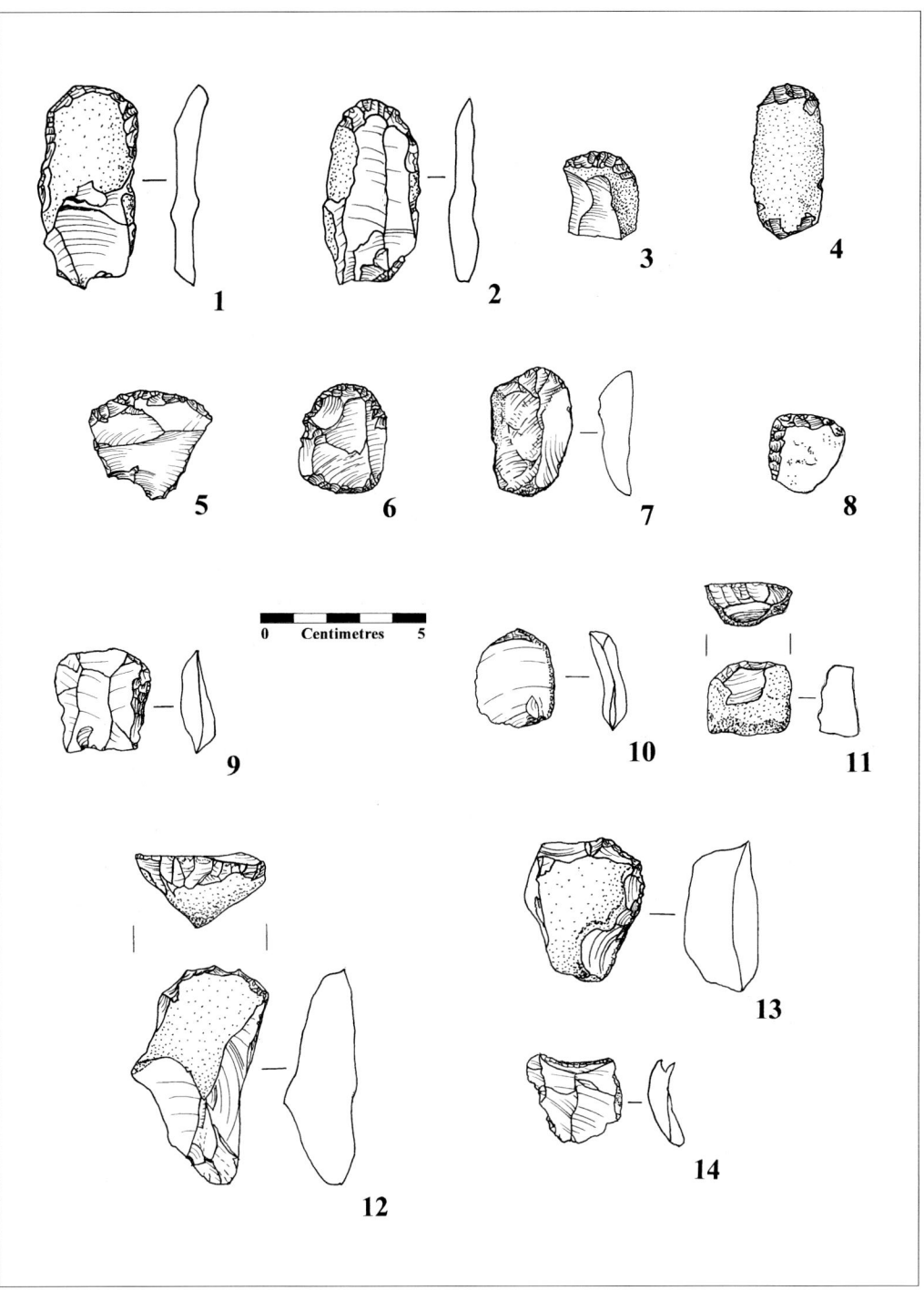

43 Mesolithic scrapers: 1-5 and 10-12) End scrapers (of which 3 is on a broken flake, and 10 and 11 are micro-scrapers); 6-7) Double-ended scrapers; 8-9) Side-and-end scrapers; 13) Side scraper; 14) Hollow scraper. From Pyecombe, Hengistbury, Rock Common, Thatcham and Streat Lane (Nos. 9 to 14). *After Butler, Barton, Harding and Wymer*

manufactured on small short flakes, and had a semi-abruptly retouched convex distal end with the retouch sometimes extending further around one or both lateral edges.

Streat Lane – A typical scraper assemblage?
On a number of Mesolithic sites it has been noticed that scrapers are comparatively simply made. For example at Streat Lane in Sussex, most of the 16 scrapers were simple end scrapers, with a few side, hollow and combined side-and-end scrapers, and all were made on flakes (*43*). Most were made on small stubby flakes, whilst two of the end scrapers were manufactured on larger flakes. Almost all of the scrapers were on hard hammer-struck flakes, and had cortex remaining on their dorsal sides, showing that there was a tendency to use primary flakes for these tools.

In most cases the convex scraping edge was at the distal end of the flake, and had been semi-abruptly retouched. The amount of retouch on some of the end scrapers was quite minimal, regularising the convex end, but for a few of the scrapers the retouch extended partially down one or both sides, which may have been to facilitate handling or hafting. A few of the scrapers had significant wear on the scraping edge, but the majority had very little indication that they had been utilised.

The surprising characteristic of this small group of scrapers is the comparative simplicity. None were made on blades, and the selection of shorter stubby cortical flakes seems to have been preferred. The impression given is that these were expedient tools, quickly made for one-off tasks and then discarded.

BURINS

Burins are frequently found in both early and later Mesolithic assemblages, often being the most common implement type after microliths, and occasionally outnumbering scrapers. However, on some sites burins are completely absent, and they are rare in Wales and the South West during the later Mesolithic. Occasionally burins can be combined on the same flake with other tool types, normally end scrapers, but sometimes having a retouched or serrated lateral edge. The flake or blade on which the burin is made will normally exhibit the typical signs of Mesolithic flintworking techniques, but is also frequently broken either by design or accidentally. The burin is then manufactured on the broken edge (*44*).

The burin spall is removed from either the distal or proximal end of the blank and only rarely from a lateral edge. Sometimes the burin spall is removed from an unmodified natural surface or break, but normally the break or surface will have been prepared or crested beforehand to provide a platform for the removal blow. The most common type of burin in the British Mesolithic is a truncation burin with the most frequent variety of a truncation burin having a single-angle removal. However there are also double-angle removals from the same prepared break, and more rarely alternate-angle removals, where the point of departure for the removals is a break or natural surface at both the distal and proximal end of the piece. The other major type of burin that is encountered is the dihedral burin, where the spall is removed from a previous burin facet, which is normally unretouched, or from a break or unmodified natural surface.

TRUNCATED PIECES

Truncated pieces are flakes, blades or bladelets that have a line of continuous regular abrupt retouch truncating the distal end of the piece, normally forming an oblique transverse truncation (*44*). More rarely a lateral edge or the proximal end is truncated, or the retouch truncates a broken flake or blade fragment. The truncation can also be concave, convex or at right angles to the main axis of the blank. The retouch is almost always direct and from the ventral surface of the piece, and the blanks have the expected traits of Mesolithic debitage. Although similar, they are larger than the simpler forms of obliquely blunted microliths.

These pieces are frequently found in Mesolithic assemblages and form an important component of the tool types found. Concave transverse truncations are found in most Mesolithic collections, and are prominent in some later Mesolithic assemblages. It is not entirely clear what function these truncated pieces had. They may have been used as tools in their own right, or may have been used in composite tools.

MICRODENTICULATES

These saw-like serrated blades are often found in Mesolithic assemblages, where they appear most often during the early Mesolithic period, becoming rare in the later Mesolithic period (*44*). They are generally made on blades with tiny continuous notches along most or part of one lateral edge. The blades are normally soft hammer-struck, but can also be hard hammer-struck, and they rarely have any cortex remaining. Although the blades can be straight-edged, most are concave, or have a curving profile. The notches are made by either using a stone tool as a compressor to apply pressure thus removing small flakes to create the notches, or by dragging another blade at right angles across the edge of the blade, which achieves the same results. Normally the point of percussion for the notch scars occurs from the dorsal side of the blade. There is rarely any backing (that is abrupt retouch to the opposing lateral edge) on microdenticulates, and they do not appear to have been hafted, although experimentation has found that most were too small to be comfortably held in the hand for long periods. Backing or additional

Prehistoric Flintwork

retouch where it does occur appears to modify the piece to make it easier to hold in the hand.

At Hengistbury Head, 64 microdenticulates were recovered during the excavations, and some were subjected to detailed microwear analysis (Barton 1992). The conclusion was that they were used in a 'general cutting/sawing motion on a relatively soft material such as bracken-type plant or green wood'.

DENTICULATIONS

Denticulates are pieces that have one lateral edge modified by large denticulations, which frequently only extend along part of that edge. Although seemingly similar to microdenticulates, the denticulations on these pieces are much bolder, and appear to have been formed by semi-abrupt retouch (*44*). They are frequently found on larger flakes or blades, and sometimes the opposite edge is cortical, presumably to facilitate handling. These pieces were likely to have been used in a saw-like action. Denticulates are more common in the later Mesolithic, especially at coastal locations in the South West and Wales.

FABRICATORS AND RODS

During the Mesolithic, fabricators have an oval, circular or diamond cross section; sometimes with one flat side, and are generally rod-shaped (*44*). They are normally flaked over their surface, and have one or both rounded ends that are abraded and worn from use. The other end and the edges of the piece may also have some wear, possibly from the tool having been hafted into a handle. They appear to have been elaborately made, and were perhaps carefully curated items.

AWLS AND PIERCERS

These are quite rare on Mesolithic sites. Both can be made on flakes or blades, normally without cortex, but sometimes with some cortex remaining on the distal surface. In the case of an awl, the point is abruptly retouched along one edge or two alternate edges (*44*). The piercer has abrupt retouch on the two lateral edges converging to form the point, which normally gives it a thicker triangular cross section (*44*). Mesolithic awls and piercers are generally much smaller, and more carefully made, than those from later periods of prehistory.

DRILL BITS (*mèche de foret*)

-These pieces turn up in small numbers on Mesolithic sites, and are referred to by their French name, *mèche de foret*. They are small bladelets that have been abruptly

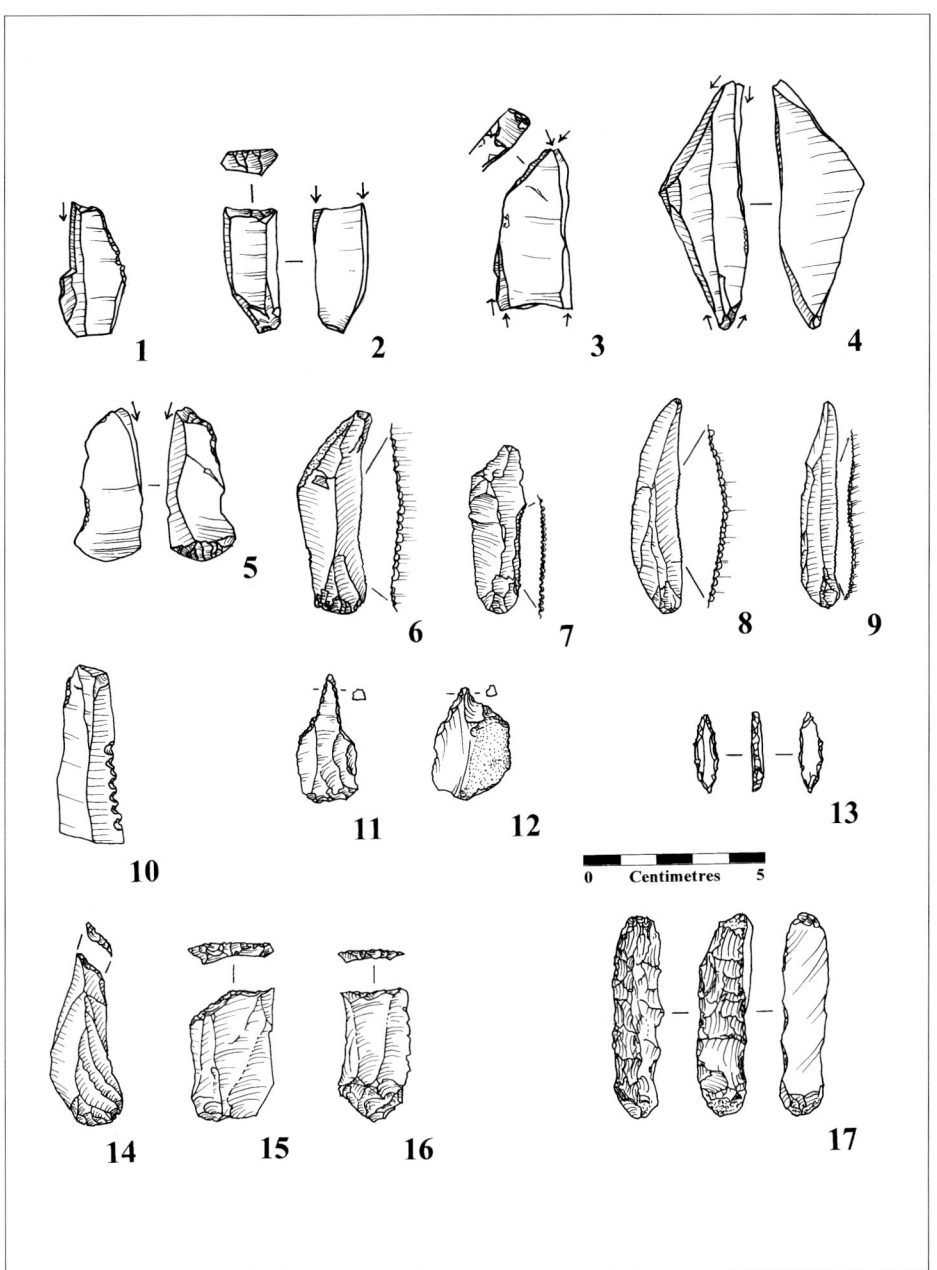

44 Mesolithic implements: 1) Single-angle burin; 2) Double-angle burin; 3) Burin with alternate-angle removals; 4) Dihedral burin; 5) Single angle burin and scraper; 6-9) Microdenticulates (detail of notched edges shown from ventral side at twice scale); 10) Denticulate; 11) Piercer; 12) Awl; 13) Mèche de foret; 14-15) Oblique truncations; 16) Right-angle truncation; 17) Fabricator. From Star Carr, Hengistbury Head, Rock Common, Oakhanger. After Clark, Barton, Harding and Rankine

retouched along both parallel lateral edges to form a lanceolate shape with a point at either end (*44*). Some pieces still retain the butt end of the bladelet, just being retouched to a point at the distal end. It is assumed by their shape and from microwear studies that they were utilised as drill bits (Barton 1992).

Over one hundred piercers were found at Star Carr (*45*), of which the majority were made on small narrow flakes or blades abruptly retouched along one or both edges to form a point at the distal end (Clark 1971). On many of these piercers, the retouch extended down the entire length of both sides, whilst on a few cases the retouch also extended around the butt end (Clark 1971). These latter pieces appear to be a more refined group of piercers than many of those found on other sites, and may have been made in this way for a particular function associated with this site. They should more correctly be called *mèche de forêt*.

NOTCHES

Most Mesolithic sites will produce a small number of flakes, and occasionally blades, with one or two notches along one or other of their lateral edges (*46*). Sometimes the notches are combined with additional retouch on one of the lateral edges. A notch is created by either a single blow, or with abrupt or semi-abrupt retouch, normally struck from the ventral side of the piece, which has removed small flakes creating a deep curved incision into the edge of the flake. On occasion, broken or smaller fragments of flakes have notches added to their lateral edges, although many of these appear to have been caused by natural damage rather than intentionally. Notched pieces seem to have a specific function and their presence on sites interpreted as hunting camps could indicate that they were used to manufacture and finally shape arrow shafts. A notch on a bladelet can be easily confused with the notch created as part of the microlith production process.

KNIVES AND CUTTING BLADES

Many flakes and especially blades could have been utilised as knives or cutting flakes, due to their naturally sharp lateral edges. However, some Mesolithic sites have produced a number of longer flakes or blades, which appear to have been specifically modified into backed knives, so that they could be used for cutting. The backed knife is a blade with one unmodified lateral edge, which would have been used for cutting (*46*). The opposite lateral edge of the blade is blunted by abrupt retouch to make it more comfortable to hold, or to facilitate its hafting into a handle. Alternatively an opposite cortical edge is left unmodified for the same reason.

Sometimes pieces with apparent retouch on one lateral edge are found, but it is possible that this is not intentional retouch designed to modify the

The Mesolithic Period

edge, but instead damage from the utilisation of the piece in antiquity. Some utilisation damage may only be seen with the aid of a microscope. These, and unmodified blades that may have been used for cutting, frequently have cortex on the opposing lateral edge to facilitate handling or hafting.

Occasionally blade segments are found, but it is not clear whether these were intended as a specific tool type. They comprise a central section of a blade missing both the distal and proximal ends (*46*). Normally there is no retouch on either lateral edge, or at the ends. It is possible that these pieces are not specific implements, and are simply a by-product or waste material. However, they could have been intended for use, hafted in composite cutting tools. It is easy to see how many blades or longer flakes, which would have been produced as by-products during the manufacture of other tools, may have been picked up and simply used as expedient tools, whether quickly modified or in their unmodified state and then discarded after use.

CHOPPING TOOLS

These are occasionally found on Mesolithic sites, and are made on rounded or oval nodules or pebbles, and also frequently made from non-flint stone. The working edge was flaked either unifacially (choppers) or bifacially (chopping tools) to create a cutting edge (*46*). They retain considerable amounts of cortex, especially on the butts, enabling them to be comfortably held in the hand for use, and were therefore probably not hafted. Another type of

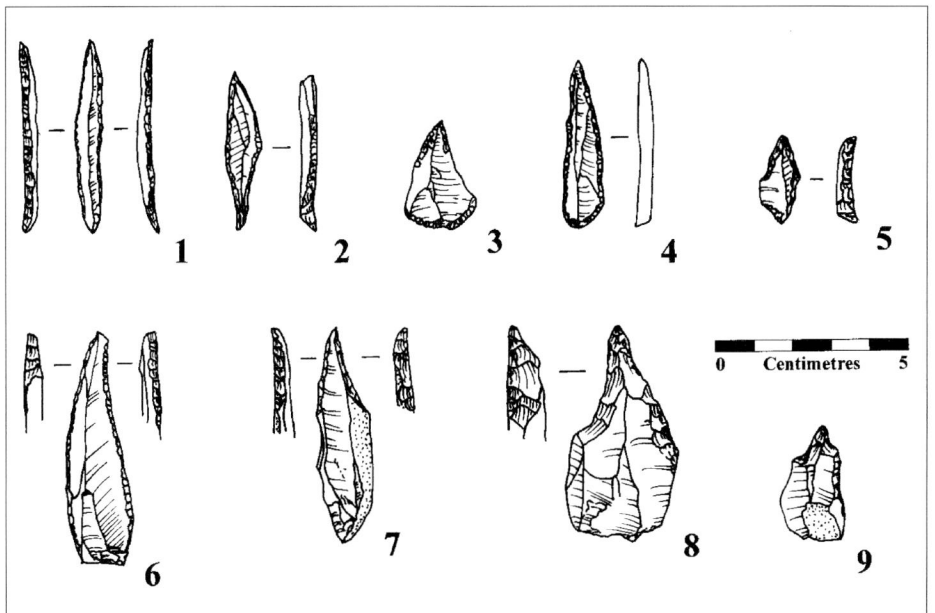

45 Star Carr piercers: 1-7) Mèche de foret; 8-9) Piercers. *After Clark*

chopping tool is frequently seen on coastal sites and in association with shell middens. These are sometimes referred to as limpet scoops or hammers and are pebbles (frequently a non-flint stone) with one or more flakes removed from either one or both ends, leaving a scoop-like scar (Palmer 1977).

OTHER RETOUCHED IMPLEMENTS

In any assemblage there are a number of diverse retouched pieces that do not fit any of the implement categories listed above. The pieces can be made on flakes, blades, bladelets, or fragments of any of these. They have areas of continuous retouch along part of one or more edges, at the distal end or on the shoulder of the piece near the butt. Many of these have no apparent function, and are probably just expedient tools that were quickly manufactured for a specific task, without following any conventional model, and then discarded.

MESOLITHIC HUNTER-GATHERER USE OF FLINT

A number of things are clear from the varied types of implements that were manufactured and used by the Mesolithic hunter-gatherer groups. They took great care in selecting the right quality flint, and then in making maximum use of the flint that they had selected. This was probably because they had to carry the flint around with them and did not want to encumber themselves with poor-quality raw material. Secondly they ensured that they were able to produce the maximum number of implements from the raw material. It is also apparent that there was a range of tool types that had specific or limited functions. The most obvious is the microlith, as clearly this was predominantly used as part of their hunting equipment. The other is the tranchet adze, and to a lesser extent the pick. These were unlikely to be used for hunting, but were more likely to be associated with activities carried out at more permanent camping locations, or raw-material procurement sites.

By looking at ethnographic and other evidence, it is possible for archaeologists to take the data provided by a flintwork assemblage from a site and use this to suggest how that site might have operated, what activities were carried out, and how the site fits into the overall Mesolithic landscape. The evidence from ethnographic sources (Binford, 1983), and research elsewhere in Europe (Jochim 1998), suggests that a system of base camps and task-specific sites may have been operated during the later Mesolithic period. Base camps would, as the name suggests, provide a base from which sub-groups of people would journey to locations within their territorial range where other 'task-specific' activities were carried out, for example short stay hunting camps. The base camps are more likely to be located at a place where food and other resources are readily available, for example beside a river or lake, whilst other task-based sites are likely to be located near to other resources, for example flint

The Mesolithic Period

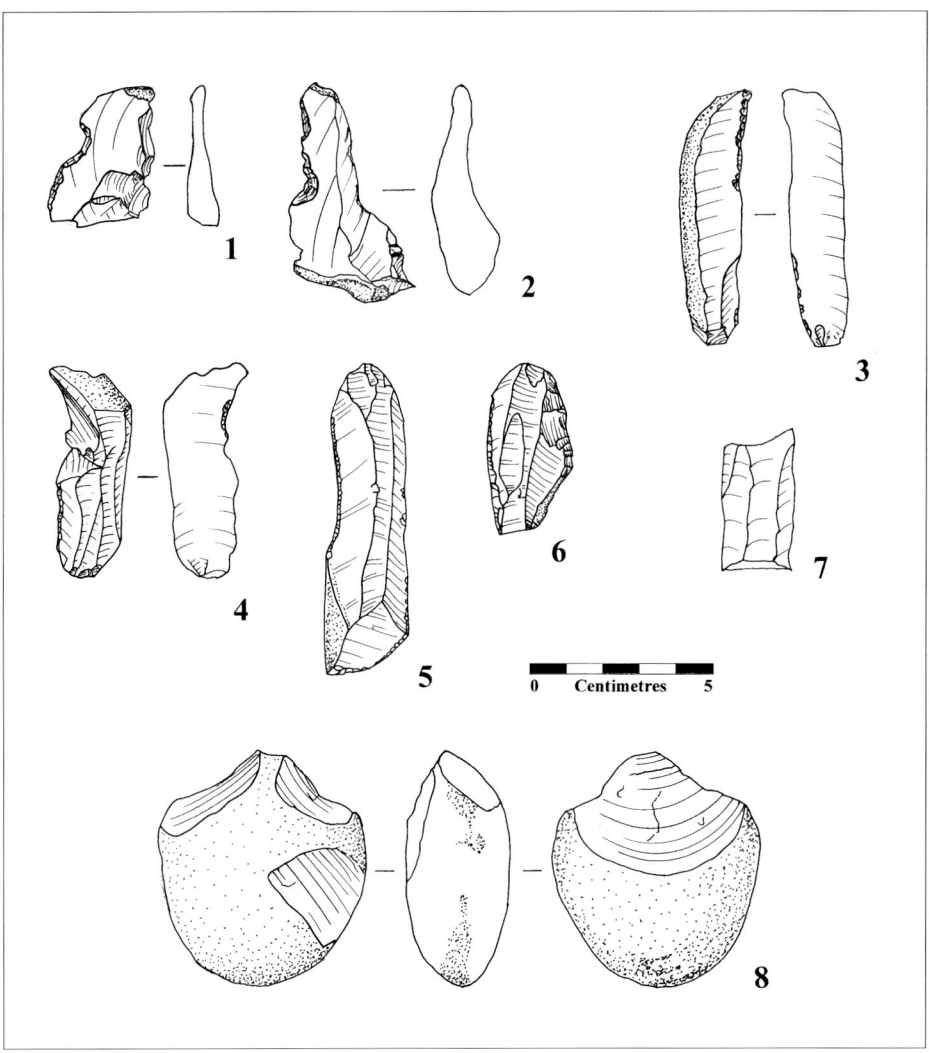

46 Other Mesolithic tools: 1-2) Notched flakes; 3-6) Knives; 7) Segment; 8) Chopping tool. From Streat Lane, St. Catherine's Hill, Star Carr. *After Butler, Gabel and Clark*

or hunting grounds. From this hypothesis it is possible to determine the type of site from the evidence we find when we locate and investigate archaeological sites from this period.

At a more permanent base camp, you would expect to find the heavy core tools like tranchet adzes, picks and adzes, a wide range of flake and blade tools (possibly in some numbers), a lot of debitage, plus evidence for the manufacture and repair of hunting equipment. The material at a base camp is also likely to be spread over a large area, and may have additional evidence such as pits or shelters (*colour plates 13 and 14*). What flint implements might you expect to find at a short stay hunting camp? The maintenance and repair of hunting equipment would mean that microliths were being manufactured, so you would expect to find bladelet cores, broken and complete bladelets and microburins, together with broken and discarded microliths. Other implements associated with the maintenance and repair of hunting equipment and the initial processing of food would include scrapers, burins and other expedient flake and blade tools. You would probably not expect to find tranchet adzes, picks and adzes and a wide range or large numbers of flake and blade tools.

There are other task-specific sites that can also be located within the landscape. For example, a flint procurement site will provide evidence for the initial working of flint nodules, discarded cores, and large quantities of debitage. If tranchet adzes were being produced some discarded preforms and roughouts would also be expected. There would be few implements, as these would have been taken away for use elsewhere, although there would be some associated with the procurement of the flint, for example picks and hammerstones. Some implements might be found if the flint procurement site also doubled up as a hunting campsite.

Within a landscape setting you may expect to find evidence of Mesolithic hunter-gatherer activity that fits this model; perhaps centred on a riverside or lakeside base camp with evidence of localised woodland clearance. Hunting camps would be located some distance away, in areas that would have supported woodland whilst also providing shelter and water; so rock shelters and streamside locations would be preferred. Other task-specific sites such as flint acquisition or coastal sites (for fishing and shellfish procurement) can also be expected. The proportion of different tools varies considerably from site to site, and the reasons for this are poorly understood. In the later Mesolithic period especially, microliths dominate some sites and there are few other tools. However, there are some sites that have no microliths, but have a range of other tools, including tranchet adzes. There is also much greater variability of tool types in the later Mesolithic period, which could be due to the variety of task-specific sites that seem to have existed then.

The following sites provide some examples of the sort of evidence that can come from excavation or other fieldwork, and will show how the evidence is used to determine site function, and how it fits into the landscape model detailed above.

Hermitage Rocks, East Sussex – A hunting camp
This south-facing outcrop of sandstone rock provided a vertical rock face some 8m high, against which a possible temporary shelter was erected (*colour plate 15*). The excavations in 1974 and 1975 produced some 4,300 pieces of worked flint, of which over 90 per cent were debitage, together with evidence for a hearth (Jacobi *et al.* 1981). The debitage included cores, flakes, blades, bladelets and core tablets, together with microburins. The implements included 141 microliths, together with 31 truncated pieces, 18 burins and four scrapers. There were also a few other retouched flake/blade tools, but no tranchet adzes or picks were found.

The excavators tentatively interpreted the site as a spring hunting camp on the basis of the excavated flintwork assemblage. The site location is also important; the south-facing rock face would have provided a suitable location for a temporary shelter, and nearby springs a source of water. The site would have been in woodland, in which animals could be hunted, and was within easy travelling distance of nearby river valleys, in which a more permanent base camp could have been located.

West Hill, Pyecombe, West Sussex – A task-specific flint procurement site
A detailed survey was undertaken at the Clay-with-flints outcrop on West Hill, Pyecombe on the South Downs (Butler 2001a). There were significant quantities of debitage: bladelet and flake cores, flakes, blades and bladelets, plus a small number of microliths and other implements, including scrapers and picks. Also found were numerous tranchet adze roughouts, preforms and a few finished tranchet adzes. The evidence shows that in the later Mesolithic period, microliths and tranchet adzes, together with a range of other implements, were being produced from flint procured from the Clay-with-flints outcrop. It is also likely that flint nodules were being collected from the Clay-with-flints outcrop and then taken to other locations where microliths and other implements were being manufactured.

It is likely that the tranchet adzes were used for woodworking activities, although some tranchet adzes, together with the picks that were found, may have been used to extract flint nodules from the Clay-with-flints. Recent fieldwork on the South Downs north of Brighton has also identified similar concentrations of Mesolithic material on other Clay-with-flint outcrops (Butler *et al.* 2002). This would confirm that the activity at West Hill was not isolated, but is an example of a widespread practice of Mesolithic hunter-gatherer groups exploiting flint sources. This activity may have been occasional, with visits to the site being made on a seasonal basis to procure the flint, which would have been easily obtained on or just below the ground surface. By its nature, this seasonal exploitation would be of low intensity, with the site being easily accessed from nearby river valleys in which a base camp could have been located.

Thatcham, Berkshire – A base camp or multifunctional site
Thatcham was excavated between 1958 and 1961 (Wymer 1962). The site was probably originally located beside a lake, and due to the peaty soil, quantities of bone and antler were preserved as well as a large flintwork assemblage of some 18,400 pieces. The debitage included flakes, blades and bladelets, together with 283 cores and 129 core rejuvenation pieces. The dominant implement type was the microlith, of which 285 were found, together with 72 microburins. Other flake implements included 132 scrapers, 61 burins, 19 microdenticulates and 15 awls/piercers. As well as the flake tools, there were also 17 tranchet adzes,

including some roughouts, together with 16 tranchet adze-sharpening flakes. A number of bone and antler tools were also found.

From the excavated evidence, it is clear that this was a longer stay base camp or multifunctional site, situated in a clearing on the edge of a lake from where the resources of the lake and the surrounding woodland could have been exploited. The huge quantity of debitage compared to implements shows that there was a significant amount of flintworking taking place. The tranchet adzes provide evidence for the building of shelters, and possibly the building of wooden boats for fishing and travel. The microliths, together with the animal bone evidence, show that hunting parties were going out into the surrounding woodland, whilst the wide diversity of other flint tool forms suggests a range of different activities being carried out at the site.

Finglesham, Kent – Not a microlith to be seen!
This site in east Kent was excavated in 1981-2, and produced an assemblage of almost 1,500 pieces (Butler, forthcoming). Although the site undoubtedly dated to the later Mesolithic (confirmed by thermoluminescence dating), there were no microliths or microburins, and virtually no bladelets, blades or their cores in the assemblage. The implements comprised scrapers, piercers, notched flakes and knives, together with tranchet adzes, roughouts and numerous tranchet adze-sharpening flakes. Analysis of the debitage, which comprised almost entirely flakes, showed that they were much larger, and were broad and squarish, rather than the smaller, longer narrow flakes normally encountered on a Mesolithic site. Comparisons with the debitage from sites with microliths showed that the debitage from Finglesham had very different attributes, but still exhibited the careful flintworking aspects expected at a Mesolithic site (crested blades, core rejuvenation flakes, platform preparation etc.).

The lack of microliths is a feature of a number of Mesolithic sites in east Kent, and probably also elsewhere in the country, and there is a great danger that unless there are other diagnostic Mesolithic items in the assemblage, they could be mis-identified as coming from a later period of prehistory.

6

EARLY NEOLITHIC FLINTWORK

It is now recognised that the change from the Mesolithic to the Neolithic period was not a sudden change brought about by incoming groups of farmers from the continent. Instead, it was more likely due to the native Mesolithic peoples taking on new ideas, and changing the way in which they lived as a response to an increasing population and the need to better manage the resources they could exploit. This change had probably already started in the later Mesolithic period, with people only slowly developing into farming communities over a very long period.

How is this reflected in the flintwork? There are some major changes in the flint tools used in the Neolithic period with new types replacing existing Mesolithic tools. The two major diagnostic Mesolithic tools both disappear from the archaeological record, although this may happen at different times in different parts of the country. The microlith and all the composite tools that were made from microliths were discarded and were replaced as a hunting tool by the leaf-shaped arrowhead. We cannot be certain why this change occurred, but possibly the opening up of the woodland by partial clearance meant that a more efficient type of arrow was required. The leaf-shaped arrowhead would have been more aerodynamic than a microlith composite arrowhead when used to engage targets over the longer ranges now required. Additionally it was almost certainly a much more efficient killing tool, having the ability to penetrate more deeply.

Similarly, the tranchet adze also mostly disappears, and is replaced by ground and flaked axes, made not just from flint but also from a greater range of other stone types. There is also a number of new tool types, which will be described below, and which were presumably introduced as a result of the change to a more sedentary way of life. From the archaeological point of view, flint and other stone tools are no longer the main source we have for understanding the Neolithic period. Pottery first appears in the archaeological record, together with monuments, and there is an increase in the number of sites with animal bones of domesticated and wild species. Because microliths were no longer being produced, the need for bladelets disappeared, which in turn resulted in some changes to the flintworking technology that was employed in the early Neolithic period. Good quality flint was still being

Prehistoric Flintwork

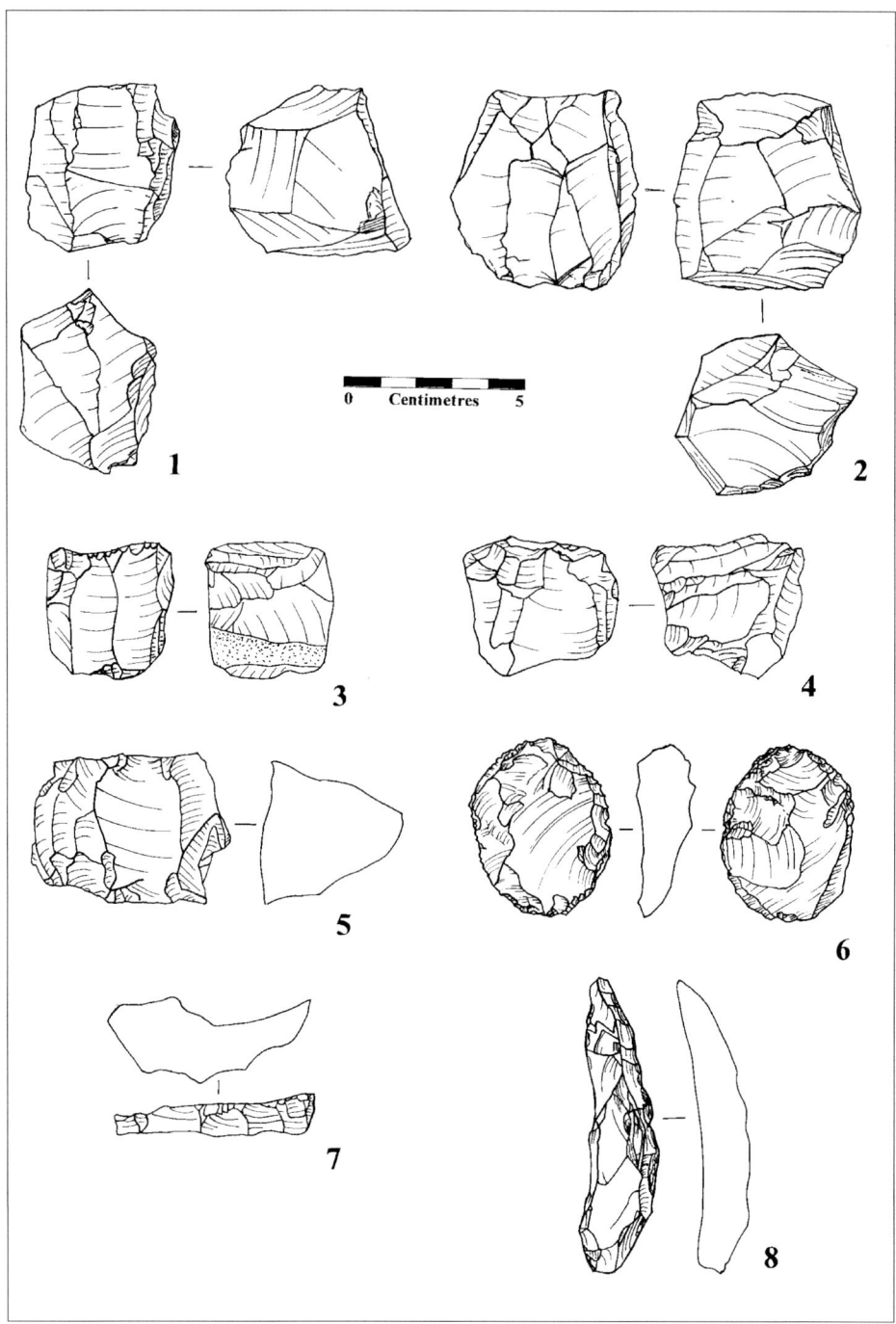

47 Early Neolithic cores: 1-2) Multiple-platform flake cores; 3-4) Two-platform blade cores; 5) Two-platform flake core; 6) Keeled (discoidal) core; 7) Core-rejuvenation flake; 8) Crested blade. *From various sites after Butler, Clark Holgate, Malone and Robertson-Mackay*

selected for flaking, and great care was being taken throughout the knapping process. However, blades were now being produced in significant numbers alongside flakes, and were the preferred choice for turning into tools. The initial steps of the knapping process were unchanged, in that most or all of the cortex was removed from the nodule, normally with a hard hammer, and a striking platform was created by removing a flake to provide a suitable surface.

As in the Mesolithic period, attention was given to the maintenance of the core and its platform(s) throughout the knapping process, including the preparation of the platform edge to remove overhangs between removing each blade or flake. When the angle between the platform and the flaking surface reached 90° and no further pieces could be removed from it, the core was rotated until a new platform could be found. Blades or flakes continued to be detached from this new platform, abrading the edge as before, and when the platform was exhausted, the core was again rotated until a new platform was found.

This represents a change from the process that was used during the Mesolithic period, as the new platform was not created, but instead was selected from the existing surfaces on the core (Holgate 1988). This new practice meant that early Neolithic cores frequently had more than two platforms, and the platforms tended to be at different angles to one another, resulting in a cube-shaped core (*47*). Where a core had only two platforms, these were frequently at 90° to one another. The negative scars on the cores were generally parallel reflecting the production of narrow flakes and blades. Occasionally, when the platforms were at acute angles to one another, a keeled or discoidal core was produced (*47*). These tended to have a triangular cross section, and although they were more common in later Neolithic assemblages, they also occurred in early Neolithic assemblages. In some parts of Britain, where flint was a scarce raw material, bipolar cores can also be found in early Neolithic assemblages. The new process also meant that core tablets were no longer produced. Instead, when the first removal was taken from a new platform that was perpendicular to the first platform, and that removal followed the edge of the first platform, the resulting blade had the appearance of a crested blade (*47*). Because of the changes in the flaking process outlined above, there were fewer rejuvenation pieces produced in the Neolithic period. However, they do occur in early Neolithic assemblages, suggesting the continued emphasis on careful working of the cores.

The soft hammer continued to be used in the early Neolithic period for removing secondary flakes and blades. This means that for recognition purposes, they have the distinctive attributes of soft hammer-produced pieces, together with abrasion scars on the dorsal side of the butt. This comes from the preparation of the platforms prior to their removal from the core. Blades produced in the early Neolithic period tended to be broader and larger than their Mesolithic counterparts, but still have parallel edges and ridges on the dorsal surface. The blades may have cortex present, and the presence of both hard and soft hammer-struck blades in most assemblages confirms that the cores were being initially worked with a hard hammer to remove the primary cortical blades before the secondary blades were removed with a soft hammer.

As in the Mesolithic period, flakes were produced in great numbers, and although blades were used for most tool types, flakes were also utilised. Through the Neolithic period there is a gradual change from blades to long flakes, so that eventually flakes predominate in Neolithic assemblages. Flakes were also produced as waste during the manufacture of axes and other tools. The flakes were removed with either a hard or soft hammer depending upon whether they were primary flakes from the initial working of a core or nodule, or from secondary working. Early Neolithic flakes tended to be larger than those produced in the Mesolithic period, but were also longer and narrower than those that followed in the later Neolithic and Bronze Age. Although most hard hammer-struck flakes had no indication of platform preparation, some did, and most soft hammer-struck flakes normally displayed the distinctive evidence of platform preparation on the dorsal side of the butt.

To summarise the early Neolithic debitage: cores are normally cube-shaped, with multiple prepared platforms, and few rejuvenation pieces. The non-core debitage is predominantly soft and hard hammer-struck blades and longer flakes, which tend to be larger than those produced during the Mesolithic period. Distinctive pieces such as bladelets, bladelet cores and core tablets are not found in early Neolithic assemblages. However, it can sometimes be difficult to distinguish between a Mesolithic and early Neolithic assemblage unless some of the relevant distinguishing pieces are present. Although most of the flake tools such as scrapers continued to be used in the early Neolithic period, there was a greater variety of tool types available than during the preceding Mesolithic period. These tools were predominantly made on blades and longer flakes, many of which were soft hammer-struck, and had prepared platforms. Ground and flaked axes, which are discussed in a later section, replaced the Mesolithic tranchet adze as the major core tool during the early Neolithic period, and new tools were introduced such as the leaf-shaped arrowhead. The early Neolithic flint tool kit comprises:

LEAF-SHAPED ARROWHEADS

Leaf-shaped arrowheads were made from flakes, which were retouched invasively into the distinctive leaf shape that gives the type its name. They can be divided into 12 types ranging from short squat types through to long slender types, based on their length/breadth ratio (*48*). They can be further subdivided dependent upon their shape and the extent of the retouch. Two shapes are recognised: (a) ogival forms, which tend to be short and have two concave upper sides and (b) kite-shaped forms which are long and slender, and have symmetrical upper and lower halves. Ogival forms have a further sub-

Early Neolithic Flintwork

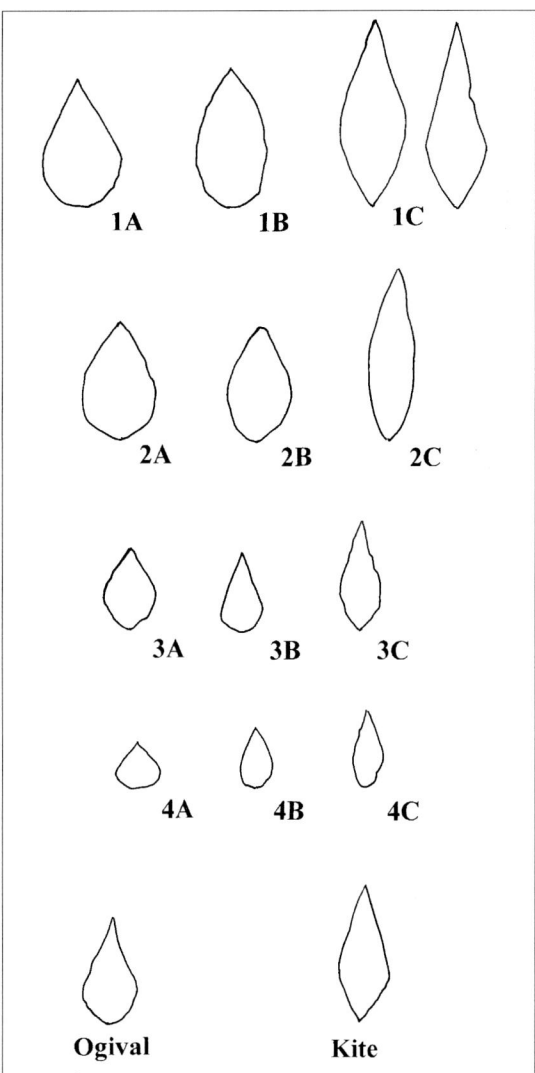

48 Early Neolithic leaf-shaped arrowhead typology. Types 1 to 4, and Forms: Ogival (Type 3B) and Kite-shaped (Type 2C). After Green

category called attenuated forms, which are small squat arrowheads with a sharp point, although these can only be defined by measurement (Green 1980).

The invasive retouch, which was executed by pressure flaking, normally covers the entire surface of both faces (bifacially) of the arrowhead, although on some the retouch only fully covers one face, with the retouch on the other face normally confined to just the tip and edges (*49*). A further sub-category has retouch on both faces confined to the tip and edges. In some cases the amount of retouch on these pieces is minimal, however, the overall leaf-shape of the arrowhead and the retouch on both faces is always present. Occasionally on some of these later arrowheads the bulb of percussion and striking platform are still present and these may be roughouts or unfinished examples. One final type is the polished or ground leaf-shaped arrowhead, but these are rare, and are mostly found in Ireland.

Prehistoric Flintwork

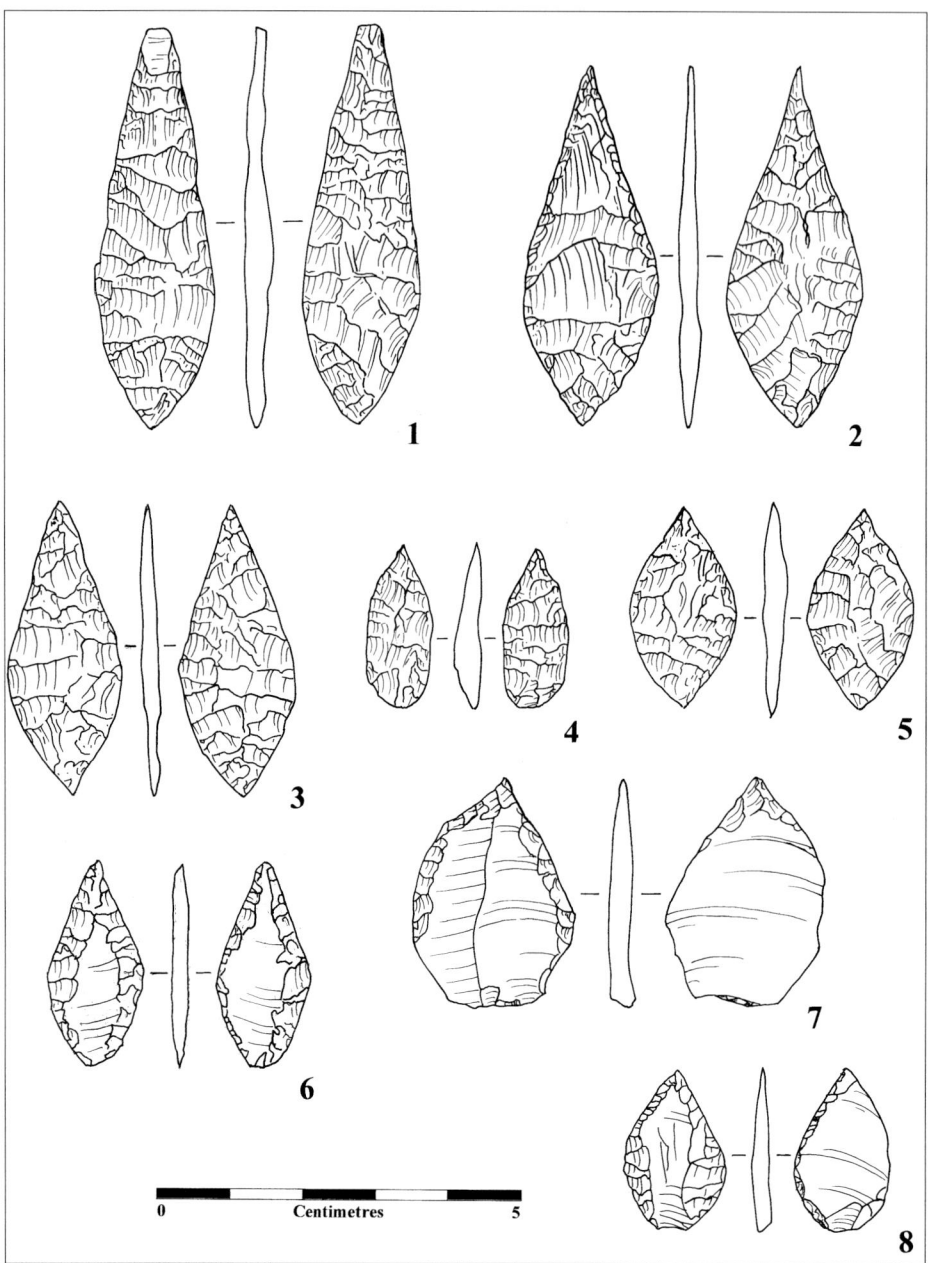

49 Leaf-shaped arrowheads from Hurst Fen. After Clark

The leaf-shaped arrowhead would have been hafted into the end of a wooden arrow shaft, and held in place with resin and twine (*colour plate 16*). Both the bifacial and partially-flaked types would have been functional arrowheads, although the bifacial varieties would have taken much longer to make and probably required a skill beyond the abilities of most individuals. It is possible that some bifacial arrowheads were 'fancy' types made for show and ritual ceremonies, whilst the partially-flaked types were quickly made and mass-produced for hunting and warfare. The numerous isolated finds of bifacial leaf-shaped arrowheads do however suggest that they were also used for hunting. This type of arrowhead is found in association with early Neolithic pottery and early and middle Neolithic monuments such as causewayed enclosures and long barrows, where it has been suggested they may have been the cause of death of some individuals. Although they have also been found in some later Neolithic and early Bronze Age contexts, there is no definite evidence to suggest they continued in use after the middle Neolithic.

SCRAPERS

Early Neolithic scrapers were manufactured on both hard and soft hammer-produced flakes and, less commonly, on blades. These normally exhibit evidence of a prepared platform on the dorsal side of the butt, together with small butts and diffuse bulbs where the blank was soft hammer-struck. The scrapers were normally produced on thicker flakes and blades, which may or may not have had cortex remaining on the dorsal side They tend to be larger than the scrapers produced during the preceding Mesolithic period, although this may be as a result of the available raw material. Occasionally scrapers were manufactured on thermal flakes, where the retouch had been applied to specifically selected thermal flakes to produce end or side scrapers (*52*). There is little evidence for any early Neolithic scrapers having been hafted.

End scrapers were made on long or, more often, short flakes, and occasionally on blades (*50* and *51*). The striking platform and bulb of percussion were normally still present, but on some smaller scrapers the butt end of the flake had been removed. Many of the end scrapers have a large negative scar on the distal side, which results in a slight depression into which the thumb fits whilst being used, thus allowing more pressure to be comfortably exerted. Other scrapers have cortex remaining on the dorsal side, which may have had a similar function when being used. End scrapers made on large rounded flakes in the early Neolithic period are sometimes called Horseshoe scrapers.

Nosed scrapers are also found in the early Neolithic period (*50*), together with double-ended scrapers, although these are quite rare. Double-ended scrapers were normally manufactured from long flakes or blades, although they were sometimes made on small flakes (*52*). Side scrapers were most frequently made on long flakes or blades, and are quite common in early Neolithic assemblages (*52*). Hollow scrapers are not often found in the early Neolithic period. They were generally manufactured on shorter flakes (*52*), and there was rarely any other retouch on the flake. Combined side-and-end scrapers are normally manufactured on shorter flakes (*53*), and are less common than the other types of scraper.

Prehistoric Flintwork

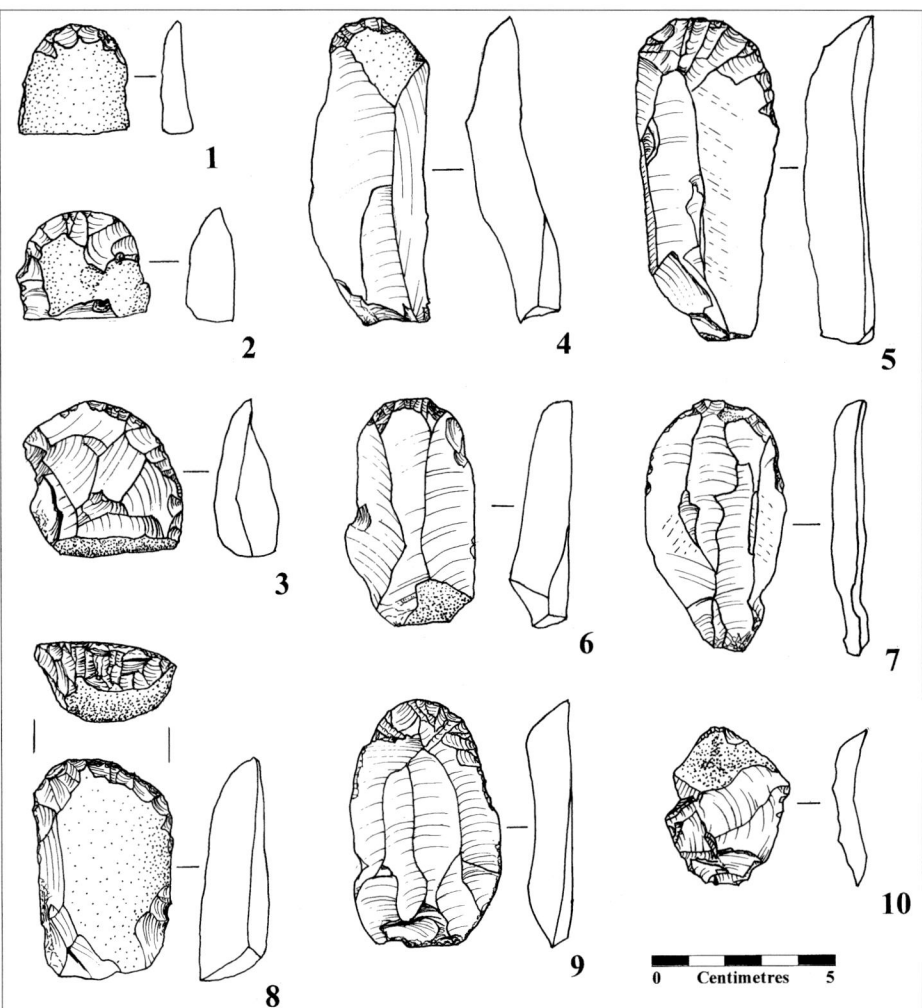

50 Examples of early Neolithic end scrapers: 1-3 are on broken flakes or blades; 4-9 are on blades or long flakes; 10 is a nosed scraper

Disc scrapers were manufactured on shorter flakes, and had abrupt or semi-abrupt retouch around the convex distal end, extending around both lateral edges, which were also convex. The retouch normally stopped near the butt end of the flake, and did not extend all the way around its circumference, but at least 75 per cent of its circumference must have been retouched. The overall shape of the finished scraper is of an almost round disc (*53*).

AWLS AND PIERCERS

Both of these types are made on hard hammer-struck short and long flakes, normally without cortex, but sometimes with some cortex remaining on the dorsal surface.

Early Neolithic Flintwork

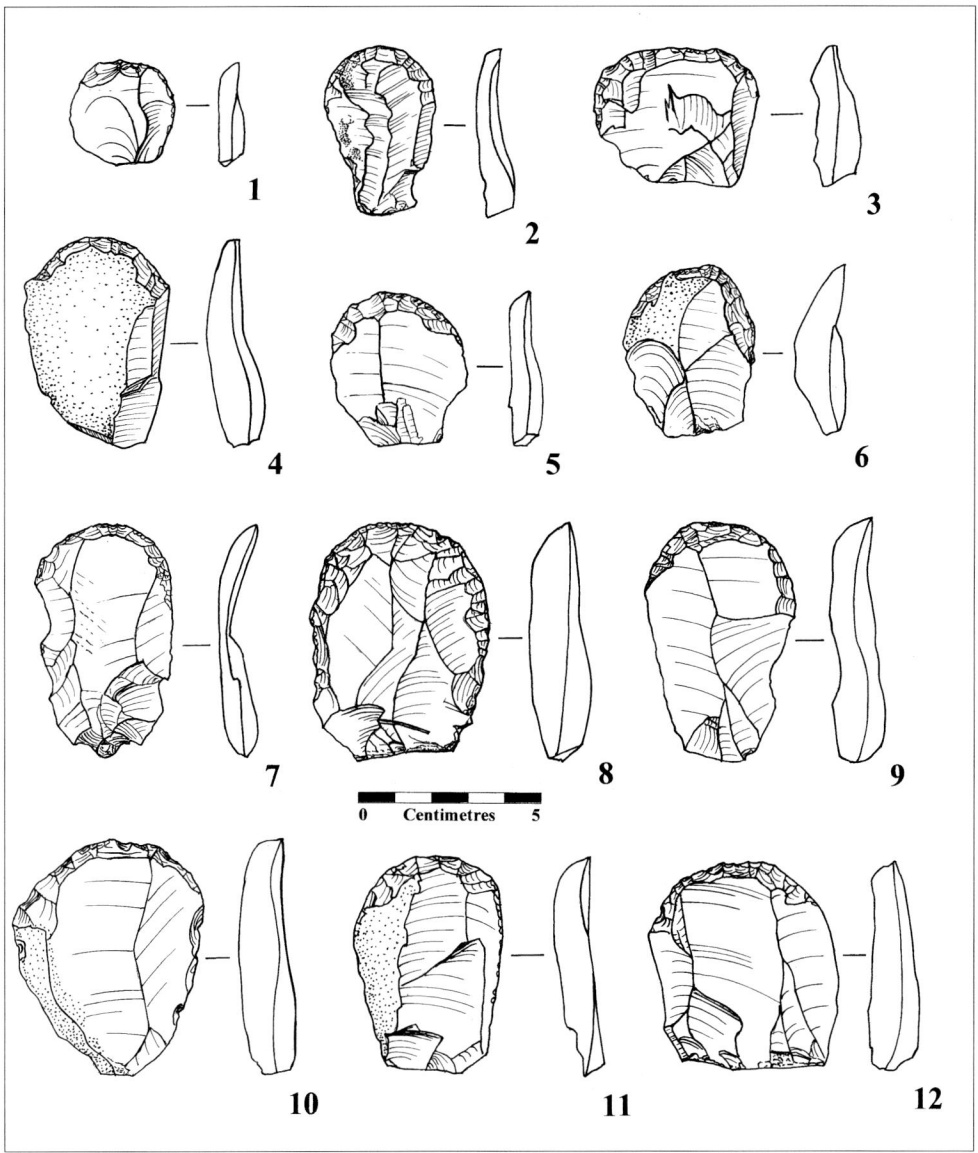

51 Examples of Neolithic end scrapers manufactured on shorter or rounded flakes (No. 8 is an example of a Horseshoe scraper)

In the early Neolithic period the points of piercers and awls were short, and they had a minimal amount of retouch (*54*). Both tool forms could have been easily used in the hand, and there is no evidence that they were hafted. Occasionally a piercer was made on an existing scraper to make a combination tool, but these are rare in this period.

Prehistoric Flintwork

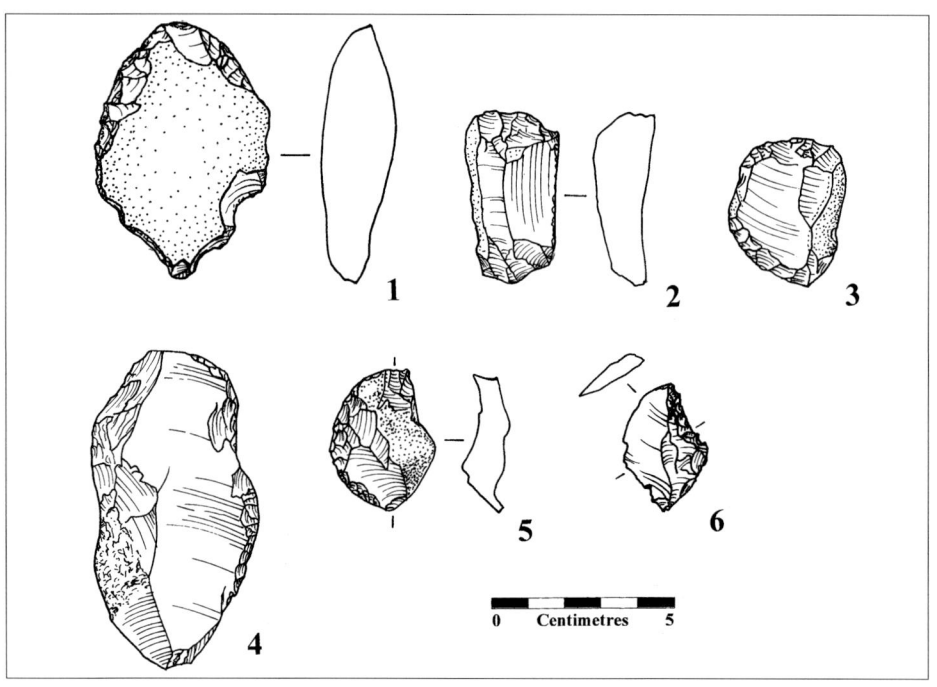

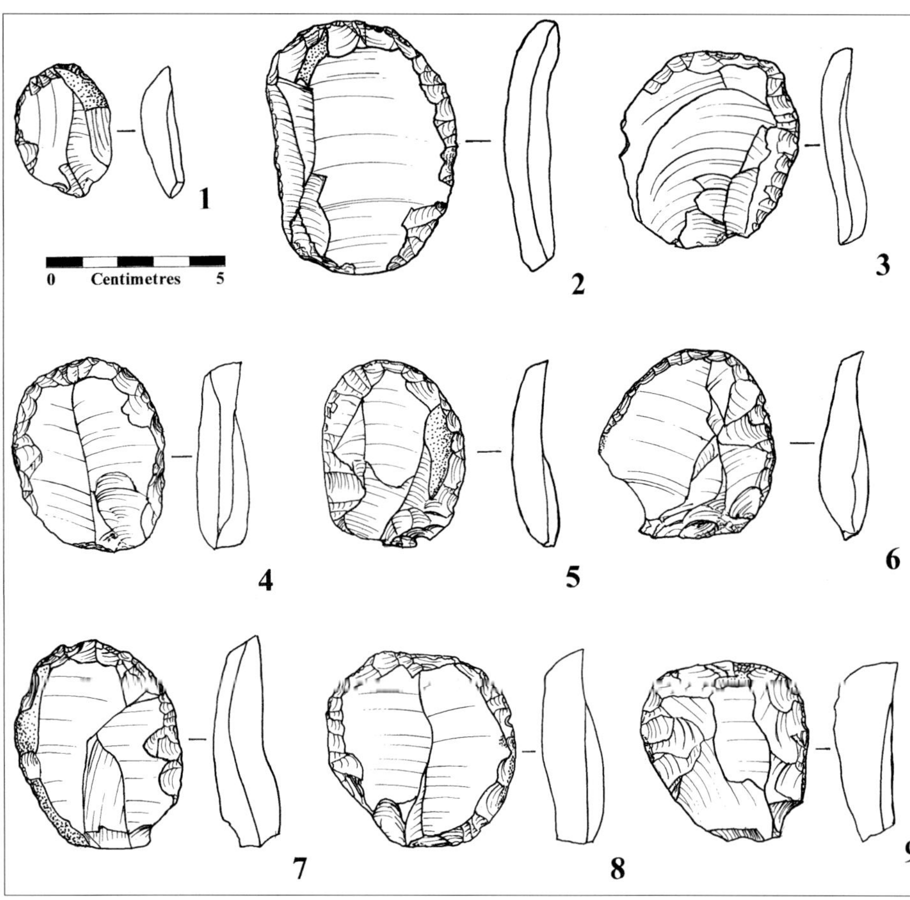

Early Neolithic Flintwork

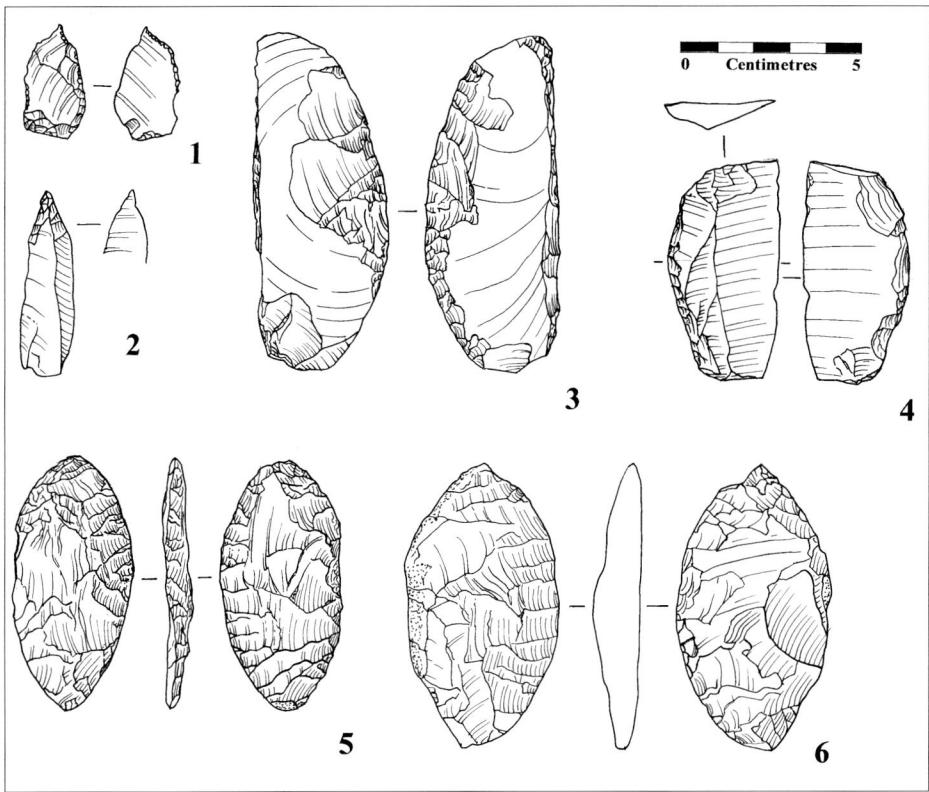

52 Opposite above: Other early Neolithic scrapers: 1) Scraper on a thermal flake; 2-3) Double-ended scrapers; 4-5) Side scrapers; 6) Hollow scraper. From various sites including Hurst Fen and Staines. *After Clark and Robertson-Mackay*

53 Opposite below: Examples of Neolithic scrapers: 1) Small end scraper; 2-3) Side-and-end scrapers; 4-9) Disc scrapers

54 Above: Early Neolithic tools: 1) Awl (note retouch on alternate sides of point); 2) Piercer (note retouch on both edges of the same side); 3-4) Backed knives; 5-6) Laurel leaves. From Hurst Fen. *After Clark*

KNIVES

Knives were made on longer flakes and broad blades, which frequently have a distinctive D shape. They normally retained their platform and bulb of percussion, and were manufactured predominantly on soft hammer-struck pieces. Occasionally the bulb and platform were removed by subsequent thinning of the butt end of the piece. Knives in the early Neolithic period were either simple knives (*54*) with unretouched cutting edges, or invasively retouched knives. Both types frequently had the opposing lateral edge backed with a convex profile, or left as an unmodified thicker edge, which sometimes had a remnant of cortex.

LAUREL LEAVES

These are small bifacially worked tools made from either small nodules or large flakes. Initially the nodule was flaked alternatively over both faces to reduce it in size and to achieve the approximate shape required; this is called a roughout. At sites where laurel leaves were produced, discarded roughouts together with broken fragments, sometimes exhibiting hinge fractures, can be found. The flaking was probably initially carried out with a hard hammer, but then finished with a soft hammer, so thinning flakes with a distinctive curved profile and multi-directional negative scars will also be found at a manufacturing site.

The finished laurel leaf has an asymmetrical form, with normally both faces pressure-flaked to achieve its final ovoid shape (*54*). On occasion only one face has been finished. One convex edge was retouched invasively, and was obviously intended as a cutting edge, while the opposite edge, which was frequently more irregularly shaped, had a more semi-abrupt retouch, perhaps to blunt it. It is not clear what laurel leaves were used for. Their use as spear or projectile points was discounted some time ago as they are not symmetrical, and do not have a point. It is likely that they were used as knives, and were perhaps hafted into wooden handles.

OVATES

Ovates are bifacially flaked oval tools, sometimes resembling Palaeolithic handaxes, which have occasionally been found in Neolithic contexts, for example at some of the Sussex flint mines. They tend to be rather roughly worked, and may have been roughouts for laurel leaves.

SERRATED BLADES OR DENTICULATES

These saw-like serrated blades are frequently found in early Neolithic assemblages (*55*). They were generally made on blades or long flakes, and had tiny continuous notches (denticulations) along part of one or, more rarely, both lateral edges. The blades and flakes were normally soft hammer-struck, but could also be hard hammer-struck. Most serrated blades were straight-edged, but a few were convex, and have a long curving profile. The notches were either made by using a stone tool to apply pressure thus removing small flakes to create the notches, or by dragging another blade at right angles across the edge of the blade, which achieved the same result. The point of percussion for the notch scars could originate from either the ventral or dorsal side of the blade, although the majority appear to originate from the ventral side. There was rarely any backing on the opposite lateral edge, however where this occurred it was finely executed abrupt retouch, probably to facilitate hafting. Sometimes cortex was left on this edge to make the tool easier to hold in the hand.

Early Neolithic Flintwork

At the Staines causewayed enclosure, 198 serrated blades were found (Robertson-Mackay 1987). Of the complete examples 106 had denticulation on one lateral edge only, whilst 49 were denticulated along both lateral edges. The number of 'teeth' per 10mm varied with a maximum of 23, and an average of 10. Only nine serrated blades were backed with abrupt retouch.

BURINS

Burins are occasionally found on early Neolithic sites, and were probably a

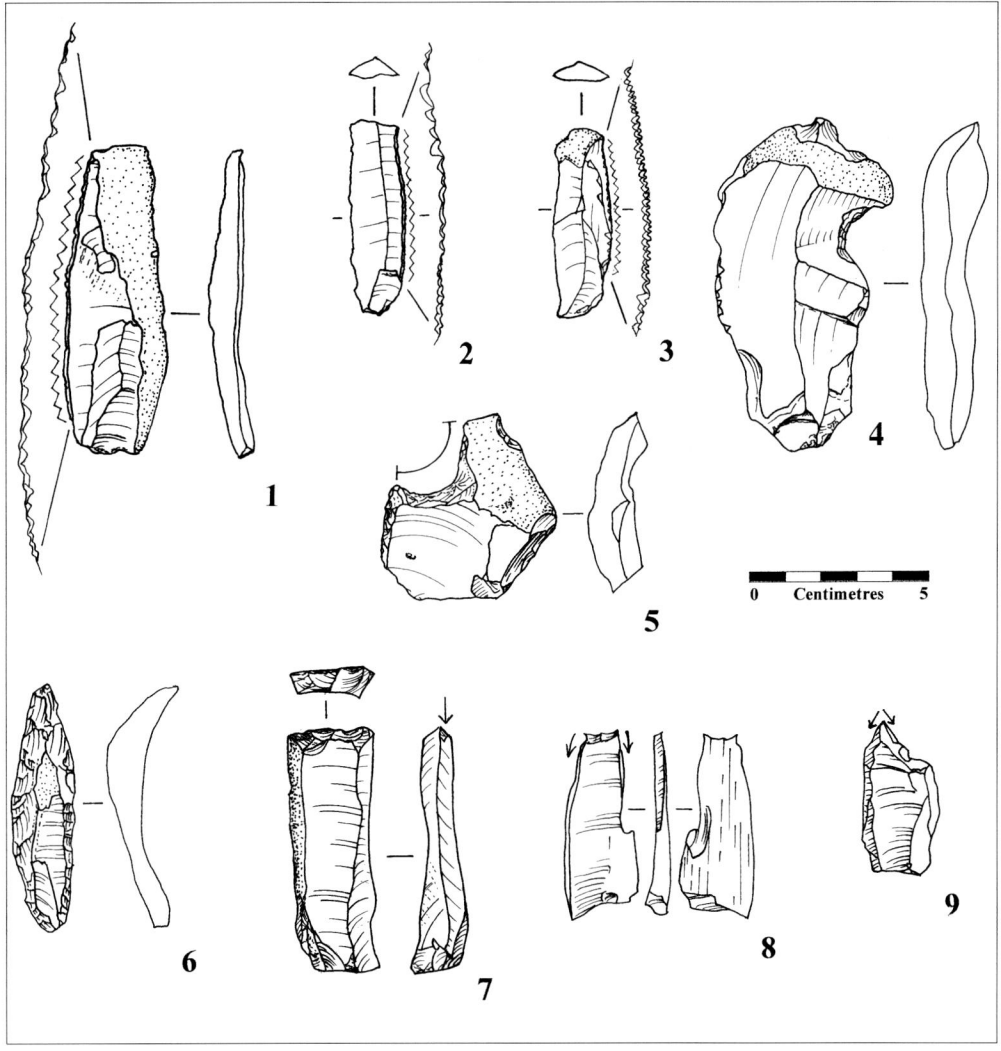

55 Early Neolithic tools: 1-3) Serrated blades (with enlarged view of serrated edges); 4-5) Notched flakes; 6) Fabricator; 7-8) Truncation burins; 9) Dihedral burin. From various sites. *After Butler and Clark*

declining element of the early Neolithic tool kit. The flake or blade on which the burin was made could be either hard or soft hammer-struck, and normally exhibited the typical signs of early Neolithic flintworking techniques. The most common type of burin is the truncation burin (*55*). The most frequent variety of a truncation burin was a single-angle removal, but there are also double-angle removals from the same prepared break. The other major type of burin encountered was the dihedral burin, (*55*) where the spall was removed from a previous burin facet, which was normally unretouched, or from a break or unmodified natural surface.

NOTCHED PIECES

Notched pieces are found in small numbers on some early Neolithic assemblages. They appear to be an expedient type of tool, as they are found on flakes and blades of all types, sizes and shapes (*55*). On occasion, even broken or smaller fragments of flakes have notches added to their lateral edges. Occasionally double-notched pieces occurred, however these may have been a crude form of denticulate.

SICKLES

Composite sickles were the main form of sickle tool in the early to middle Neolithic period. They were made from a number of separate flake or blade sections, which were hafted into a wooden handle to form a cutting edge. The flakes and blades used in composite sickles were generally short and square in shape. Bulbs and platforms were frequently removed, and one edge blunted with abrupt retouch for hafting. The cutting edge was normally left unretouched, but is sometimes found with invasive retouch.

FABRICATORS

Fabricators were made on thick flakes, or on a fragment of a nodule or core. They had an oval, triangular or rectangular cross section, sometimes with one flat side, and are normally flaked over both surfaces, sometimes retaining some cortex (*55*). They have one rounded end that was abraded and worn from use, whilst the other end and adjacent edges of the piece may also have had some wear, possibly from the tool having been hafted into a handle.

ADZES AND PICKS

Adzes and picks that were used during the early Neolithic resemble those from the Mesolithic period, and it would be very difficult to tell them apart. Most early Neolithic sites that produced adzes and picks had a Mesolithic component as well,

Early Neolithic Flintwork

and therefore it is possible that these items may have been residual pieces from the Mesolithic activity. Picks tended to be large and fairly roughly made with a pointed working end, whilst adzes were quite rare in early Neolithic contexts. Some rough looking adzes with a tranchet removal creating a cutting edge (*56*) have been found in early Neolithic contexts (Gardiner 1990). It is possible that these too may be intrusive, or a continuation of later Mesolithic techniques, but in a simplified and reduced form as they were replaced by the more efficient ground forms in the Neolithic. See Chapter 7 for Duggleby polished adzes.

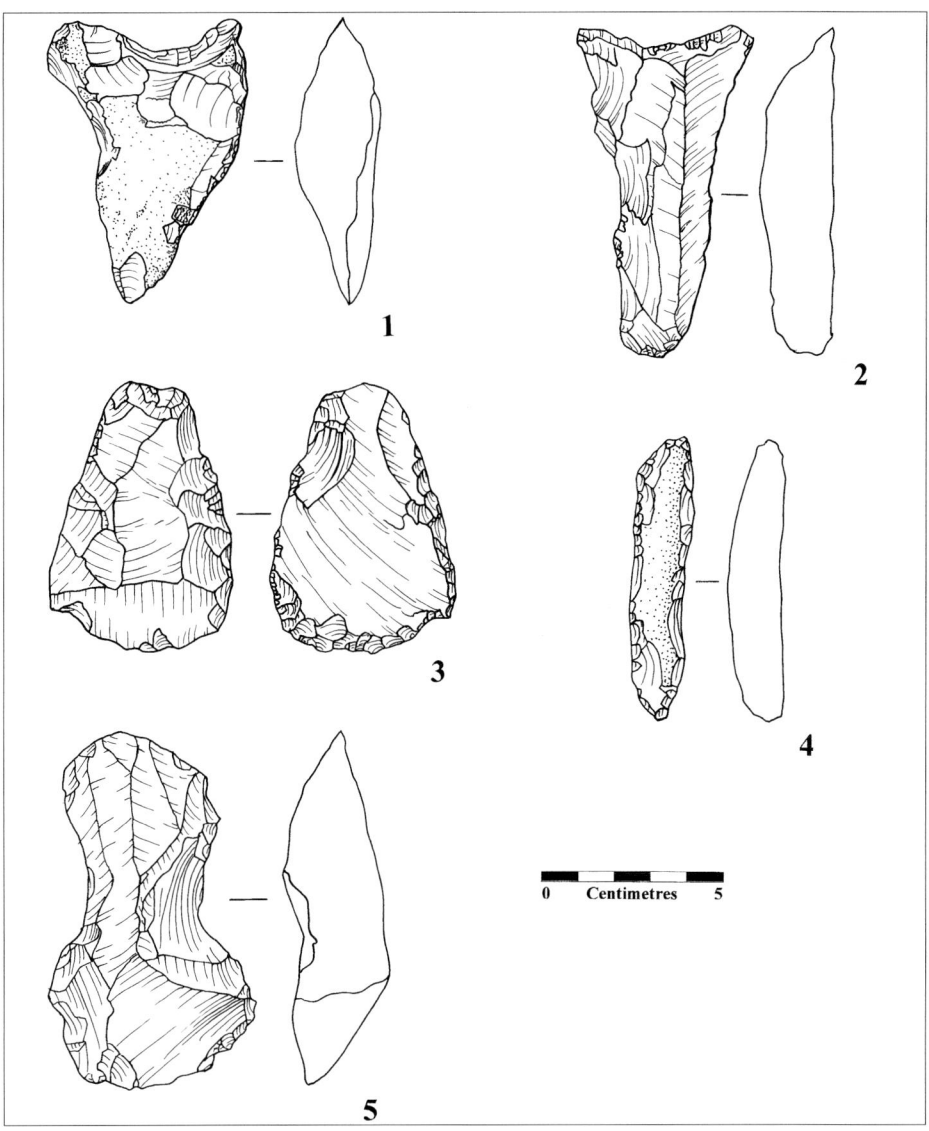

56 Neolithic tools: 1-2) Y-shaped tools; 3) Tranchet tool; 4) Rod; 5) Waisted tool. *After Butler and Gardiner*

Y–SHAPED PIECES

These tools were made on smaller elongated nodules or large thick flakes (*56*). The tool comprised a long body, almost square or oval in section, sometimes shaped to a point at the butt end, which broadened at the distal end. Some were flaked all over, but most were quite crudely made with extensive areas of cortex remaining. All three sides of the tool were normally concave with the shorter side at the distal end frequently being more concave than the other two sides, giving it a distinctive Y-shape. The points of the Y were frequently worked and abraded, as is the shorter side between the two points, confirming that this was the working end of the tool. Although the Y-shaped tool could be held in the hand, the butt end could have been hafted into a handle. Their function is unclear; some may have been used as axes and had transverse flakes removed to form a cutting edge, whilst others may have been used as scraping tools.

RODS

Rods are elongated tools made on segments of large flakes, with steep bilateral or multilateral retouch (*56*). They usually had an oval or plano-convex section, and frequently had cortex remaining on the dorsal surface. There is little evidence of abrasion at the ends of the rod, although occasionally some abrasion is found on the lateral edges, and it is not clear what function they had.

CHISELS

These are very similar to flaked axes (see below), and resemble modern day chisels in shape. They were bifacially flaked long thin pieces of flint, which were normally lenticular in cross section. They had roughly parallel sides, with the butt end normally narrowing, and may have been hafted into a handle. The cutting edge is also frequently narrower than the body of the tool, and was bifacially flaked to form a cutting edge, which was more often than not ground. Chisel roughouts are occasionally found, suggesting that the manufacturing process was similar to that used for making axes.

UTILISED AND RETOUCHED FLAKES OR BLADES

During the early Neolithic many waste flakes and blades were semi-abruptly retouched partly along one lateral edge, and utilised for various cutting and scraping tasks. Many others had one lateral edge left unretouched, whilst the opposite edge was either blunted or retained some cortex. Examination of the unretouched edge often reveals edge damage, suggesting that these were also utilised. These pieces do not fall into any specific tool type, and were probably expedient tools that were quickly made, used and then discarded. Blades or longer flakes tend to have been used, and exist both with and without cortex. They can be found in large numbers on some sites.

EARLY NEOLITHIC USE OF FLINT

The range of flint tools used in the early Neolithic period reflected the transition that was being made from living entirely on natural foodstuffs to cultivated cereals and domesticated animals. The whole knapping strategy suggests that, away from the Upper Chalk, flint was still being carefully curated, and the maximum use was being made of each nodule. This fits with the view that early Neolithic communities were not fixed in one place, and were still moving through the landscape during the different seasons, but now with managed crops and domesticated animals incorporated into the annual cycle. There were still familiar elements of the hunter-gatherer tool kit, such as arrowheads, burins and denticulates. Combined with this change, a range of new flint tools was being produced that suited the activities of the farming communities. These new tools included sickles for cutting crops and ground axes for clearing the woodland.

Another feature of the early Neolithic period is the large monuments that were constructed across the landscape, such as causewayed enclosures, long barrows and chambered tombs. These must have required enormous numbers of people to build them, as well as hinting at a level of organisation and control hitherto not seen. Evidence of where these people lived is hard to find, as most of the known early Neolithic settlement sites are characterised by just a few postholes and pits. However, these sites have usually produced large quantities of worked flint.

Hurst Fen, the first of three representative early Neolithic sites we will look at, is characteristic of these so called 'settlement sites' and produced a typical assemblage of early Neolithic flintwork. The other sites are causewayed enclosures, which also produced a classic range of early to middle Neolithic flintwork, but are thought to have been used as communal places for gathering together, and were not settlement sites.

Hurst Fen, Suffolk – An early Neolithic 'settlement' site

The site of Hurst Fen in Suffolk was excavated between 1954 and 1958 (Clark 1960). Although the excavation found only a few postholes, pits and ditches, a large assemblage of early Neolithic flintwork was recovered. However, there was no definite evidence of houses or structures that you would normally associate with a farming settlement. The analysis of the flintwork assemblage by J.G.D. Clark, and his subsequent report, provided the type-site for early Neolithic flintwork in this country. Clark divided the cores into five classes, some with sub-categories:

Class A:	One platform	
1) flakes removed all round		12
2) flakes removed part of the way round		206

Class B:	Two platforms	
1) parallel platforms		1
2) one platform at oblique angle		101
3) platforms at right angles		10

Class C:	Three or more platforms	26
Class D:	Keeled – flakes struck from two directions	78
Class E:	Keeled – but with one or more platforms	98

Of the 532 cores in a sample that were subjected to a detailed analysis, 160 had evidence of platform preparation, although Clark mistakenly identified this as subsequent use of the core as a scraper. Other flint specialists, in analysing cores from Neolithic assemblages and those of other periods, have subsequently used Clark's classification, although some consider it to be too complex and simplify it, normally omitting the sub categories and merging the keeled cores (discoidal cores) into a single group. Scrapers at Hurst Fen were sorted and classified into five groups:

Class A	End scrapers	502
Class B	Double-ended scrapers	8
Class C	Disc scrapers	14
Class D	Side scrapers	19
Class E	On broken flakes	83

Thirty per cent of the scrapers were on longer flakes or blades, whilst 11 per cent were made on thermal flakes. The numbers shown above give an idea of the proportions of each type of scraper on the site, and their relative importance and therefore the frequency at which they may be expected on other early Neolithic sites. This shows the rarity of double-ended scrapers, and the relative insignificance of side and disc scrapers. Scrapers made on broken flakes (fragments missing their proximal or bulbar end) make up a significant part of the assemblage. Other implements at the site included 58 leaf-shaped arrowheads, 356 serrated flakes, 18 laurel leaves, 16 awls and piercers, 11 burins and 10 backed knives. There were also six polished flint axes, eight fabricators and a single sickle fragment.

The Hurst Fen assemblage includes examples of most of the different implement types that were manufactured during the early Neolithic period. The very broad range of different implement types would suggest that there were many different activities being carried out at the site. These vary from hunting, as represented by the arrowheads, through processing activities (using scrapers, knives and piercers/awls) to farming activities as evidenced by the sickle. These early Neolithic sites are also often associated with examples of the first pottery, which helps in the dating. Yet at many sites pottery is absent, and only careful analysis of the flintwork can provide us with both a date for a site, and an indication of the activities that were being undertaken.

Windmill Hill – The flint assemblage from the causewayed enclosure
The flintwork assemblage from Keiller's excavations at the early Neolithic causewayed enclosure of Windmill Hill was published in 1965 (Smith), and is another good example of a typical early Neolithic flintwork assemblage. Smith used Clark's classification for the 271 cores, and found that there were similar proportions of the types to those found at Hurst Fen. The unbroken waste flakes from the primary levels were analysed, and it was found that 25 per cent were true blades, whilst only 13.5 per cent of the flakes were broad. Some 52 per cent of the flakes were non-cortical. The discarded waste flakes were considerably smaller than those used to make serrated or utilised flakes.

The 218 scrapers were classified in the same way as those from Hurst Fen, with the proportions of the different scraper forms showing many similarities. Amongst the other tools recovered were 627 serrated flakes, 414 utilised flakes, 132 leaf-shaped arrowheads, 84 knives, 68 piercers and awls, 25 laurel leaves, two fabricators, two one-piece sickle fragments plus 21 sickle-flakes from composite sickles, and some polished axe fragments. Burins were noted as being completely absent. The 132 leaf shaped arrowheads found at Windmill Hill were divided into two types, those that were bifacially retouched (109), and those which had retouch confined to just the tip and edges (23). The complete arrowheads ranged in length from 22mm to 42mm.

Although this assemblage of flintwork resembles that from the Hurst Fen settlement site in many ways, the two sites have very different functions. The common denominator is the flintwork and pottery, which together confirm the cultural affinities of the two sites.

Staines Causewayed Enclosure
The causewayed enclosure at Staines was excavated between 1961-63 (Robertson-MacKay 1987), and an assemblage of 24,562 pieces of worked flint was recovered. The 738 cores were classified according to Clark's scheme:

Class A1	10
Class A2	453
Class B1	4
Class B2	104
Class B3	39

Class C   39
Class D and E   43
Unclassifiable   46

The proportions of each type are similar to those at Hurst Fen, with Class A2 dominating, and Class B2 next most common. There are however fewer Class D and E cores at Staines. There was little evidence of platform preparation, but numerous core rejuvenation and core-trimming flakes were present. Unretouched flakes made up around 80 per cent of the assemblage, but relatively few could be classed as blades. The small size and high proportion of cortical flakes reflected the small nodular raw material that was being used. The 389 scrapers were classified using a modified version of Clark's Hurst Fen scheme:

A	End scrapers	169
A/D	Side-and-end scrapers	136
C	Disc scrapers	7
D	Side scrapers	35
E	Broken scrapers	5
F	Unclassifiable	2
G	On thermal flakes	36

End scrapers dominate the assemblage, but with significant numbers of side-and-end scrapers, which were not separately identified at Hurst Fen, also present. A single hollow scraper was also present, but not separately identified in the table. The number of scrapers made on thermal flakes was quite high (9.2 per cent). Although scrapers were the most common implement type, there were also over 195 serrated flakes, 160 piercers and awls, 118 notched pieces, 103 knives, 66 laurel leaves, 34 leaf-shaped arrowheads, 21 axes and 12 fabricators. Thirteen transverse and triangular arrowheads and a one-piece sickle were also found.

Apart from a few pieces, which suggested continued activity in the later Neolithic and early Bronze Age, the composition of this assemblage is typically early Neolithic. The lack of blades, and the small flake size, was associated with the local raw materials that were being exploited, which were predominantly river-gravel flint nodules.

A recent study has shown that the most common flint implements found at causewayed enclosures were scrapers, serrated flakes, piercers and retouched flakes, with smaller numbers of leaf-shaped arrowheads, axes, laurel leaves, knives and fabricators (Saville 2002). It was concluded that these assemblages did not indicate that there were specialised production or craft activities being carried out at the causewayed enclosures.

7

NEOLITHIC FLINT AXE PRODUCTION

During the Neolithic period a new type of axe was produced in huge numbers. The ground and polished flint axe, together with similar ground and polished axes made from other types of stone, represents a major change in flintworking technology, and also symbolises the clearance of woodland that had begun to take place. Axes were made from flint that had been extracted from the chalk by mining or quarrying, or collected from surface deposits, such as the Clay-with-flints on the South Downs. Not all flint axes were ground or polished (*colour plate 17*). Many were used in an unground state as flaked axes, whilst others had only the cutting edge of the axe ground or polished.

THE AXE PRODUCTION PROCESS

The axe production process varied slightly depending upon the type of raw material that was being used. As well as nodules, large flakes were also frequently used as the blanks for making axes, and at some flint mining sites, flakes may have been the primary raw material used. The process for making an axe was broadly as follows. The first part of the process was to select a suitable nodule, or suitably sized flake. The initial flaking was carried out with a hard hammer, probably removing flakes from one face of the blank first, and then from the opposite face, ensuring that the overall shape of the intended axe was maintained throughout to form the roughout (*57*). The preparation flakes from this initial flaking have the expected broad butts and pronounced bulb of percussion resulting from the use of a hard hammer. The initial flakes would either have cortex on the dorsal side, or have multi-directional negative scars, reflecting the removal of flakes from that surface from both edges of the blank. Many roughouts are found abandoned on axe manufacturing sites, normally either because of a misdirected blow that broke the roughout, or because too large a flake was removed, thus making continued flaking impractical. Flaws, which were often encountered in the flint nodules, could also lead to the roughout being discarded.

The next stage was to shape the roughout into a preform. All of the remaining cortex was removed, any high ridges were reduced in size and the

Prehistoric Flintwork

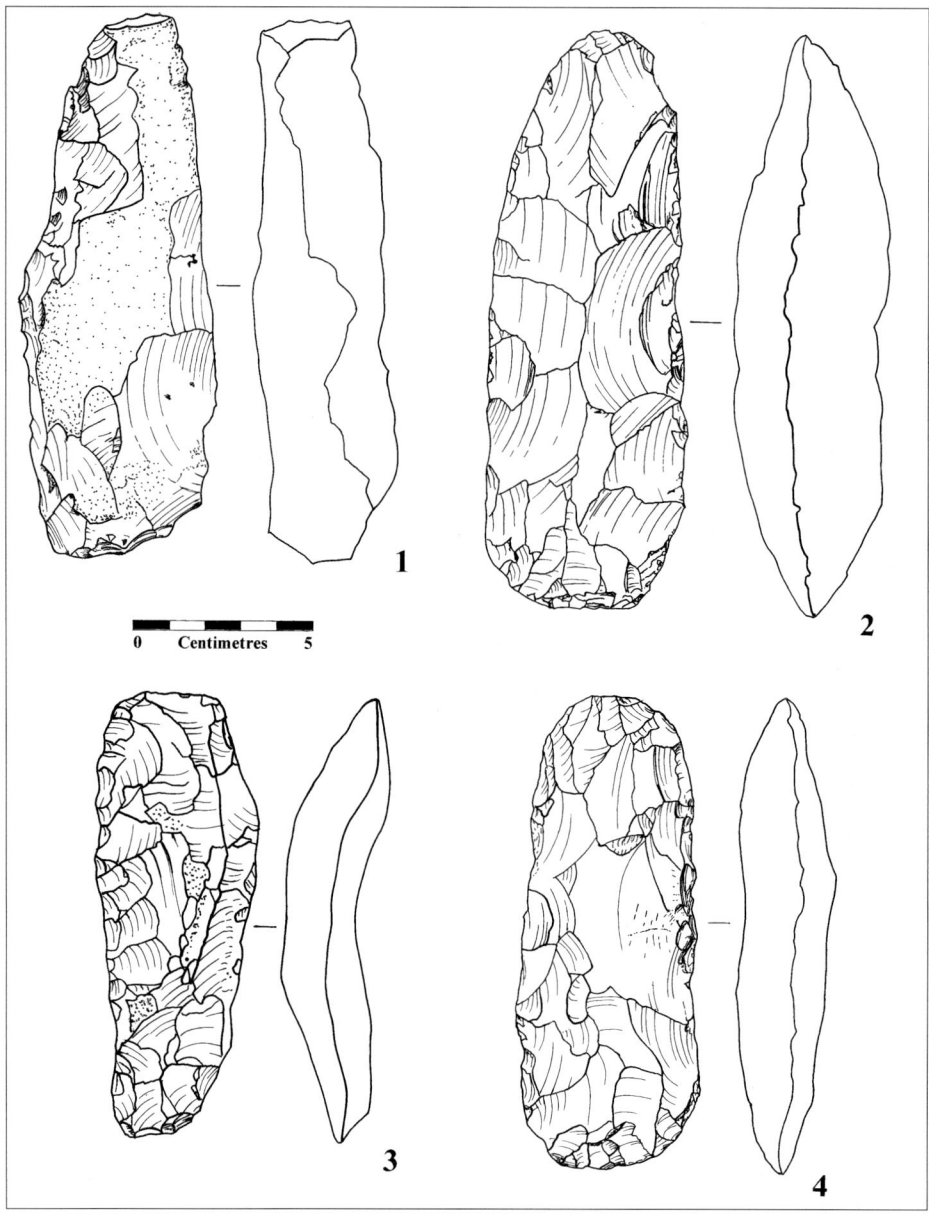

57 Neolithic axe production: 1) Roughout; 2) Preform; 3) Axe preform on a flake; 4) Cissbury axe preform. From Pyecombe, Long Down and Cisbury. *After Butler and Holgate*

cutting edge was carefully retouched with shallow flake removals to form a straight and sharp edge (*57*). The finishing flakes during this shaping process were removed with a soft hammer, and so have thin curving profiles, narrow butts, a diffuse bulb and small lip associated with soft hammer production, together with multi-directional negative scars on the dorsal side (*58*). Having achieved the intended shape of the axe, some final retouching was carried out

Neolithic Flint Axe Production

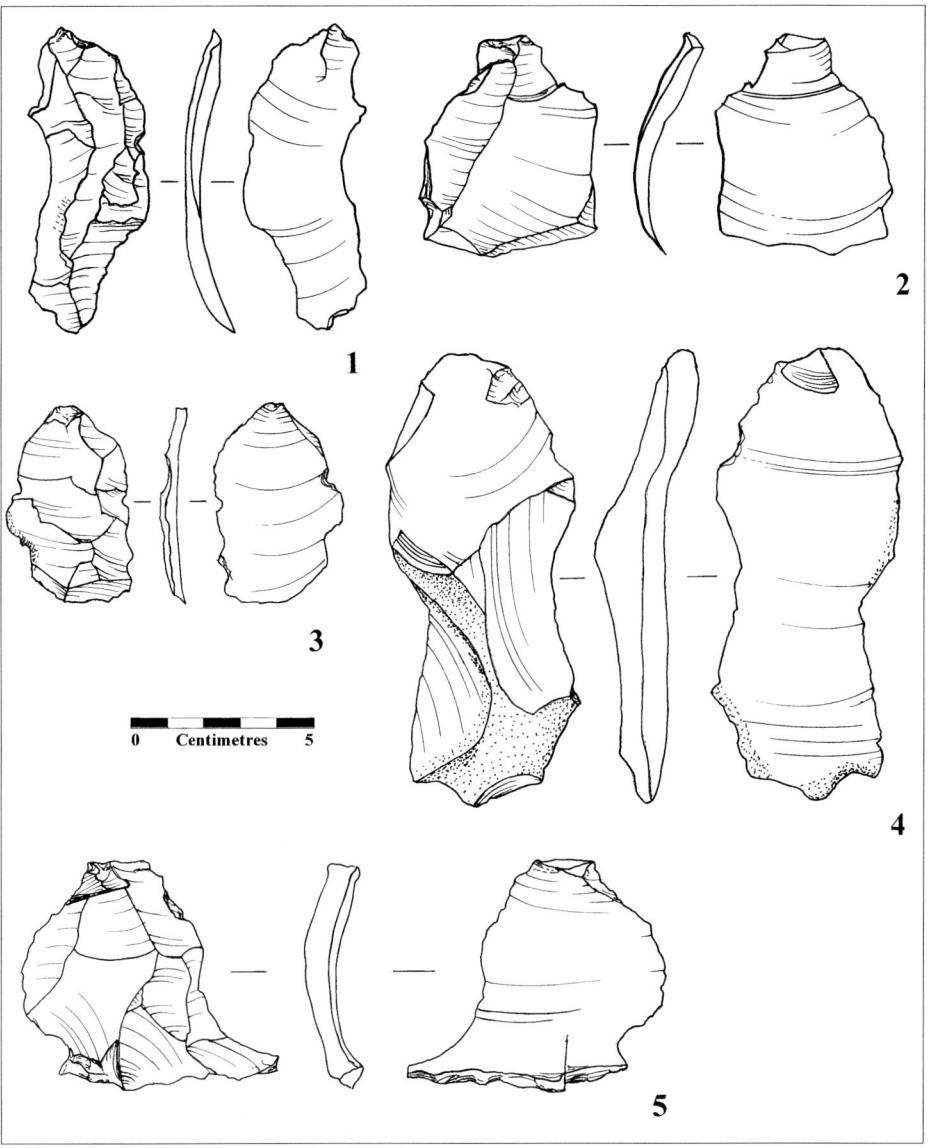

58 Examples of axe-thinning flakes from Cissbury. Note: thin curving profiles, narrow butts, a diffuse bulb and small lip, together with multi-directional negative scars on the dorsal side

around the edges to prepare it for grinding. Discarded preforms are also found on axe-manufacturing sites. Some have been broken during the final stages of production, but others seem to have been abandoned due to flaws or simply because they cannot be shaped into the required form.

The process up to this point was fairly straightforward and not too time consuming. An experienced knapper could have taken the axe to the end of the preform stage in under 20 minutes. The axe was also perfectly useable in this form, and many were used without any further work or grinding. However, other axes were then ground, sometimes over their entire surface, and sometimes only at the cutting edge. The grinding and polishing of the axe was a laborious process, requiring the continual grinding of the surface with a handheld sandstone rubber stone, or against a piece of sandstone rock (*polissoir*). Water was used as a coolant, and loose sand may have been used as a medium to speed up the process, but it would still have taken a long time to completely grind and polish an axe. Various times have been quoted for grinding an axe, but these very much depend upon its size and how much of it is to be ground. Smaller axes may have only taken some five hours (Olausson 1982), whilst larger axes could have taken up to 40 hours (Harding 1989).

Various types of *polissoir* were used. Some were small and could be transported to wherever axes were being produced. In Sussex it is likely that small pieces of sandstone, which were available from local Wealden sources, were used as small hand-held *polissoirs*, otherwise the sarsen erratics found over the South Downs may also have been used. In Wiltshire, large sarsen stones were used to polish axes, with one example on Fyfield Down (*colour plate 18*) near Avebury, and another incorporated into West Kennet long barrow. In each case the long grooves resulting from the polishing or sharpening of axes can clearly be seen.

If the finished axe was to be used for woodworking, then it would have been hafted into a wooden handle. A small number of axes, still set into their wooden handles, have been found in anaerobic conditions, and have helped us to understand how they were hafted. Sometimes the axe was first set into an antler sleeve, to cushion the shock during use, before being fixed into the handle. The axe would have been inserted into a hole in the handle and secured in place with leather and fibre thongs (*colour plate 19*). Where the handles have survived, they have been made from a variety of wood types including alder, birch, and pine.

FLINT AXES

Axes can be divided into categories based on aspects of their shape, and a number of typological schemes have been devised in different parts of the country (Clough *et al*. 1979). One typology divides axes into thick or thin-butted varieties. Thick-butted axes had a thick oval section with a broad butt end, whilst the thin-butted axe had a squashed oval section, and was generally narrower than the thick-butted variety. From the side thin-butted axes had a much thinner profile, narrowing to a point at the cutting end, and having a rounded butt end. The categorisation of thick- and thin-butted axes was first introduced from Scandinavia, and although lithic specialists in Britain often use it, it may not be entirely appropriate for establishing British typologies.

Neolithic Flint Axe Production

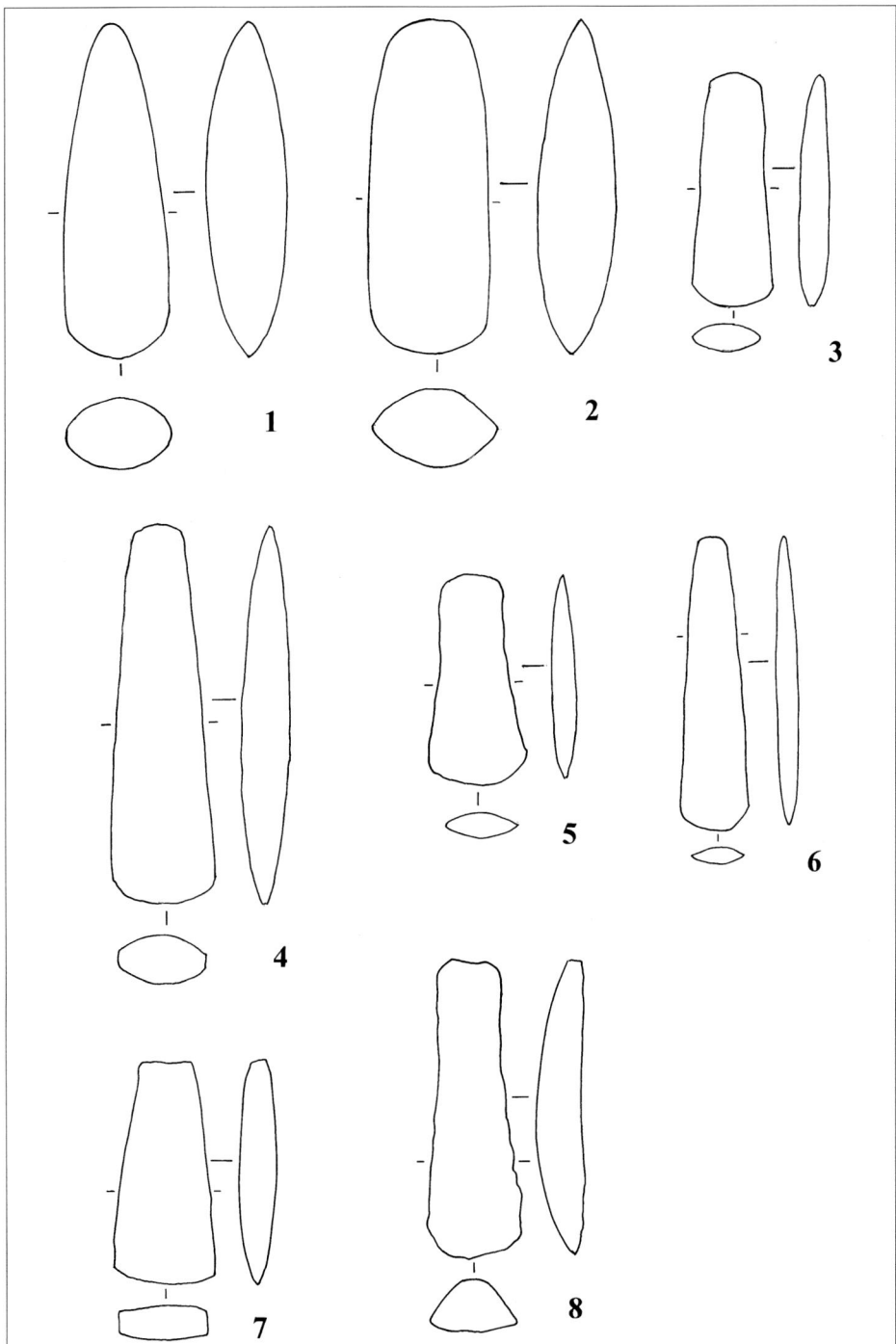

59 Neolithic axe types: 1-2) Thick-butted (Type A); 3) Thin-butted (Type B); 4) Elongated axe with facetted sides (Type C); 5) Thin-butted (Type B) with concave sides; 6) Chisel; 7) Rectangular section (Type D); 8) D-shaped section (Type E). *After Holgate and Clough* et al.

Prehistoric Flintwork

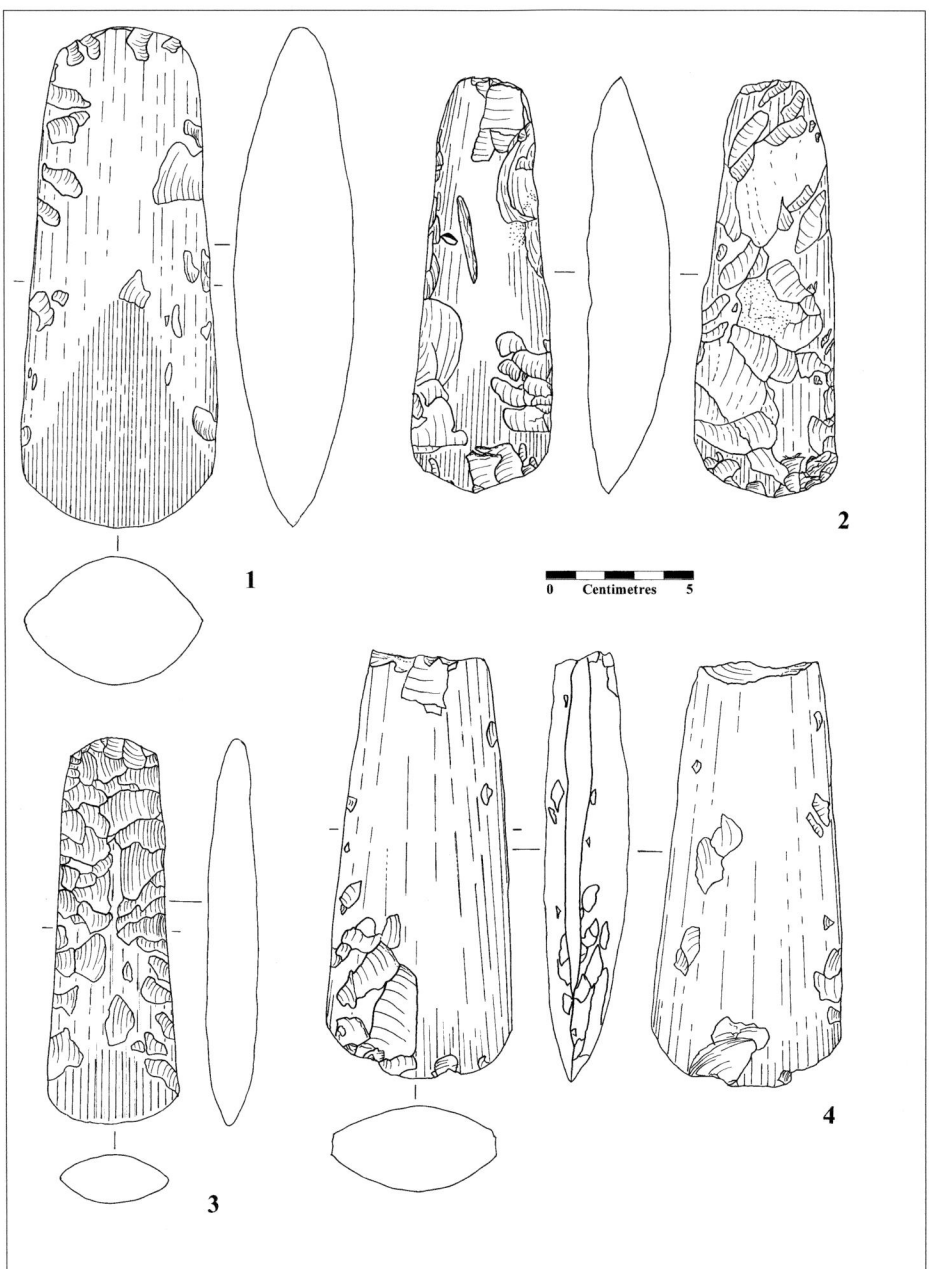

60 Polished axes: 1) Thick-butted (Type A) axe polished all over; 2) Polished axe with use-damage and re-flaking; 3) Thin-butted (Type B) axe polished at cutting end; 4) Thick-butted axe with facetted edges (Type C). *After Butler and Holgate*

A second typology divides axes into five categories based on their cross section (Field *et al.* 1984) (*59*), and with occasional variation is the most commonly used method for categorising Neolithic axes.

A	Oval varying between nearly circular to elliptical
B	Lenticular or double-convex
C	Lenticular with facetted sides
D	Rectangular
E	D-shaped

Using one or other of these typologies, axes are also divided between those that are ground and those that have been left unground.

Polished/ground axes

These axes were normally polished or ground over their entire surface (*60*), but are also frequently found with just the cutting edge ground (called edge-ground axes). Sometimes the grinding was not sufficiently deep to remove all of the flaking scars. When viewed from the side their profile narrowed towards the cutting edge. At the butt end the profile also narrowed, but was more rounded, and occasionally flat. The butt end was often left in a flaked state, which may have helped to haft the axe into a handle as it created friction and made the fit into the handle more secure. Occasionally the sides of the axe are facetted: the flat side probably being achieved by grinding. They were normally less than 200mm long.

During the latter part of the Neolithic period, some ground axes were produced with concave sides and very broad and pronounced rounded cutting edges. These are often referred to as Seamer axes, and are often very highly polished, making it unlikely that they were used for utilitarian purposes. They were also frequently made from fine-quality coloured flint – in red, yellow, orange and mottled varieties (Manby 1979). The Duggleby type adze, which has a slightly curved profile with a D-shaped section and one flat face, was also manufactured from coloured flint and had a similar fine-polish finish.

Ground chisels were much thinner and narrower forms of the ground axe, normally between 75mm and 125mm long and less than 25mm wide, although in areas where flint is common they can be larger. Chisels can also be ground over the entire surface or just at the cutting edge, and tended to be more common in the later Neolithic.

Broken ground axes were frequently re-flaked, but rarely re-ground. If the cutting edge was damaged or broken during use, it would be re-sharpened by removing a number of small flakes, and then retouched so that a new cutting edge was created. Other common breaks were at the point where the axe was hafted into its handle. A break here would result in some re-flaking, sometimes using the break as a platform, to reshape it so that it could be re-hafted into the handle.

Flaked axes

Flaked axes and chisels were also utilised in their final flaked form without

Prehistoric Flintwork

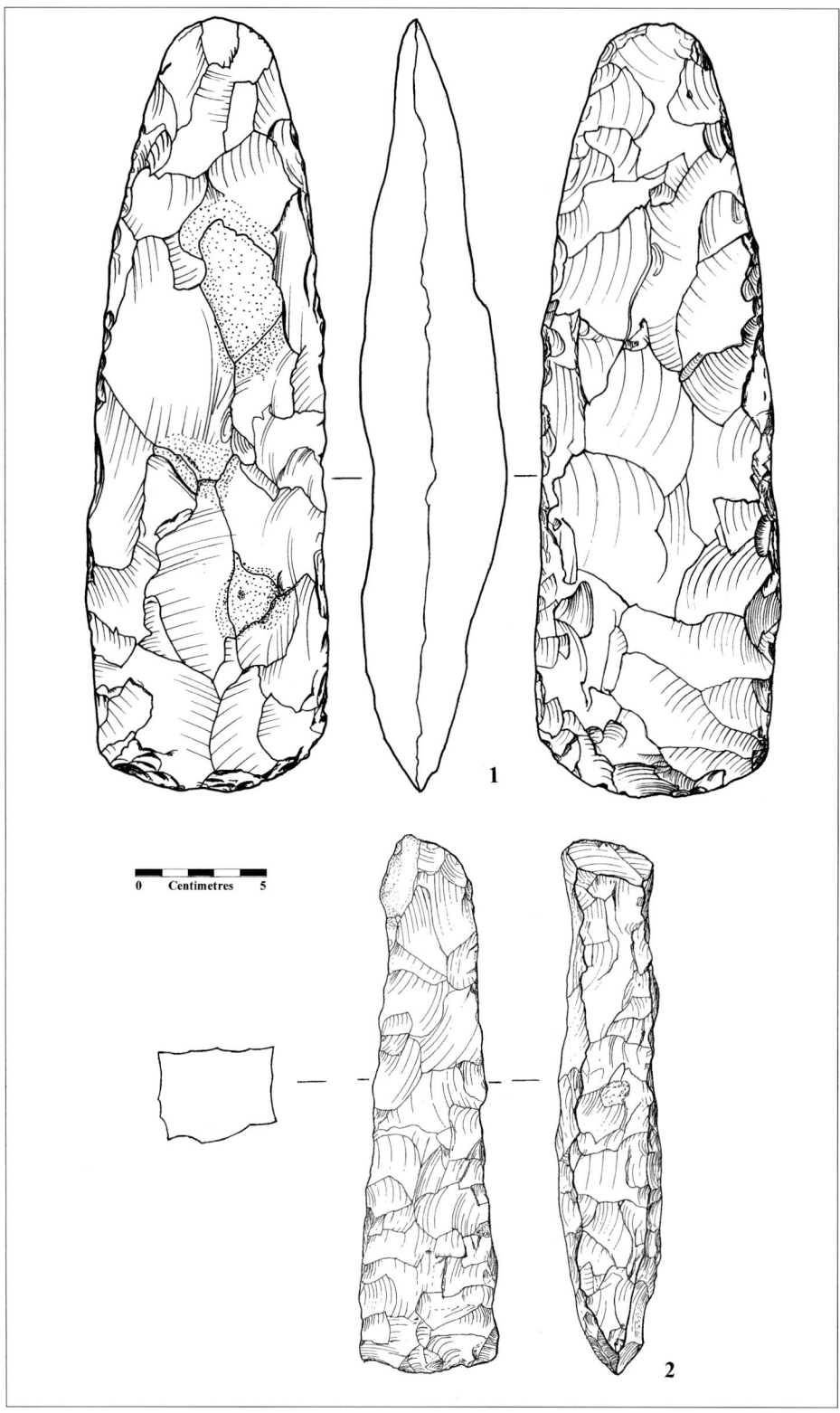

any polishing or grinding (*colour plate 20*). The cutting edge of the preform was finished by careful flaking and retouching to form a slightly convex shape. They vary considerably in size and shape, with the largest in the region of 300mm in length (*61*), but most being around 200mm long. If the axe had been hafted, then there would frequently be evidence of abrasion on the upper lateral edges.

Scandinavian axes
These axes were probably originally imported into Britain from Scandinavia, and occasionally the flint raw material from which they have been made can be sourced to Scandinavia. They have a distinctive type of flake that is created during the final stages of production (Vemming Hansen 1981). These flakes were removed with a soft hammer alternately from both faces along the edge of the axe, and then using the edge as a platform, flakes were removed across each face. The butt ends of the latter flakes therefore exhibited flaking scars from the earlier side removals. The final sharpening flakes were removed from the cutting edge of the axe. These finishing flakes are rarely found in Britain, but are common in Scandinavia, suggesting that these axes were probably mostly imported in a finished form. It is however possible that some may have

62 Gallery IIa, Mineshaft 21, Harrow Hill, The Curwen's excavation 1924-5. *Copyright: The Sussex Archaeological Society*

61 Opposite: Neolithic axes: 1) Large Neolithic flaked axe found in a cache of flaked axes at Clayton, Sussex; 2) Scandinavian axe. *After Butler*

been copied and made in Britain. They are distinguished by their rectangular section with facetted sides, and were either completely flaked, or ground only at the cutting edge. Another recognition point is that the negative flake scars tend to be smaller and deeper than those from British flaked axes. Scandinavian axes can be up to 200mm long (*61*).

OTHER TYPES OF NEOLITHIC AXE

Numerous other stone types were exploited for the production of ground axes during the Neolithic. These rocks (including dolerite, tuff, greywacke and greenstone) originated in Wales, Scotland, the Lake District, the South West and Ireland, where the stone was quarried, frequently from quite remote and inaccessible upland places. Whereas flint axes were used in both flaked and ground forms, other stone axes were mostly utilised in a pecked or ground form, although some types of stone could also be flaked. The study of the distribution of axes of these other types of stone, and their petrological analysis (Woodcock *et al.* 1988), has shown that they were traded or exchanged over long distances with, for example, axes sourced to the Lake District and Cornwall found all over southern and eastern Britain. In addition, there are axes made of jadeite (which probably came from the Alps) found in British early Neolithic contexts, which indicate that a much wider pattern of exchange was taking place throughout Europe at this time. A full review of these non-flint stone axes is beyond the scope of this book, but discussions of the sources, production and trade of these axes can be found in other volumes (Malone 2001, Edmonds 1995 and Clough *et al.* 1988). As well as axes and chisels, other similar tool types were made from stone including wedges and gouges (Darvill 1989), and some stone types were also used for flake tools and arrowheads.

NEOLITHIC FLINT MINES AND QUARRIES

During the Neolithic period a number of different flint sources were exploited for the manufacture of axes and other tools. As well as surface deposits such as Clay-with-flints, river and beach gravels, and other secondary sources, some primary seams of flint in the chalk were directly exploited by mining and quarrying. A recent survey of flint extraction sites in England by English Heritage (Barber *et al.* 1999) suggests that there are 10 confirmed and a further 10 possible flint mining and quarrying sites in England, plus two in Scotland and one in Northern Ireland. The largest group of flint mine sites is clustered on the chalk downland of southern England, of which those on the Sussex South Downs have been investigated archaeologically over the last century or so (Russell 2001a) (*62*). Here, flint mines at Cissbury, Harrow Hill, Blackpatch, Church Hill and Long Down were exploited for flint during the early Neolithic and are amongst the earliest 'monuments' created in this country (radiocarbon dates ranging from before 4000 BC through to around 3000 BC). Mining then seems to have stopped at the Sussex flint mines, and during the later Neolithic period only Grimes Graves in Norfolk (radiocarbon dates of 3000-2500 BC) appears to have been used, although on a grand scale. On the continent, flint mines have been found in a number of countries; notably France, the Netherlands, Scandinavia and Poland.

The method of extraction seems to have been the same at all sites. First the seam was quarried in an open cast manner, but as the seam became deeper within the hillside it was necessary to dig shafts. A vertical shaft was then dug into the chalk until the required seam of flint was reached (*63*). The shafts were between 4m and 8m in diameter, and up to 14m deep, and were generally dug through two or more seams of lesser quality flint until the preferred seam was reached (Holgate 1991). Once the seam was reached, radiating galleries were excavated following the seams of flint (*colour plate 21*), leaving pillars to support the roof. The excavation was carried out with very basic tools, namely antler picks (*colour plate 22*) and shovels made from the shoulder blades of cattle. The flint nodules were probably lifted out of the mineshaft in wicker baskets or leather bags by ropes, or carried up wooden ladders. Initial working of the flint nodules seems to have taken place close to the mines, as numerous 'working floors' covered with thousands of waste flakes have been found around the mineshafts. Here the flint nodules were worked into roughouts and preforms, but were then taken elsewhere to be worked into their finished forms. Once the flint from one shaft was exhausted or the shaft abandoned, another was excavated nearby. The chalk rubble extracted from the new mine was usually thrown downhill of the shaft where sometimes it partly filled earlier shafts situated there. Normally it was left in huge spoil heaps around the shaft on the downhill side. The flint extracted from the mines was not only used for producing axes as there is evidence from some sites that other tools were also being made. In fact at Grimes Graves there is very little evidence for the manufacturing of axes at all!

The flint mines varied in size from smaller ones such as Long Down with about 20 shafts, through Cissbury with around 100 shafts, to Grimes Graves, with over 360 shafts. However, Martin's Clump in Hampshire is likely to be the largest in terms of number of shafts (Barber *et al.* 1999). At Den of Boddam in Scotland the geology is different from the chalk downland of southern Britain. Here, over 450 mine shafts/quarry pits were cut up to 3.5m deep through a barren glacial till to get at the flint pebbles below (Ashmore 1996). On the County Antrim coast in Northern Ireland, there appears to have been only casual exploitation of the flint at coastline exposures, although open cast mining took place at Ballygalley Hill. The ground and polished flint axes, which are frequently quite small and only partially polished, were a minor

Prehistoric Flintwork

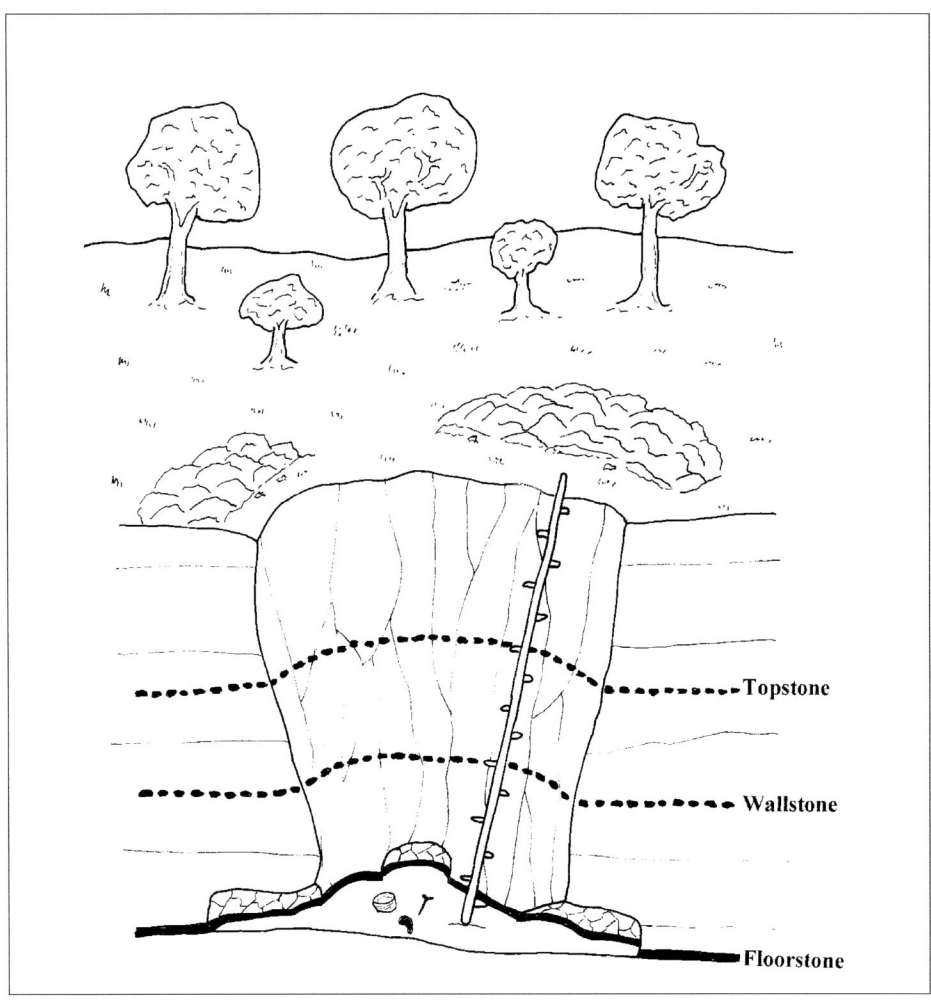

63 Section through a typical flint mine. After Holgate

product of the flintworking sites, and do not occur in large numbers in Ireland (Woodman 1992).

Although we do not fully understand how the flint mining industry was organised, it was clearly a large and structured activity. It is possible, considering the long period of time during which the mines were in operation, that only a single shaft was open and exploited on a seasonal basis at any one time. It has been calculated that a typical shaft at Grimes Graves would have produced some 40 tonnes of flint, which (if used to its maximum potential) would have produced 50,000 implements (Holgate 1991).

THE GROUND FLINT AXE IN NEOLITHIC SOCIETY

If flint and stone axes were useable in their flaked form, then why go to all the extra work and bother of grinding them? There are two answers to that question, one or both of which may have applied. The first is a practical reason, which is that a flaked flint axe has many angular facets at and around its cutting edge. If the axe is used in its flaked form then each of these facets can effectively act as a platform. A blow at the wrong angle could break the axe. However, if it has been polished, then the cutting surface of the axe is smooth and there are no angles, and consequently fewer breaks (Olausson 1982).

Ground axes almost certainly played a symbolic and ritual role, although this is not easy to demonstrate. A finely-ground or polished flint axe must have been an impressive and prestigious item to own. Maximum use was made of colour and inclusions within the stone, and surviving examples often have swirling patterns or even fossilised molluscs incorporated into their surface. Numerous axes have been recovered from locations such as pits, burials (Manby 1979, 69) or wet places, where they may have been deposited as offerings or during the enactment of rituals. Although many of these are whole, others have been found that appear to have been 'ritually killed'; that is, deliberately broken in two prior to deposition. Almost all of these ritually deposited axes are in mint condition (7), having no damage to their cutting edge, and no wear from hafting, and must therefore have been procured specifically for this purpose. Flaked axes are also found in possible ritual deposits, frequently as hoards (Butler 1999) deposited in pits or ditches, or with burials.

These ritual aspects do not just apply to the axes themselves, but also extend to the mines from which they were extracted. It is not clear why all the time and effort was expended in digging mines when perfectly acceptable flint could be obtained from surface deposits and by simple quarrying. Perhaps there was a ritual aspect to the extraction process, possibly connected with the act of digging into the earth to get to the flint. This may have been as important as extracting the flint itself. In the Sussex flint mines there was also significant evidence of ritual depositions, including pottery, animal bones and burials, which suggests that ceremonies may have been taking place in and around the mineshafts (Russell 2001b, Topping 2004).

Neolithic axe production at West Hill, Pyecombe, Sussex
A landscape survey at West Hill to the north of Brighton in Sussex showed that a Clay-with-flints outcrop was being exploited as a source of raw material during the Neolithic period (Butler 2001). A total of 55 Neolithic flint axes at various stages of production were recovered. This included 38 roughouts and six preforms, together with nine polished-axe fragments and two re-flaked polished axes. All of the roughouts and preforms were manufactured on flint that originated from the Clay-with-flints outcrop on West Hill. Most of the roughouts were abandoned due to flaws in the flint or breakage during the removal of the primary flakes. Some had been abandoned at a very early stage

in the flaking process, although in at least one case, flaking continued after a bad break. All of the roughouts had varying amounts of cortex remaining.

Only six preforms were found at the site, of which three had their cortex fully removed, whilst the remaining three still had some cortex remaining. Two of the preforms were broken cutting-end fragments, and it is possible that these were broken during the final stages of flaking. However, they may have been intended, and perhaps utilised as flaked axes, and were broken during use, although the cutting edge does not have any wear or damage from use. Analysis of the complete abandoned roughouts and preforms shows how there is a reduction in size and weight from the roughout stage through to the preform stage, demonstrating how the manufacturing process was reducing the size of the nodule.

TABLE 2
Analysis of Neolithic roughouts and preforms–(averages)

TYPE	WEIGHT g	LENGTH mm	BREADTH mm	THICKNESS mm
Roughouts	356	143	55	42
Preforms	202	118	50	30

Of the polished axes found during the survey, five had been manufactured on flint that had almost certainly originated from a Sussex flint mine whilst the remaining four fragments and two re-flaked polished axes had been manufactured on flint derived from the West Hill Clay-with-flints.

It is likely that most of the ground axes produced at West Hill were removed from the site for use elsewhere, whereas some axes that had been manufactured on mined flint were being brought onto West Hill and, when broken, abandoned there. Although there is a high concentration of flint mines on the South Downs, it is interesting to note that there are no known flint mines on the Downs to the north of Brighton, despite the high quality flint occurring there. It is interesting to note that the Brighton Downs area also has a higher density of non-flint stone axes than the area of Downs around the flint mines.

Harrow Hill Flint Mines, Sussex
Harrow Hill is located on the South Downs to the north of Worthing and comprises about one hundred flint-mine shafts. The uppermost seams had also been quarried from the ground surface. The first excavations at Harrow Hill (*64*) were carried out by the Worthing Archaeological Society in 1924-5 (Curwen *et al.* 1926). The Curwens excavated a single mine shaft which was found to be 7m deep, and cut through four different seams of flint. During the excavations, flintworking debris and a variety of antler picks and ox shoulder blades were recovered. Further excavations of mine shafts followed in 1936 (Russell 2000).

Neolithic Flint Axe Production

64 The Curwens' excavation 1924-5 at Harrow Hill. *Copyright: The Sussex Archaeological Society*

In 1982 a further mine shaft was excavated (*colour plate 23*), while some additional trenches were excavated in 1984 to establish whether flintknapping had occurred close to the mine shaft (McNabb *et al.* 1996). The excavations found seven possible axe roughouts and a finished axe, together with 650 flakes, including 262 axe-thinning flakes, in a knapping area just to the north of mine shaft 13.

Fieldwalking on the southern part of the site in 1984 revealed a dense concentration of axe-thinning flakes and axe roughouts covering an area of 50m^2. Further excavations in 1986 established that there was a large flintworking area, which produced large numbers of hard and soft hammer-struck flakes, axe-thinning flakes, chips, tested nodules, cores and axe roughouts. In addition, a number of open-cast mines were encountered (*colour plate 24*). These were pits and short galleries that had been excavated into the side of the hill slope to exploit seams of flint that were exposed there (Holgate *et al.* forthcoming).

The 1986 excavations recovered a total of 4,800 pieces of worked flint. These included over 1,600 soft hammer-struck axe-thinning flakes and 22 axe roughouts, together with over 2,500 other flakes, 100 finishing flakes and three axe preforms. The evidence from these excavations appears to confirm Neolithic working practices at flint mine sites. The flint nodules that had been extracted from the mine were initially flaked close to the mine shaft to remove surplus flint. Although occasionally some further flaking of nodules may have also been carried out close to the mine shaft, the majority of the nodules were taken to the edge of the mining area and were here flaked to produce roughouts and preforms.

8

LATER NEOLITHIC AND EARLY BRONZE AGE FLINTWORK

The change from the early to later Neolithic at around 3000 BC is marked by a number of new monument types such as henges together with timber and stone circles. There are new burial rites that focus more on individual burial rather than the earlier communal burial. There are also changes in pottery types with the introduction of Peterborough and Grooved Wares and Beakers, the latter most frequently found in individual graves under round burial mounds (*colour plate 25*). Coinciding with these changes is the first introduction of metal tools, which marks a fundamental change in society, and the beginning of the Bronze Age. Although the later Neolithic and early Bronze Age can be separated into two distinct phases by these changes in pottery and the introduction of metal tools, it is more difficult to separate the flintwork from these two periods. Apart from a few tool types which can be more closely dated by association with specific pottery types and metalwork, the majority of the flint tools, the debitage and general flintworking technology does not change throughout this time, and therefore tends to be labelled collectively as 'later Neolithic/early Bronze Age' flintwork.

Around the start of the later Neolithic, flintworking technology changed quite dramatically, with the whole process from the selection of raw material through to the end of the knapping process seeing a general decline in care and quality. There are however exceptions, with a number of finely made implements matching the quality of anything that went before. Almost any flint, irrespective of quality, was now used, except in areas where flint was still being mined. Once selected, any suitable surface on the nodule or pebble was used as a striking platform for the removal of flakes, and there was no attempt to prepare the platform. Once a platform was exhausted, the core was either rotated until another suitable platform was found, at which point knapping recommenced, or the core was simply discarded. For this reason later Neolithic cores tend to be larger than the cores of earlier periods and are rarely worked-out, frequently having just a few removals from each platform. They will also generally have some cortex remaining. The cores of this period are therefore generally either single platform, or multiple platform with the platforms at

Prehistoric Flintwork

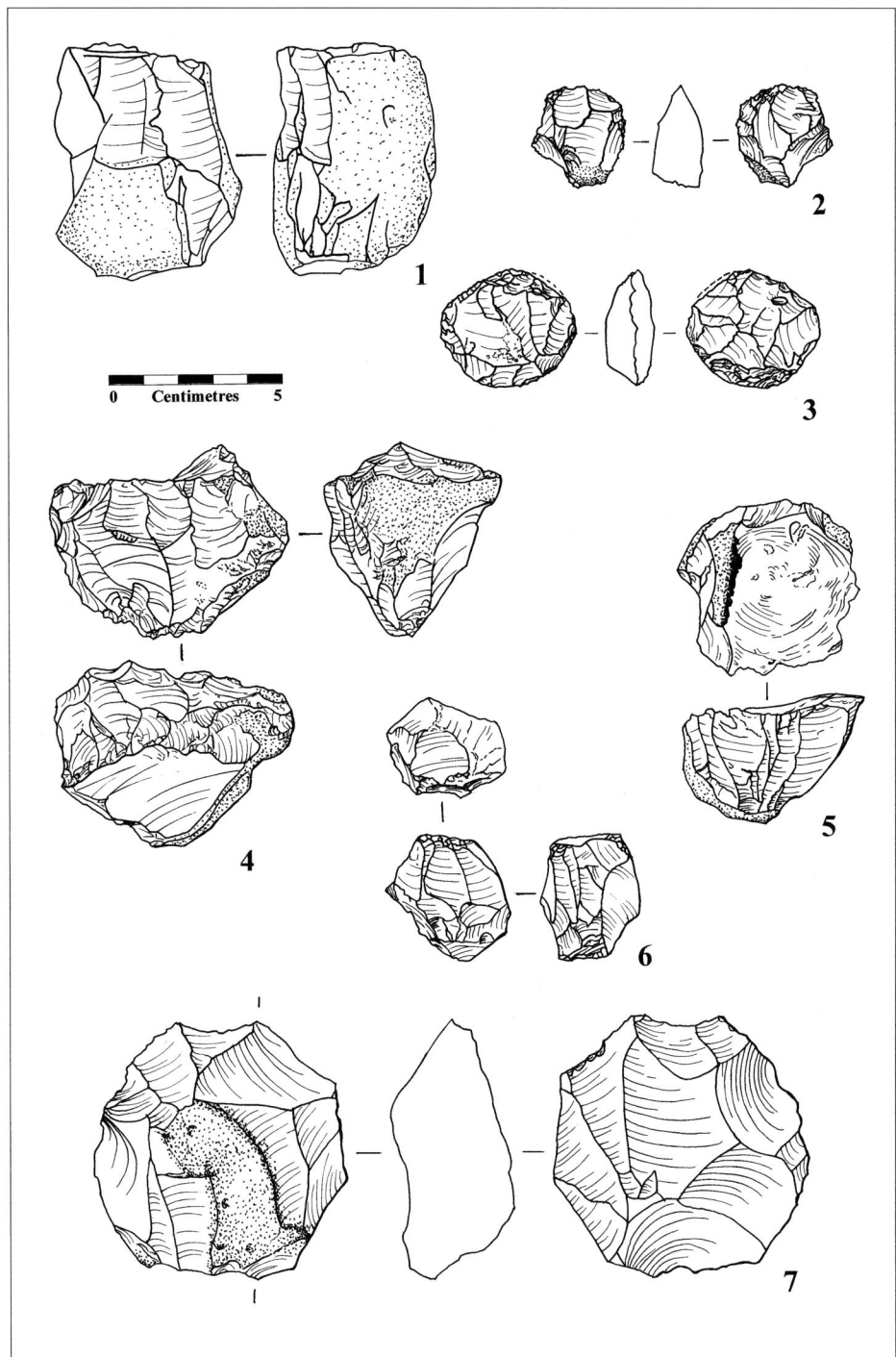

65 Later Neolithic/early Bronze Age cores: 1 and 5) Single-platform flake cores; 4) Two-platform flake core; 2 and 6) Multiple-platform flake cores; 3 and 7) Discoidal cores. Note small size of raw material used for Brean Down examples (Nos. 2 and 3) Various sites including Brean Down and Green Park. *After Bell, Butler, Holgate and Brossler* et al.

different angles to one another, and show few signs of any platform preparation (*65*).

One specialist form of core was produced during the later Neolithic, and resembles the Levallois-style of core produced in the Palaeolithic. Sometimes called a tortoise core, or more commonly a discoidal core (*65*), it was used to produce thin blanks for arrowheads and knives. A disc-shaped core was flaked from two platforms, with one surface being carefully flaked until it was almost flat. The core was then turned on its side and a single thin Levallois-type flake running parallel with the flat surface was removed (Holgate 1988). The production of these flakes suggests that some measure of skill was retained by some later Neolithic flint workers; perhaps by individuals who specialised in producing these more complex items.

The discoidal core was also commonly called a keeled core (named after the keel of a boat) until recently, and the two terms are still used interchangeably. The definition of a keeled core was that the platforms were at acute angles to one another, with a triangular cross section. However, some keeled or discoidal cores were not intended for the removal of Levallois-type flakes, but were simply well worked-out multiple platform cores.

Flakes were removed from the cores with a hard hammer, and blades were rarely produced. Although blades were frequently present in some numbers in later Neolithic assemblages (see Rackham below), they were more likely to have been made accidentally, and would therefore not have the parallel lateral edge and dorsal ridges of true blades. Soft hammers were rarely used during the later Neolithic period, except perhaps in the finishing of one or two specific tool types (see below). The flakes produced during this period therefore had the attributes of hard hammer-struck pieces, with a prominent bulb, wide butt, overhangs, and with frequent miss-hits and hinge fractures. Later Neolithic and early Bronze Age flakes were generally shorter than those of the earlier Neolithic period. They were also broader and thicker due to the hammer blow being struck further into the body of the core. Because fewer flakes were being removed from each core, there was a greater chance that the flakes would have some cortex remaining on the dorsal side.

Due to the changes in core reduction, the core rejuvenation pieces of the earlier periods were almost non-existent, however it is possible that they may have occurred accidentally as a result of the use of multiple platform cores. For example, one of the first flakes removed from a new platform that was at right angles to a previous platform may resemble a core rejuvenation flake or large core tablet. Many cores appear to have been reused as hammerstones once they had outlived their usefulness as a core.

In addition to the hard hammer-struck flakes, other pieces of debitage in a later Neolithic/early Bronze Age assemblage include flake fragments and shattered pieces which resulted from the use of a hard hammer, and will be present in some numbers. The change in the methods of flintworking was

Prehistoric Flintwork

not simply due to the use of poorer quality raw material, as there were many sites where good quality flint was available and was being used. However, the technology used for knapping reflects the changes discussed above (Holgate 1988). The change must therefore have been a reflection of the background changes in society, perhaps the move to greater emphasis on a sedentary lifestyle, and eventually the introduction of metal which began to replace some of the tools previously made from flint. Having stated earlier that there was an overall decline in the quality of flintworking during this period, they were still able to produce a number of very finely worked tools. There must have been individuals within their communities who were still able to work with flint to the same degree of control and skill as their Neolithic predecessors.

ARROWHEADS

During the later Neolithic period a wide range of arrowheads was produced (*colour plate 16*). They were originally classified by Clark (1934b), and then more recently by Green (1980). Although termed 'arrowheads' a number of these types have never been found hafted (e.g. chisel and oblique), so at present there must remain some doubt as to their true function. The largest group of arrowheads are termed transverse arrowheads and are divided into three major types (*66*). They have a distinct association with later Neolithic Grooved Ware pottery.

Chisel arrowheads
Chisel arrowheads were manufactured on Levallois flakes by truncating the butt end with invasive retouch to form a triangular or sub-rectangular shape (*67*). The tranchet or primary flake edge does not normally have any retouch. They were probably hafted into a wooden shaft at the retouched butt end, thus presenting the broad unmodified edge. These correspond to Clark's classes B to D.

Petit tranchet arrowheads
These are similar to chisel arrowheads and were probably used in the same way. The main cutting edge was parallel to the main axis of the flake or blade from which it was made, and its sides were blunted with abrupt retouch. One edge was normally one of the original lateral edges of the blank, and there was no retouch on either face of the finished piece (*67*). These correspond to Clark's class A.

Oblique arrowheads
These are sub-rectangular in shape, with semi-abrupt or invasive retouch on one or both edges to form a point. The retouch can be extended down

Later Neolithic and Early Bronze Age Flintwork

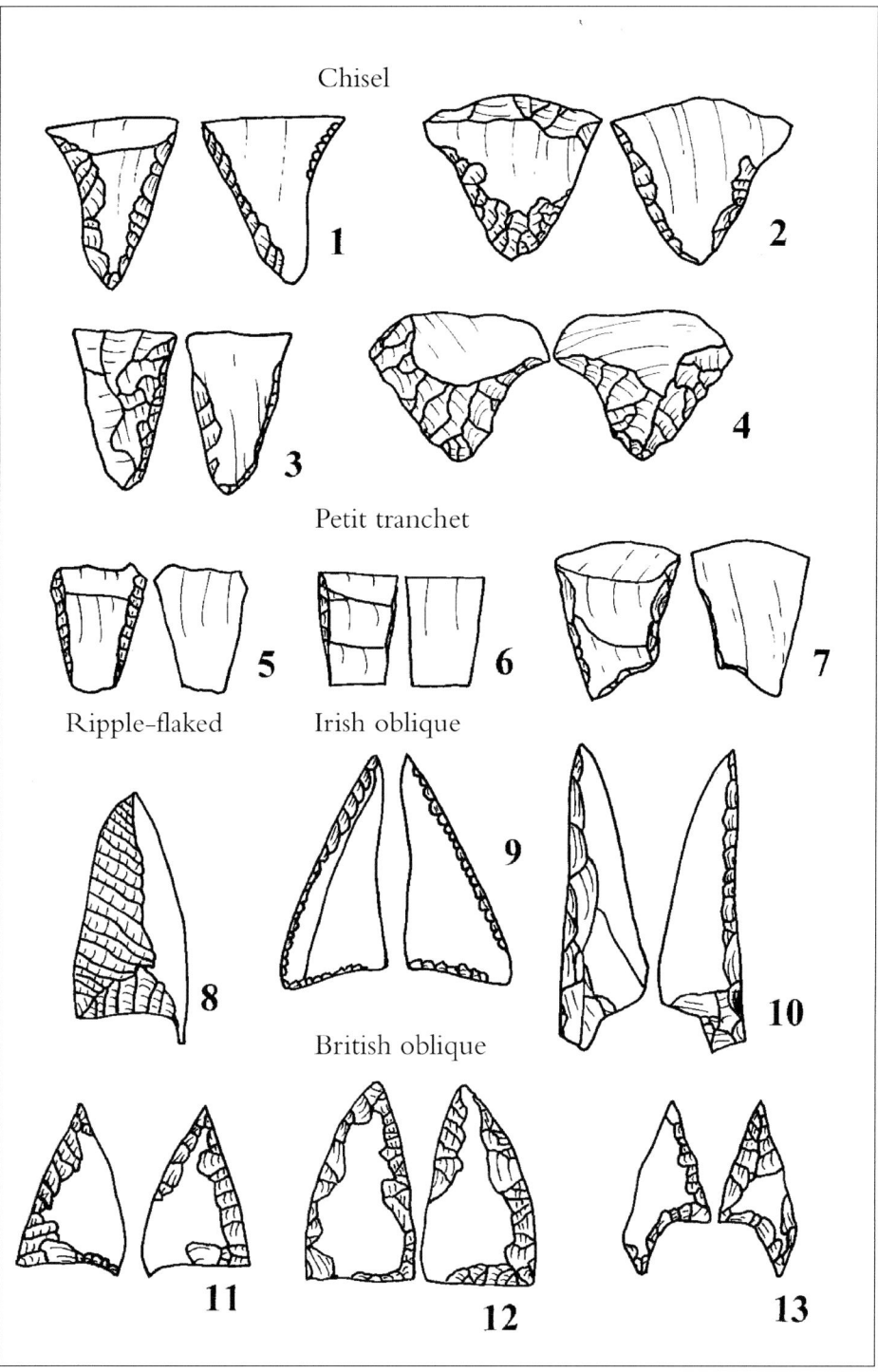

66 Later Neolithic arrowhead types: 1-4) Chisel arrowheads; 5-7) Petit tranchet arrowheads; 8) Ripple-flaked arrowhead; 9-10) Irish oblique arrowheads; 11-13) British oblique arrowheads. *After Clark and Green*

the entire edge, or is sometimes just below the point. Occasionally oblique arrowheads may have a retouched hollowed base to form a deliberate single barb. They are frequently found associated with Grooved Ware pottery. Oblique arrowheads correspond to Clark's classes E to I. Green classified them into three sub types (*66* and *67*):

(a) Ripple-flaked oblique arrowheads

This type had invasive retouch on one face, along one edge, and sometimes around the base, forming a small barb. The manufacture of these arrowheads may have involved the grinding of the edge to ensure that the subsequent removals ran true.

(b) British oblique arrowheads

These typically had the primary flake edge as the longest side, which commonly continued to form a barb. Retouch could be semi-abrupt and invasive, and normally extended along the convex secondary flake edge and the concave base on one side, whilst on the other side the retouch could be along the same edge, sometimes below the point and also at the base.

(c) Irish oblique arrowheads

Irish oblique arrowheads are normally longer than the British types, and rarely have a well-defined barb. They were generally semi-abruptly or invasively retouched along the longest edge and along the base, with the retouch being on both faces. The primary flake edge was normally on the shortest edge. Irish oblique arrowheads have been subdivided into pointed and elongated types (Flanagan 1966).

Triangular arrowheads
This type of arrowhead occurred in Neolithic assemblages alongside transverse, barbed-and-tanged and leaf-shaped arrowheads, and its use may extend further into the Bronze Age. They are triangular in shape, and had pressure-flaked invasive retouch over one or both faces of the piece. Occasionally one face was fully-flaked whilst the other may have some retouch just around its edges. It is not clear whether they are variants of some of these types or a type in their own right (*67*). Some were possibly intended as blanks for barbed-and-tanged arrowheads or broken leaf-shaped arrowheads, whilst the extent of the retouch and transverse cross section of some suggests that they were variants of the transverse arrowhead.

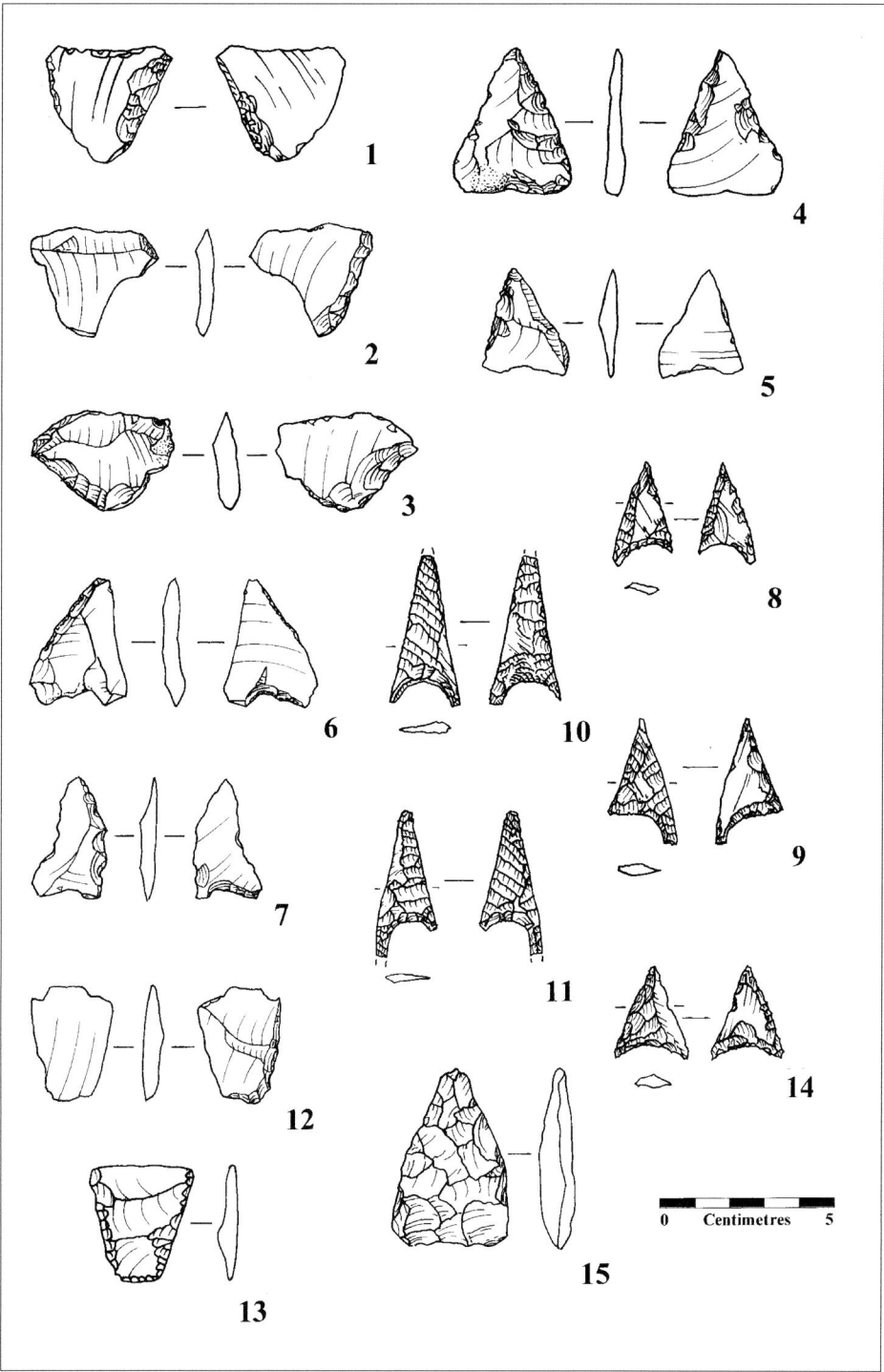

67 Examples of later Neolithic arrowheads: 1-3) Chisel arrowheads; 4-9) Oblique arrowheads; 10-11) Ripple-flaked arrowheads; 12-13) Petit tranchet arrowheads; 14) Hollow-based arrowhead; 15) Triangular arrowhead. Various sites

Prehistoric Flintwork

Hollow-based arrowheads
Hollow-based arrowheads are similar to oblique arrowheads, but had two equal length barbs and more regular distribution of retouch (*67*) around the edges. The retouch was limited to the edges of the piece and rarely extends over either face. They are quite rare in British contexts, but were almost certainly a later Neolithic type.

Barbed-and-tanged arrowheads
The barbed-and-tanged arrowhead is one of the distinctive pieces that can be linked with the early Bronze Age or Beaker period, being commonly found in association with sites throughout the period 2500 to 1500 BC. Barbed-and-tanged arrowheads are frequently found in graves containing Beaker vessels. The term includes arrowheads with both barbs and a tang, and those with only a tang. Green (1980) divided barbed-and-tanged arrowheads into two major types – fancy and non-fancy – depending upon whether the form had been carefully shaped (*68*). These two types are then further subdivided into sub-

Table 3
Barbed-and-tanged arrowhead sub-group classification

Group	Description	Shape
A	Pointed barbs	 V
B	Squared barbs	⊔
C	Base of barbs obliquely shaped	 ⊔\
D	Rounded barbs	 U
E	No barbs present	
F	Squared tang	⊔
G	Rounded tang	 U
H	Pointed or triangular tang	 VU

Later Neolithic and Early Bronze Age Flintwork

groups according to the shape and size of the barbs and tangs.

They were manufactured using pressure-flaked invasive retouch which, on the fancy types and better-made non-fancy types, normally covered both faces of the piece. The less well-made types were sometimes only retouched around the edges, which resulted in a thicker arrowhead (*69*). The tang and barbs were formed by pressure flaking, which created a notch between the tang and each barb, before the final flaking to shape the tang and barbs. Barbed-and-tanged arrowheads are frequently found with one or both barbs broken, but it is not always clear whether this is a result of a break during manufacture or through use.

Fancy barbed-and-tanged arrowheads
These arrowhead types were generally finely worked, with pressure-flaked invasive retouch covering the entire surface of both sides. Good-quality flint was almost always used for these types.

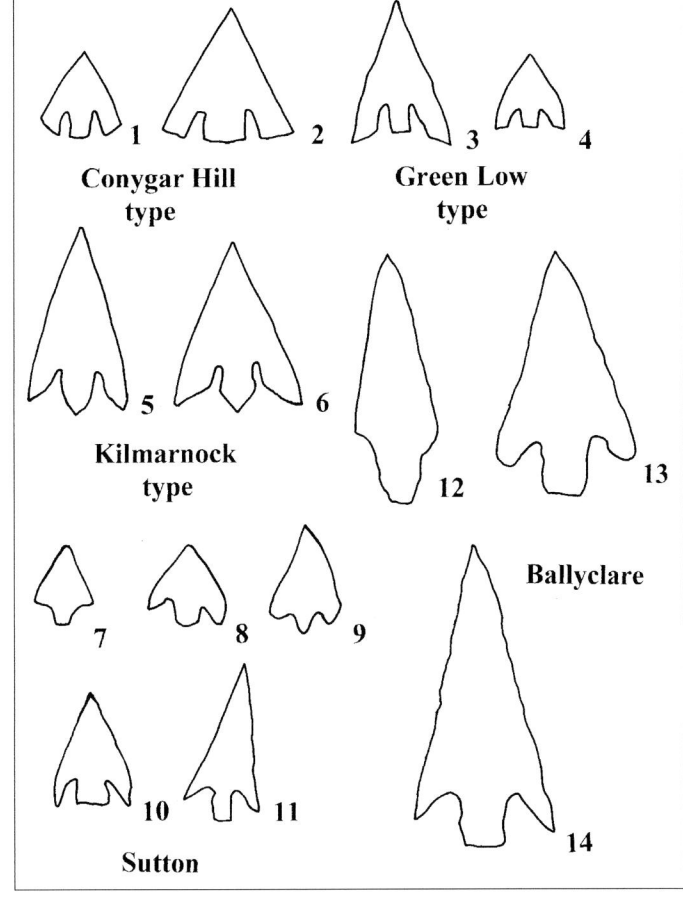

68 Barbed-and-tanged arrowhead types. 1-2) Conygar Hill type; 3-4) Green Low type; 5-6) Kilmarnock type; 7-11) Sutton type; 12-14) Ballyclare type. *After Green*

Prehistoric Flintwork

Conygar Hill type:

Barb-and-tang group BF
The barbs are the same length or shorter than the tang
The base of the arrowhead is convex or flat

Green Low type:

Barb-and-tang groups CF, CG or CH
The barbs are always longer than the tang
The base of the arrowhead is concave

Kilmarnock type:

Barb-and-tang groups AH, BH or CH
The barbs are the same length or shorter than the tang

Non-fancy barbed-and-tanged arrowheads
These are organised into two groups, both of which can be further divided into three subdivisions comprising those with no barb (E), rounded or square barbs (BG, DF, DG), and pointed barbs (AF, AG). The quality of these arrowheads can vary enormously, with some having been carefully worked, with pressure-flaked invasive retouch covering the entire surface of both sides. Others were manufactured on poor-quality flint with a minimal amount of retouch, which was normally restricted to the edges of the piece.

Ballyclare type:

These are larger arrowheads that weigh more than 8g and have a large length/breadth ratio.

Sutton type:

This is a smaller arrowhead type, weighing less than 8g with a small length/breadth ratio.

Ground and polished arrowheads
Later Neolithic ground arrowheads are very rare in British prehistory, although a few examples are known, including partially-polished oblique arrowheads from the Yorkshire Wolds. A single example of a polished barbed-and-tanged arrowhead (*69*) has recently been found in Sussex (Butler 2001d).

Later Neolithic and Early Bronze Age Flintwork

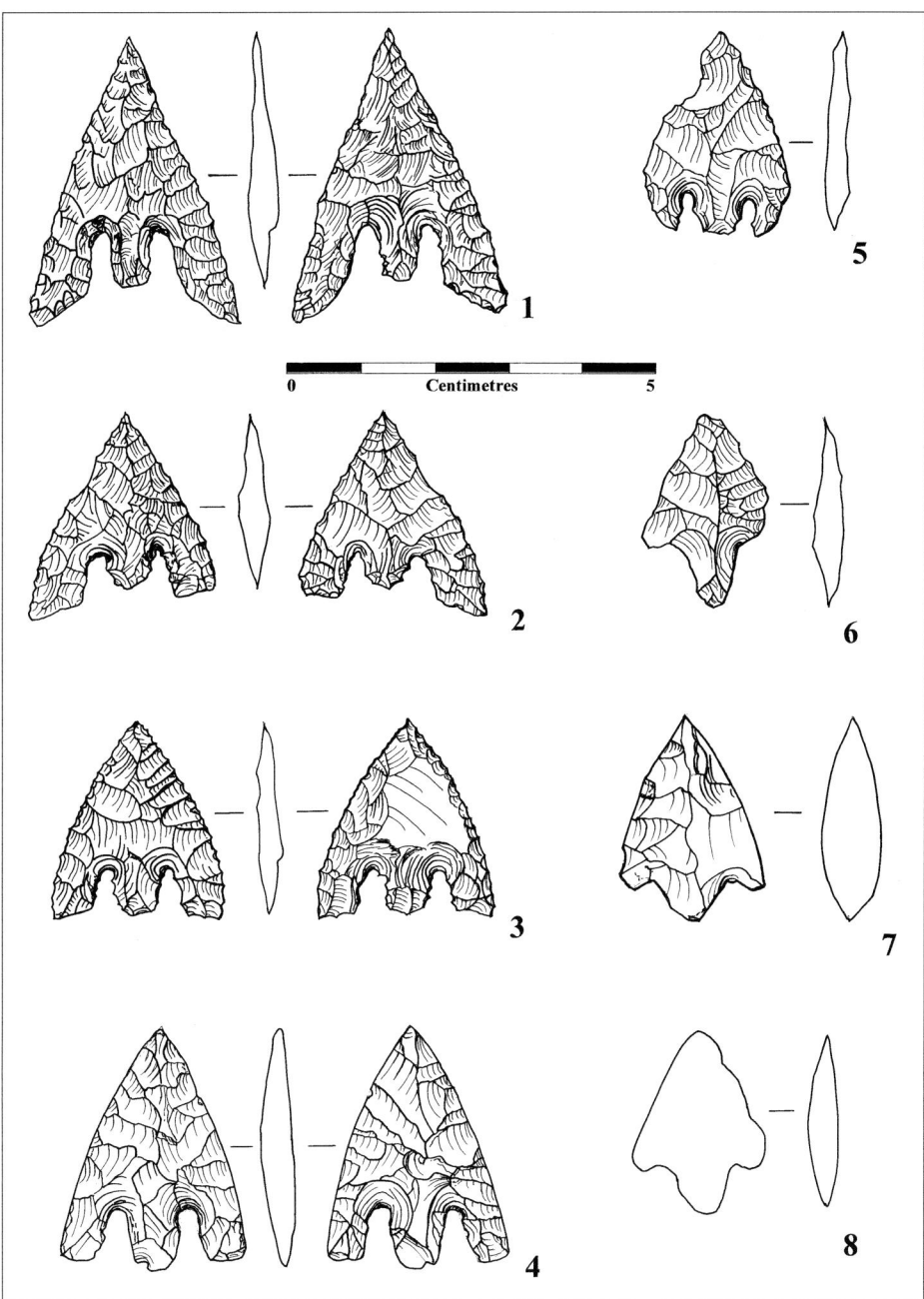

69 Examples of barbed-and-tanged arrowheads: 1-3) Green Low type; 4) Conygar Hill type; 5-7) Sutton type; 8) Polished barbed-and-tanged arrowhead. Various sites. *After Butler and Priestley-Bell*

Prehistoric Flintwork

SCRAPERS

During the later Neolithic period scrapers were no longer manufactured on blades and only very rarely manufactured on longer flakes. Instead there was a tendency to use shorter and broader hard hammer-struck flakes, together with broken flakes and thermal flakes. Retouch was normally abrupt or occasionally semi-abrupt. However, there were small numbers of very carefully made scrapers, some of which were invasively retouched or had ground edges. Scrapers are almost always the most common type of tool found on later Neolithic and early Bronze Age sites.

Apart from the differences that result from changes in the underlying flintworking technology, later Neolithic scrapers were very similar to those of

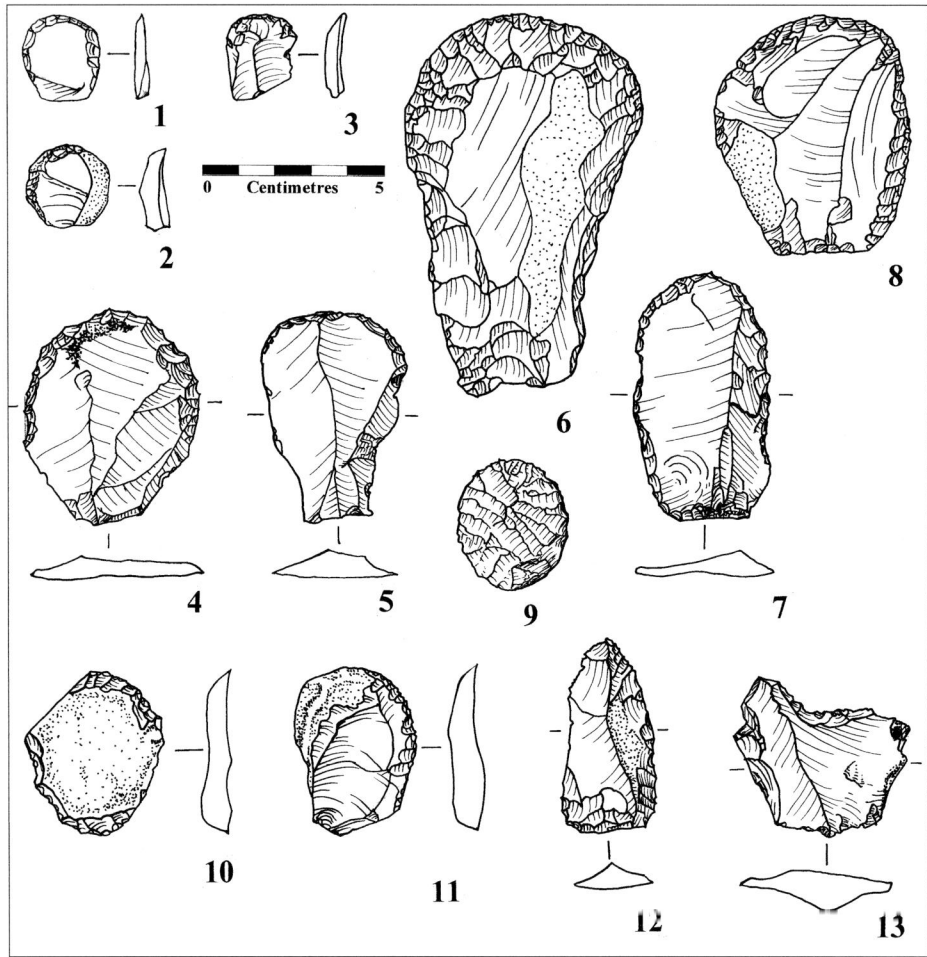

70 Later Neolithic and early Bronze Age scrapers: 1-2) Button or thumbnail scrapers; 3-7) End scrapers; 8) End and side scraper; 9) Invasively retouched scraper; 10) Double ended scraper; 11-12) Side scrapers; 13) Hollow scraper. From various sites including Durrington Walls, Belle Tout, Rackham, Brean Down. *After Wainwright, Bradley, Holden and Bell*

the earlier Neolithic period, although they were generally broader and thinner. The following comments are intended to highlight those differences, and describe the new types of scraper that emerged in the later Neolithic and early Bronze Age (*70*).

Many of the end scrapers had cortex remaining on the dorsal side, which may have facilitated handling, whilst some scrapers were narrower at the proximal end, where sometimes abrasion can be seen on the lateral edges. This may result from the scraper having been hafted into a handle. Large end scrapers, manufactured on thicker flakes, with steep abrupt retouch on a straight distal end, may have been used as planes for woodworking. Some double-ended scrapers are also found on later Neolithic sites (*70*). End scrapers made on large rounded flakes with abrupt or semi-abrupt retouch around the convex distal edge, and extending partway along each lateral edge, are sometimes called Horseshoe scrapers.

Discoidal scrapers were manufactured on short rounded flakes, and had abrupt or semi-abrupt retouch around the convex distal end, which extended around both convex lateral edges (*53*). The retouch normally stopped near the butt end of the flake, and therefore did not extend all the way around its circum-ference. Side scrapers were sometimes made on flakes and occasionally flake fragments of any size, but were normally made on longer blanks. They had semi-abrupt retouch along one lateral edge of the piece, sometimes resulting in a slight convex shape, but more usually had a straight edge. The opposite lateral edge often had cortex, or could have been retouched to ensure that it was blunted.

Many of the later Neolithic and early Bronze Age end scrapers have retouch that continues down one or both of the lateral edges (*53*). Horseshoe and discoidal scrapers also have retouch extending around the distal end and down the lateral edges. Therefore it can be difficult to separate side-and-end scrapers from these. However, the term can be used to classify those scrapers where the retouch around the distal end is separated from the retouch along the lateral edge by a short length of edge with no retouch.

Hollow scrapers were frequently found in later Neolithic and early Bronze Age assemblages. They were normally manufactured on larger flakes, and had a broad concave area of abrupt or semi-abrupt retouch along one lateral edge of the flake, or at the distal end of a flake. Occasionally there was additional retouch elsewhere on the flake. Some hollow scrapers, especially those with a concave area of retouch at the distal end, may have been hafted.

Edge-ground scrapers

A small number of scrapers have been found with all or part of their edge ground or polished. The blunted edge, and rounded shape of the piece tends to suggest that these were intended as scrapers and not as cutting tools. They occur in both later Neolithic and early Bronze Age contexts.

Invasively-retouched scrapers

These were either end scrapers or discoidal scrapers, which had invasive retouch around the worked edge. They were normally manufactured on thin flakes that may have been carefully selected for their size and shape. There was rarely any remaining cortex on their distal side. These are most commonly found associated with early Bronze Age burials or as possible ritual deposits.

Button/Thumbnail scrapers

Small scrapers that were circular in shape are normally referred to as either button or thumbnail scrapers. They had semi-abrupt retouch, which extended around all or most of the edge, and were usually under 20mm in diameter (i.e. about the size of a man's thumbnail, from where they get their name). They are a distinctive early Bronze Age type.

COMBINATION TOOLS

Combination tools appeared in the Neolithic period and continued in use into the early Bronze Age but are most common in the later Neolithic assemblages. They never occurred in large numbers, and were used alongside ordinary scrapers, piercers and notched flakes. The term can be applied to a number of different tool type combinations, although most incorporate a scraper. They were manufactured on hard hammer-struck flakes, or more rarely flake fragments, and had two distinctly different tool types manufactured on the same blank. Typical combinations were a scraper and notch, scraper and piercer, or notch and piercer (*71*). The two tools were normally created on different parts of the flake, for example one at the distal end and the other along a lateral edge, or alternatively on the two opposing lateral edges.

AWLS AND PIERCERS

These tool types continued to be made on hard hammer-struck flakes. The size and shape of later Neolithic piercers and awls varied considerably, with large flakes having both large and small points, and small flakes with very small points (*71*). Occasionally the length of the piercer point was longer than the remaining body of the flake. Although the majority were intended for use in the hand, there is some evidence that a minority of these tools were hafted.

DENTICULATES

Later Neolithic denticulates were simply-made tools on hard hammer-struck flakes. The denticulation was normally along part of one lateral edge, but could also be around the distal end of the flake. Occasionally there was additional abrupt retouch on part of the flake, perhaps to facilitate holding. These were

Later Neolithic and Early Bronze Age Flintwork

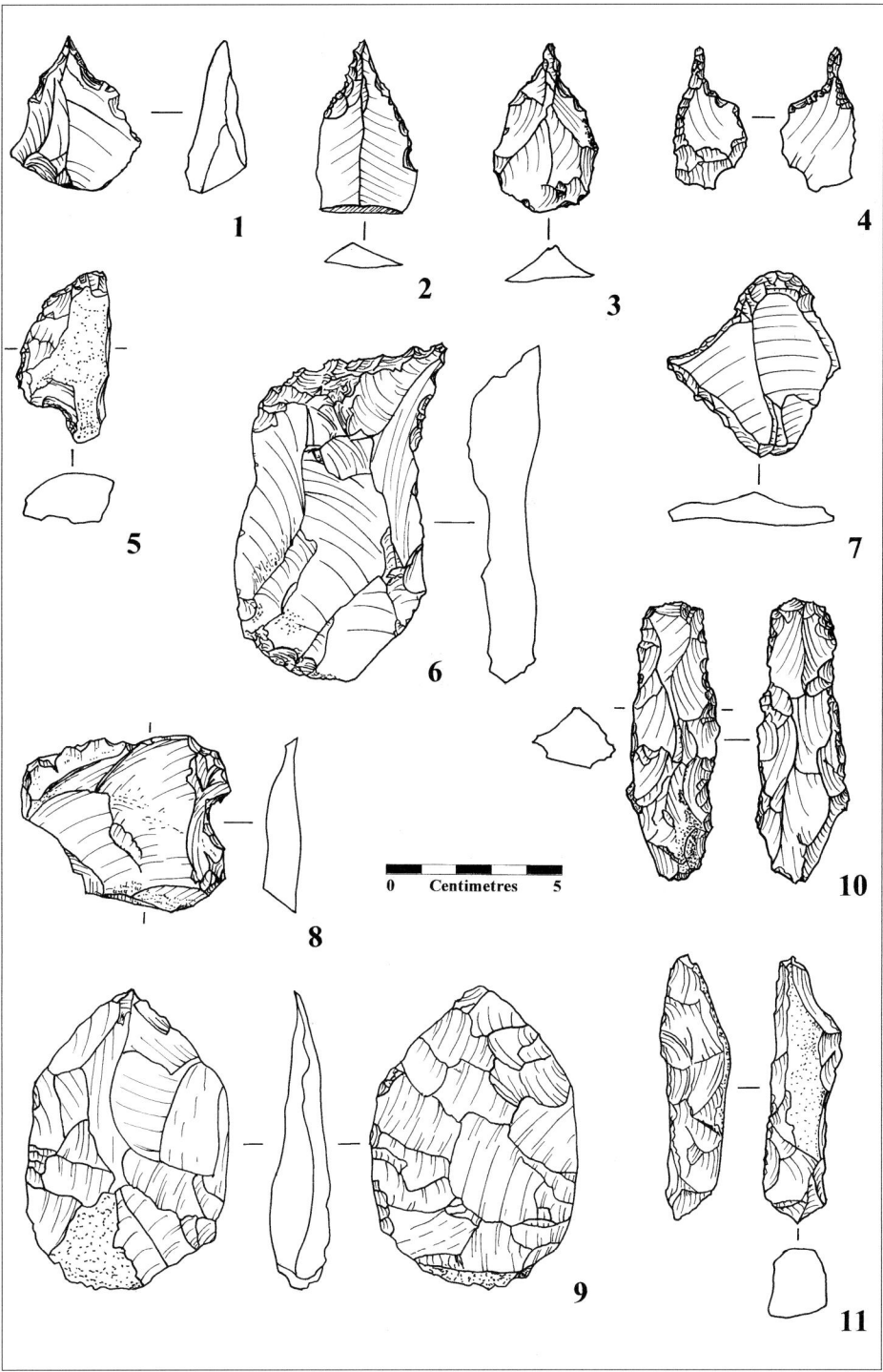

71 Later Neolithic and Early Bronze Implements: 1-4) Piercers; 5) Combination tool – scraper/notch; 6-7) Combination tools – scraper/piercer; 8) Notched flake; 9) Ovate; 10-11) Fabricators. From various sites including Durrington Walls, Belle Tout, Rackham, Thetford and Seaford. *After Wainwright, Bradley, Holden, Robins and Butler*

Prehistoric Flintwork

not common tools in later Neolithic assemblages.

NOTCHED PIECES

Notched pieces are frequently found on later Neolithic and early Bronze Age sites. They were manufactured on flakes of all sizes and shapes, together with broken or smaller fragments of flakes (*71*).

OVATES

Ovates were bifacially-flaked oval-shaped tools that resemble Palaeolithic handaxes, and have often been found in later Neolithic contexts (Robins 2002). They were made on large flakes, or sometimes nodules, and occasionally had areas of cortex or original flake surface remaining (*71*). Bifacial ovates were amongst the tools produced at the Grimes Graves flint mines (Mercer 1981). These may have been roughouts for discoidal knives, but could easily have been used as simple choppers.

KNIVES

Simple knives continued to be used, and were manufactured on longer flakes which had an unretouched straight cutting edge. Invasively retouched knives were also still used (*72*), but tended to be manufactured on smaller flakes than during the earlier Neolithic period. Some knives had edge polish along the cutting edge. Two further types of finely retouched knives (discoidal knives and plano-convex knives) appeared during the later Neolithic period, and continue in use into the early Bronze Age. These represented a survival of technical complexity in their manufacture, at a time when the majority of flint tools were declining in quality.

DISCOIDAL KNIVES

These were flat bifacially-retouched flakes with all or part of the edge blunted or bevelled by grinding and polishing. Both the bulb and platform of the original flake were removed during the flaking of these tools. Occasionally one or both faces of the knife were ground, although more frequently only the flake scar ridges on the surface(s) had been ground, as the grinding did not extend fully into the flake scars themselves. The ground edges were sometimes blunt, and cannot always have made efficient cutting tools, so therefore they were perhaps multi-purpose tools rather than knives *per se*.

Clark (1932a) divided discoidal knives into four forms: rounded, triangular, lozenge and rectangular (*72*). He also suggested that they were a development from scrapers. It is possible that there could be regional variations defined by

Later Neolithic and Early Bronze Age Flintwork

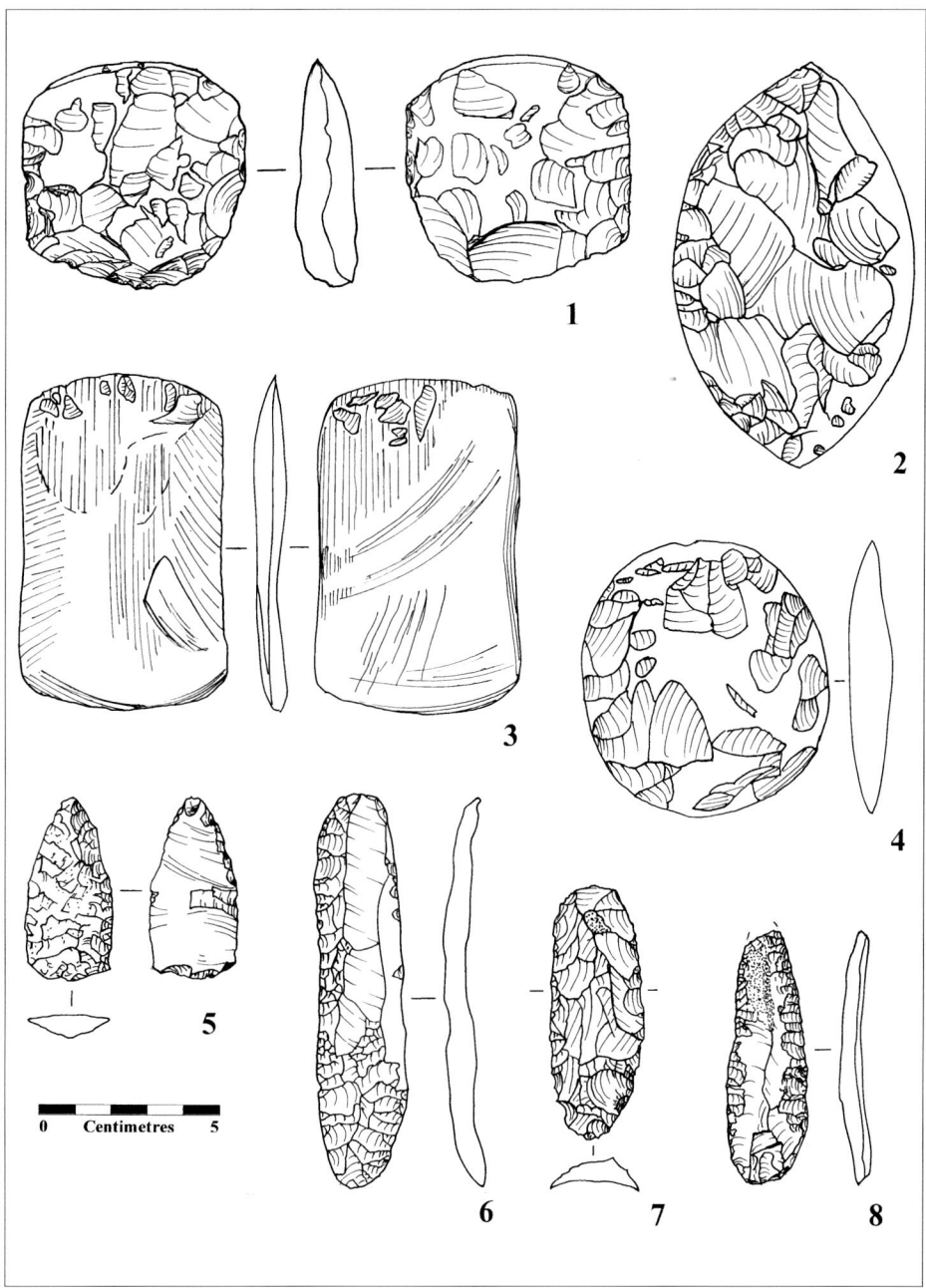

72 Later Neolithic and early Bronze Age Implements: 1-4) Discoidal knives; 5) Plano-convex knife; 6) Ground edge plano-convex knife (right lateral edge is ground); 7-8) Invasively retouched knives. From various sites including Mount Pleasant, Durrington Walls and Brean Down. *After Clark, Wainwright, Bell and Gardiner*

these different shapes. Discoidal knives are frequently associated with Grooved Ware pottery.

PLANO-CONVEX KNIVES

These were blades or long flakes of plano-convex cross section that had unifacial pressure flaking over the dorsal side, while the ventral side was left unflaked (*72*). Normally the bulb and platform were left intact on the flake or blade, which had a distinct longitudinal curve. The whole dorsal side was normally flaked, but sometimes the central part of this face retained its original surface. The commonest form was an elongated oval shape (which occasionally had serrated edges) with either a rounded or obtuse-shaped point. More rarely they had a blunted scraping end or a chisel-like end (Clark 1932b). Plano-convex knives could be up to 150mm long, but most were much shorter than this. They were mostly associated with Food Vessels and Beakers, suggesting an early Bronze Age date.

DAGGERS

Flint daggers were very rare in Britain, and are normally only found in Beaker graves, although there have been occasional chance finds, some of which may have been ritual deposits (Field 1982). They were made on large blades from which the bulb and platform had been removed. The blades were bifacially pressure flaked so that none of the original blade surface remained. They could be either leaf-shaped or lozenge-shaped (Smith 1919-20), and were often between 150-180mm long, and around 60mm wide (*73*). The point end was normally broad before narrowing to a point, giving a convex profile, while the basal end was generally narrower towards the rounded base, thus resulting in straight lower sides. They often had one or more notches on each lateral edge, close to the basal end, to facilitate hafting.

It is thought that these early Bronze Age daggers may have been copying the early forms of copper-alloy daggers. On the continent, especially in Denmark, the flint daggers were very developed, and almost exactly replicated copper-alloy daggers. They could exhibit features such as a handle and pommel, and some even copied a stitched seam on the handle, all replicated in the flint. Modern experimentation has shown that this type of dagger could take some 12 hours to produce, and could generate 3-4,000 individual pieces of debitage (Stafford 1998). Furthermore, evidence was found for the use of a copper-tipped pressure-flaking tool during the most intricate part of the process.

SICKLES

Single-piece sickles are known from some later Neolithic sites, and their use

Later Neolithic and Early Bronze Age Flintwork

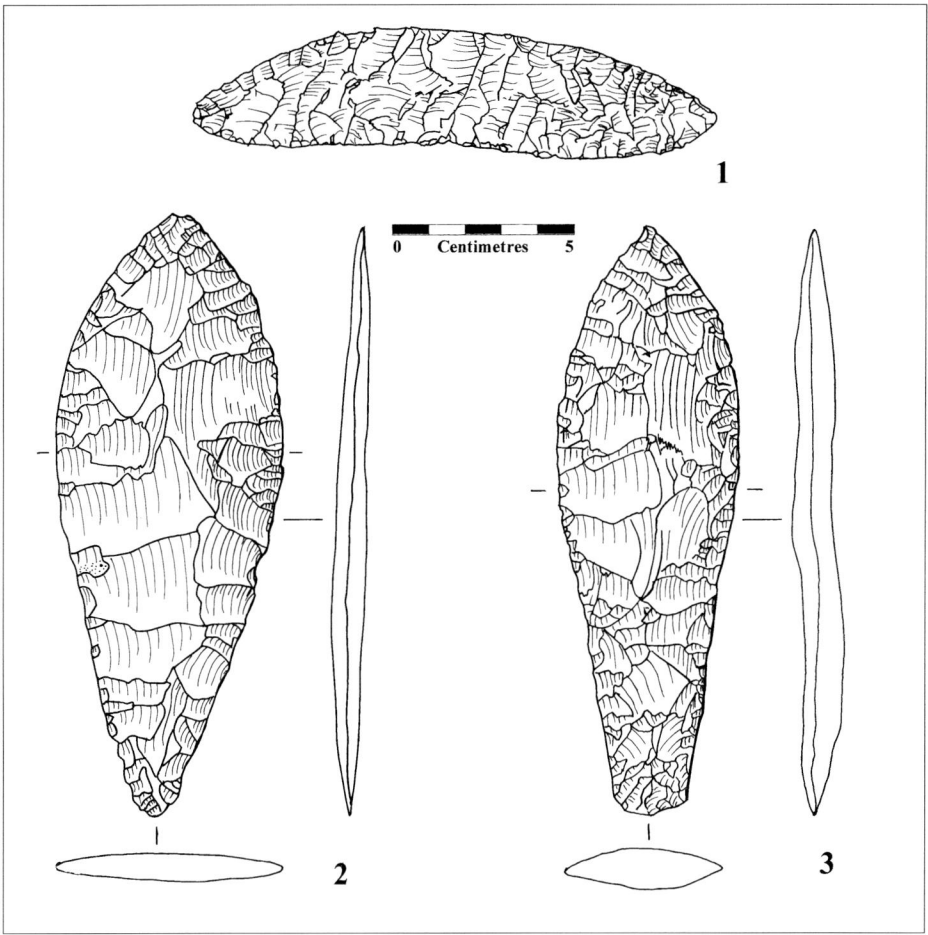

73 Later Neolithic and Early Bronze Age Implements: 1) One-piece sickle; 2-3) Daggers. *After Malone and Field*

may also extend into the early Bronze Age. They were manufactured on large blades or flakes, or more rarely on elongated nodules, with bifacial retouch covering the whole of one or both faces (73). The initial flaking would have been carried out with a hard hammer, probably from each face alternately along each lateral edge, to produce a preform. The bulb and part of the platform may sometimes still be visible on the sickle, even after the final flaking, as well as small areas of cortex. The final invasive retouch was carried out using pressure flaking from both lateral edges of the piece, and more rarely grinding or polishing was used to remove protuberances (Clark 1934c). Both ends of the sickle were usually worked to a tapering point by invasive retouch, so that the piece ended up with a convex outer edge and a slightly concave or straight inner edge. Very rarely, single-piece sickle roughouts are found, abandoned at an early stage in their production, and before the final retouching. The outer convex edge was normally thicker than the inner cutting edge, and they were probably hafted with the thicker edge fitting into a curved wooden handle (*colour plate 26*). Use-wear analysis has shown that some examples have a 'use-gloss' on the cutting edge resulting from the cutting of fibrous plant material.

TRIBRACHS

This is an extremely rare form, with only a handful of examples known from Britain. It had three roughly equal length arms, finely bifacially flaked to form three concave edges between the arms, and was normally quite slender. One arm is normally slightly longer than the other two (Evans 1897). Their function is unknown, but they are thought to date from the Neolithic period or early Bronze Age.

FABRICATORS

Fabricators were made on thick flakes, or from a fragment of a nodule or core, and tended to be larger than those from earlier periods, but were otherwise similar to those used in the earlier Neolithic period (*71*).

CORE TOOLS

Transverse cutting tools were normally large and crudely-worked core tools. They were pointed at the butt end, and broaden out towards the cutting edge forming an elongated triangular shape. They were roughly flaked over their entire surface, although occasionally a small area of cortex may have survived. A tranchet-like transverse blow from a lateral edge that removed a flake formed the cutting edge. The pointed butt end may have been designed as a tang so that the tool could have been hafted into a handle. These were not very common tools, and may have originated in the earlier Neolithic, but most associations are with later Neolithic assemblages.

Waisted core tools were crudely-made core tools that had been wholly or mostly flaked over their surfaces with one end modified into a cutting blade or a scraping edge (*56*). The central part of the tool was additionally flaked to create a narrow waist. Abrasion around the waist suggests that this was to enable the tool to be hafted.

FLINTWORK IN THE LATER NEOLITHIC AND EARLY BRONZE AGE

The changing attitude to flintworking during the later Neolithic and early Bronze Age appears to reflect the changes that were taking place in society at that time. The clearance of woodland and expansion of farming led to a more sedentary community who probably now lived in permanent settlements. This would have led to a different attitude towards flint procurement and the subsequent manufacturing of tools. A settled community, especially those with easy access to flint raw material, did not need to curate flint. Instead they could have simply picked up a piece of flint when a tool was required and made the tool, which could then be stored for later use, or discarded. Primary working of flint nodules at procurement sites may still have taken place, with numerous small secondary knapping areas created in and around the settlement sites as tools were made. The resulting debitage was then discarded into pits and ditches.

Religion and ritual seems to play a significant part in later Neolithic and early Bronze Age society. Henges, stone circles and avenues, together with individual burial mounds, sprang up across the country. Associated with these monuments, and especially those related to burial, was a range of carefully made and beautifully crafted flint tools, including the fancy barbed-and-tanged arrowheads, invasively-retouched scrapers, discoidal and plano-convex knives, and daggers. These tools were manufactured with a skill not apparent on the vast majority of tools made during this period. This would suggest two things. Firstly, that these tools were being specifically manufactured, perhaps by specialists (Durden 1995) for ritual purposes, primarily burial, and were never intended as functional tools. Secondly, it is clear that the knowledge and ability to manufacture items of quality still existed, but the majority of tools were not made with this care, simply because they did not need to be.

The introduction of metal tools in the early Bronze Age began to have an impact on the flint tools that were needed. Although this is not as pronounced as during the later Bronze Age, it can almost immediately be seen in the disappearance of the ground-flint axe from the early Bronze Age tool kit, as the more efficient copper-alloy axe replaced it. The association of ground-flint axes with ritual sites is phased out, and axes and other tools made from copper-alloy began to appear with burials or as votive deposits instead. On occasion though, some flint tools (for example daggers) were being made as copies of the new copper-alloy tools. Perhaps this was to replace the more valuable copper-alloy tool in the grave, with the flint copy accompanying the burial into the afterlife, whilst their ancestors kept the metal tool.

Durrington Walls – A later Neolithic Henge
A large assemblage of 11,472 pieces of worked flint was recovered during the 1966-8 excavations at Durrington Walls (Wainwright *et al.* 1971). These comprised 11,082 flakes, 57 cores and a mere 333 implements. Durrington Walls is dated by radiocarbon dating to around 2500 BC, and the predominant pottery is Grooved Ware. A sample of flakes was analysed in detail, and found to be generally broader and shorter than those from early Neolithic sites, although 11 per cent were blades. The cores were classified in accordance with

Clark's scheme from Hurst Fen, which showed that 63 per cent were single-platform cores, 21 per cent were two-platform cores, and 16 per cent were keeled.

Scrapers were the predominant type of implement, making up 62 per cent of the implements found. These too were classified according to Clark, showing that although end scrapers are the predominant type, side and disc scrapers are also important:

Class A	End scrapers	133
Class B	Double-ended scrapers	2
Class C	Disc scrapers	12
Class D	Side scrapers	48
Class E	On broken flakes	8
Class F	Hollow scrapers	4

It was noted that although there were similarities between the scrapers from Windmill Hill and Hurst Fen, the scrapers from Durrington Walls were broader and thinner, but on the whole much larger, than those from the earlier Neolithic sites. The 58 transverse arrowheads mostly comprised oblique types (84 per cent), with a single petit tranchet type, and the remainder chisel arrowheads. Apart from a small number of retouched flakes, the next most frequent tool type were knives with 14 examples, which included two fragments from plano-convex knives. Ten piercers, together with five fabricators, a sickle blade fragment, two axe fragments and three adzes were also found.

A later Neolithic site at Rackham, West Sussex

This site was excavated in 1970, and produced an assemblage of 13,062 pieces of worked flint in two large concentrations, connected with hearths and possible stake holes. The site produced an uncalibrated radiocarbon date of 2000 ± 140bc (Holden *et al.* 1975). The flintwork assemblage included 11,855 flakes, of which a sub-sample of 1,000 flakes was analysed in more detail. Although the blades and longer flakes made up over 20 per cent of the assemblage, the great majority of flakes fitted into the medium and broad categories, with 27 per cent being broader than their length. A further 14 per cent of the flakes were wholly cortical showing that primary working of cores was taking place here. A large number of flakes had been utilised, and it was noted that there was a preference for longer and larger flakes to be used.

The 170 cores were mostly small, which was seen to be a reflection of the poor-quality raw material available. There was little evidence of platform preparation. The cores were classified according to Clark's scheme, which found that 52 per cent were single platform, 29 per cent two-platform, 8 per cent three-platform, and 11 per cent keeled. There was a ratio of 70 flakes to each core. Scrapers were the predominant implement type, making up 94 per cent of the 928 implements, and were classified as follows:

Aa	End scrapers	134
Ab	Side-and-end scrapers★	238
B	Side scrapers	147
C	Disc scrapers	6
D	Double-ended scrapers	9
E	On small cortical flakes	166
F	On small irregular flakes	134
G	Broken scrapers	60

(★ End scrapers with retouch extending down the lateral edges)

The scrapers were mostly made on hard hammer-struck flakes, which retained large areas of cortex. The complete scrapers were measured, and this showed that there was a great deal of uniformity in their size and shape. The remaining implements included 38 knives (including plano-convex and discoidal types), three barbed-and-tanged arrowheads, a single transverse arrowhead, three fabricators, three burins and a flaked axe fragment. These implements made up 7 per cent of the assemblage.

All elements of the knapping process were identified at this site, confirming that the raw material was being brought to the site and knapped, with selected flakes then being used for the production of implements. It was suggested that due to the high proportion of implements, this site might have had a specialised function, probably related to the use of scrapers. The presence of some burins and the blades indicates that there is a residual earlier Neolithic element mixed with this assemblage.

FLINTWORK WITH BEAKER BURIALS

Carefully made flint tools such as knives, daggers and arrowheads are often found associated with Beaker burials. Normally just one or two of these flint items are found with the burial, and, with a Beaker pottery vessel, copper-alloy dagger and stone wristguard they make up a typical Beaker grave group. In rare cases, a large number of flint artefacts have been found with a burial. For example with the 'Amesbury Archer', as well as 16 barbed-and-tanged arrow-heads, there were two flint caches that included flint knives, scrapers, a fabricator and flakes (*colour plate 27*). Perhaps this is an example of a typical flint tool kit *in situ*. The artefacts placed in the grave frequently appear to have been specifically made for that purpose. They are not damaged through use, and are normally of much higher quality than similar items found on domestic sites or as casual finds.

At Radley, near Abingdon, an inhumation burial accompanied by a Beaker vessel had a barbed-and-tanged arrowhead embedded in the body. This arrowhead, which may have been the cause of death, was a short stubby example with minimal barbs. However, a set of superbly worked barbed-and-tanged arrowheads in mint condition (larger in size and with good barbs) had been placed near the feet of the body. This shows clearly the distinction between arrowheads used for routine tasks and those used for ceremonial or funerary purposes.

Not all Beaker burials have flint artefacts buried with them, but flintwork is frequently found associated with the burial monument. At Pyecombe in West Sussex, the Beaker burial had no flint artefacts buried with him, although his grave group comprised a copper-alloy dagger, beaker pot and wristguard. However, in the ditch around the barrow was a group of five unused invasively-retouched scrapers that represented a carefully-placed deposit (Butler 1991). When excavated, the ditches around barrows usually have numerous pieces of flintwork (normally mostly debitage) found in them. Although occasionally some of this flint was associated with ritually-placed deposits such as at Pyecombe, the vast majority of this flintwork seems to be related to later Bronze Age activity taking place around this focal location (see Chapter 9).

9

LATER PREHISTORIC FLINTWORK

The middle and later Bronze Age saw intensification in farming activities, with large numbers of small farming settlements covering the landscape. The increase in population meant that there must have been intense pressure to maximise the use of the available land, and there was expansion of settlements onto marginal land on the South Downs and elsewhere. Combined with this was evidence for territorial boundaries and the emergence of early hillfort enclosures. The quantity of metalwork circulating during the middle and late Bronze Age had greatly increased, and there was a wider range of metal tools that were available to replace the existing flint and stone tools. As the requirement for implements manufactured from flint reduced (Ford *et al*. 1984), this led to a further decline in the quality of flintworking techniques.

During the later Bronze Age there was an increasing trend towards the production of shorter and squatter flakes, which were almost entirely produced with a hard hammer. There was little care taken in the selection of the flint for knapping, so we see raw material of varying quality being used even when better quality flint is available locally. On the Sussex Coastal Plain small rough nodules of beach pebble flint were collected and utilised for the production of scrapers and other tools, even though high-quality flint could have been obtained from the adjacent South Downs. In Aberdeenshire a similar situation occurred, with small flint pebbles being used despite the fact that larger good-quality nodules were available not far away (Wickham-Jones *et al*. 1999).

Another result of this expedient selection strategy was the reuse of flakes that had been produced and discarded in an earlier period of prehistory. During the later Bronze Age flint was frequently scavenged from earlier barrow mounds or spoil heaps (Butler 2001c). It is sometimes possible to identify these reused flakes as the later Bronze Age retouch cuts through the patina revealing the true colour of the underlying flint. At Grimes Graves, flint nodules and previously discarded flakes from the later Neolithic flint mine spoil heaps were used as the source of raw material during the Middle Bronze Age (Longworth *et al*. 1991).

The decline in flintworking technology led to an increase in the frequency of miss-hits, hinge fractures and broken flakes (generally described as fragments and shattered pieces by lithic specialists – see Glossary), and within a later

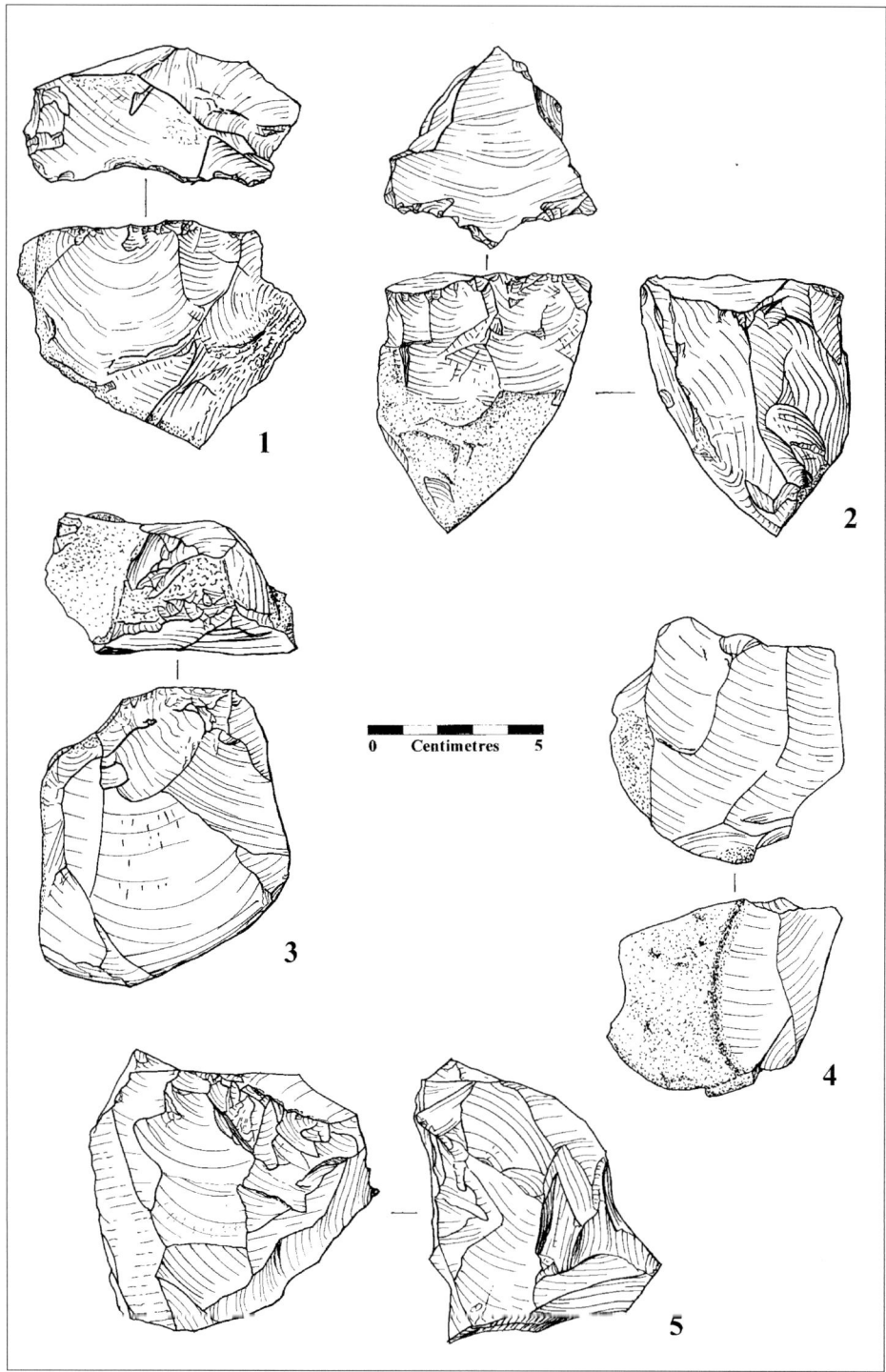

74 Later Bronze Age cores: 1-3) Single-platform flake cores; 4) Two-platform flake core; 5) Multi-platform flake core. From Grimes Graves and Crowlink. *After Longworth* et al. *and Butler*

Bronze Age assemblage these can make up a significant proportion of the debitage found. The deliberate lack of control during core reduction also led to a wide variation of flake size and shape, resulting in the possibility of large, small, broad, narrow, thick and thin flakes all coming from the same core during the same knapping episode. Other attributes of later Bronze Age flakes are broad platform remnants, obtuse flaking angles and prominent and multiple bulbs (Ballin 2002). The presence of almost blade-like flakes was common amongst Bronze Age assemblages, but a more detailed inspection of the dorsal surfaces will quickly show that they do not have the parallel ridges and edges that a true blade would have, and are therefore just the result of this more relaxed knapping strategy.

The cores of the later Bronze Age can seem quite crude, and many field workers find them difficult to recognise. They tended to be very irregular in shape, with no obvious relationship between the different platforms, as any suitable flat surface on the core could have been used as a platform (*74*). There was no evidence of platform preparation, so the edges of each platform will have frequent overhangs. Cores were generally larger than in earlier periods, although this depended upon the raw material size. The cores could have one, two or multiple platforms, with frequently only a few flakes having been removed from each platform, before the core was discarded. Many cores were reused as hammerstones. The variety of different-shaped flakes that were removed from a core would leave a confused pattern of negative scars on its surface.

Because a small number of flakes were removed from each core, and they tended to be primary flakes removed from the outer cortical part of the nodule, this resulted in a higher proportion of flakes on a later prehistoric site being covered with cortex. This can be a useful indicator for dating an assemblage, as flintworking in earlier periods, when greater numbers of flakes were removed from each core, would have resulted in fewer with cortex.

There were of course exceptions to the general points raised above, and these were usually as a result of the available raw material. Where the raw material resulted in smaller-sized cores, the resulting flakes would also be smaller, and there may have been a tendency towards more regularity in the shape and size of the flakes. In parts of the country where flint is rare, there was evidence for curation of flint cores in the later Bronze Age, and even occasionally the use of platform preparation to ensure that the maximum number of flakes could be obtained from each core.

The later Bronze Age knapping strategy is simple and straightforward: when a flint implement was needed, a suitably-sized nodule or pebble was picked up or scavenged. Flakes were then removed from any suitable flat surface with a hard hammer (another flint nodule or pebble perhaps picked up at the same time) until a suitably-sized flake came off that could be used to make the required implement. As there was such a wide variation in the size of various implements during the later Bronze Age, there was no real predetermined size of flake required for a tool, therefore the number of flakes that needed to be removed from the core before a suitably-sized one was obtained is likely to have been small, and probably mainly determined by the quality of the flint, and the individual's ability to remove a complete flake. Once a suitable flake had been removed, the remains of the nodule and any unsuitable flakes (and the fragments, chips and shattered pieces that would have been produced at the same time) would then have been discarded, as would the hammerstone. The implement would be utilised for the task in hand, and then it too would have been discarded. This type of knapping and disposal process would explain the dispersal of cores, flakes and other debitage, together with the implements, in small numbers around Bronze Age settlement sites, and would perhaps be typically associated with farming and other activities around a settlement, possibly in the associated fields. Within a settlement, the disposal and activity areas are likely to be more controlled, which would result in concentrations of debitage close to flint-manufacturing areas. There would perhaps be slightly more curation of cores, hammerstones and implements within a settlement area, leading to higher concentrations of implements that were discarded close to their place of use, whilst the debitage was likely to have been disposed of into pits and ditches adjacent to the knapping areas.

LATER BRONZE AGE IMPLEMENTS

The reduction in quality of flintworking during the later Bronze Age can also be seen in the tools that were made. The number of different tool types had reduced significantly, so that by the end of the Bronze Age the only tools that were consistently appearing in assemblages were scrapers, piercers and notched pieces. There were few standardised tool forms with most types simply being made on whatever flakes were to hand. The quality and application of retouch also diminished, with some tools being utilised after only being roughly shaped. Implements, especially scrapers, were frequently made on scavenged flakes of earlier prehistoric date; these were probably selected due to their shape being suitable for conversion into a tool. The tools that were still manufactured in flint during the later Bronze Age were as follows:

SCRAPERS

Scrapers continued to be the most common type of tool manufactured, and on later Bronze Age sites normally make up in excess of 50 per cent of all implements present. End scrapers are the most common form of scraper found in later Bronze Age assemblages. The range and variety of end-scraper forms is considerable, with small flakes, large thick flakes, fragments, and occasionally longer flakes or blades being utilised as blanks (75). On a number of sites it has been noted that short end scrapers are the predominant form of end scraper present. Cortex was frequently present, and often covered all or most of the dorsal side except where it had been removed by the retouching of the convex scraping end. Abrupt, and more rarely semi-abrupt, retouch was normally used. On some scrapers the retouch was minimal, the blank having been roughly shaped to provide a convex end, and then utilised so that abrasion damage can be seen on the scraping end. Some larger end scrapers that had been manufactured on thick flakes narrow towards the proximal end of the piece. Abrasion on these scrapers on the lateral edges at the proximal end suggests that they may have been hafted into a handle for use.

Longer hard hammer-struck flakes or fragments were most frequently used as blanks for side scrapers. Most have cortex present on the dorsal side opposite the retouched edge, or covering most of the dorsal side. Abrupt or semi-abrupt retouch was used to modify one straight lateral edge (75). The opposite lateral edge was hardly ever retouched. Hard hammer-struck flakes and fragments were used as blanks for hollow scrapers. Abrupt retouch was used to form a concave scraping area on a lateral edge or at the end of the blank (75). The retouched area could extend along part or the whole of the edge. There was no uniformity as to the location of the retouched area, and they were frequently made on the distal or proximal ends as well as on the lateral edges.

HORNED SCRAPERS

Horned scrapers were first recognised by Evans (1897) although he classified them as hollow scrapers. Clark (1927) originally gave them the name of horned scraper, and discussed their distribution and possible function. Although all horned scrapers had a similar profile, the size of each, and the extent and location of the retouch differs (75). The horned scrapers were manufactured on thick hard hammer-struck flakes. A deep concave area, usually at the distal end, was removed, leaving two projecting 'horns'. The horns generally narrowed almost to a point at their extremity. The proximal end of the flake was rounded, and there was some abrasion evidence suggesting that the longer examples were hafted. The horned scraper was clearly a ubiquitous implement, almost certainly being multi-functional. However, the variety of types suggests that although they may have a specialised primary function, there was not necessarily a single model type which was being copied in each case. The horned scrapers found in Sussex have recently been divided into four types based on the extent and location of the retouch (Butler 2001c):

Type A: Retouched between the horns and along one lateral edge only
Type B: Retouched between the horns and along both lateral edges
Type C: No retouch between the horns, although sometimes abraded. Retouched at the convex proximal end and sometimes along one or both lateral edges

Prehistoric Flintwork

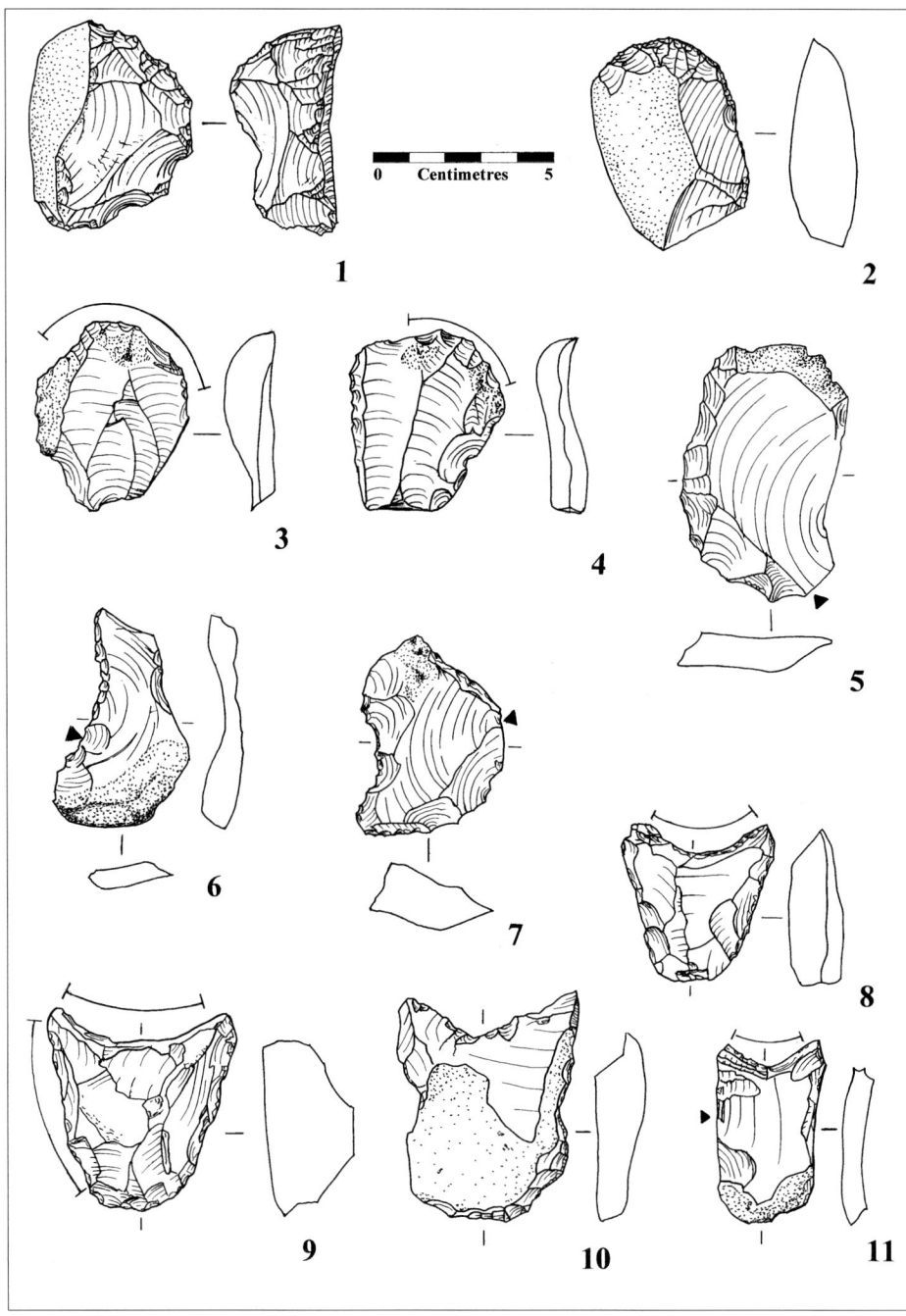

75 Later Bronze Age scrapers: 1–4) End scrapers; 5) Side scraper; 6–7) Hollow scrapers; 8) Horned scraper Type A; 9) Horned scraper Type B; 10) Horned scraper Type C; 11) Horned scraper Type D. From Grimes Graves, Crowlink and Alfriston. *After Butler and Longworth* et al.

Type D: Manufactured on a thinner flake with retouch between the horns, which were located on one lateral edge of the flake rather than at the distal end

It is clear from the above descriptions that the concave area at the distal end was the primary scraping edge for Types A and B, These scrapers also had some abrupt retouch along one or both lateral edges, which could also have been used for scraping. However, it is possible that this retouch was designed to make the pieces easier to handle during use. The horns could have been utilised for piercing, and were similar in size to some of the large Bronze Age piercers. With Type C, the rounded proximal end appears to have been the primary scraping edge, having a similar profile to an end scraper.

The evidence from the few excavated examples suggests that the Horned Scraper was a later Bronze Age implement type. Its restricted distribution to the Seaford/Alfriston area of the Sussex Downs (although a small number are known from elsewhere) could indicate a locally specialised function.

PIERCERS

Piercers were normally the second most common tool type on later Bronze Age sites, and also had considerable variety in their shape and size (76). They were manufactured on hard hammer-struck flakes or fragments, many of which retained some cortex. The retouched point was normally at the distal end of the blank, but could also be on a lateral edge, or even at the proximal end. Occasionally the retouch is only along one edge of the point, with the other edge using the natural edge or a break. Some piercers seem to have a burin-type removal to form the point, which was then abruptly retouched. The points were frequently quite long especially those formed on the distal end of the flake, but those formed on the lateral edge of a piece were normally short. Awls were almost totally absent in later Bronze Age assemblages, probably having been replaced by its bronze equivalent.

NOTCHED PIECES

These pieces were normally manufactured on smaller stubby hard hammer-struck flakes or fragments, with occasional pieces on longer flakes. The notch was normally on one lateral edge (76), or more rarely at the distal end. There was rarely any other retouch on the piece. Cortex is frequently present.

KNIVES AND CUTTING FLAKES

These are rare in later Bronze Age assemblages, and it is possible that many are residual pieces from earlier activity. Longer flakes or blades were selected for

Prehistoric Flintwork

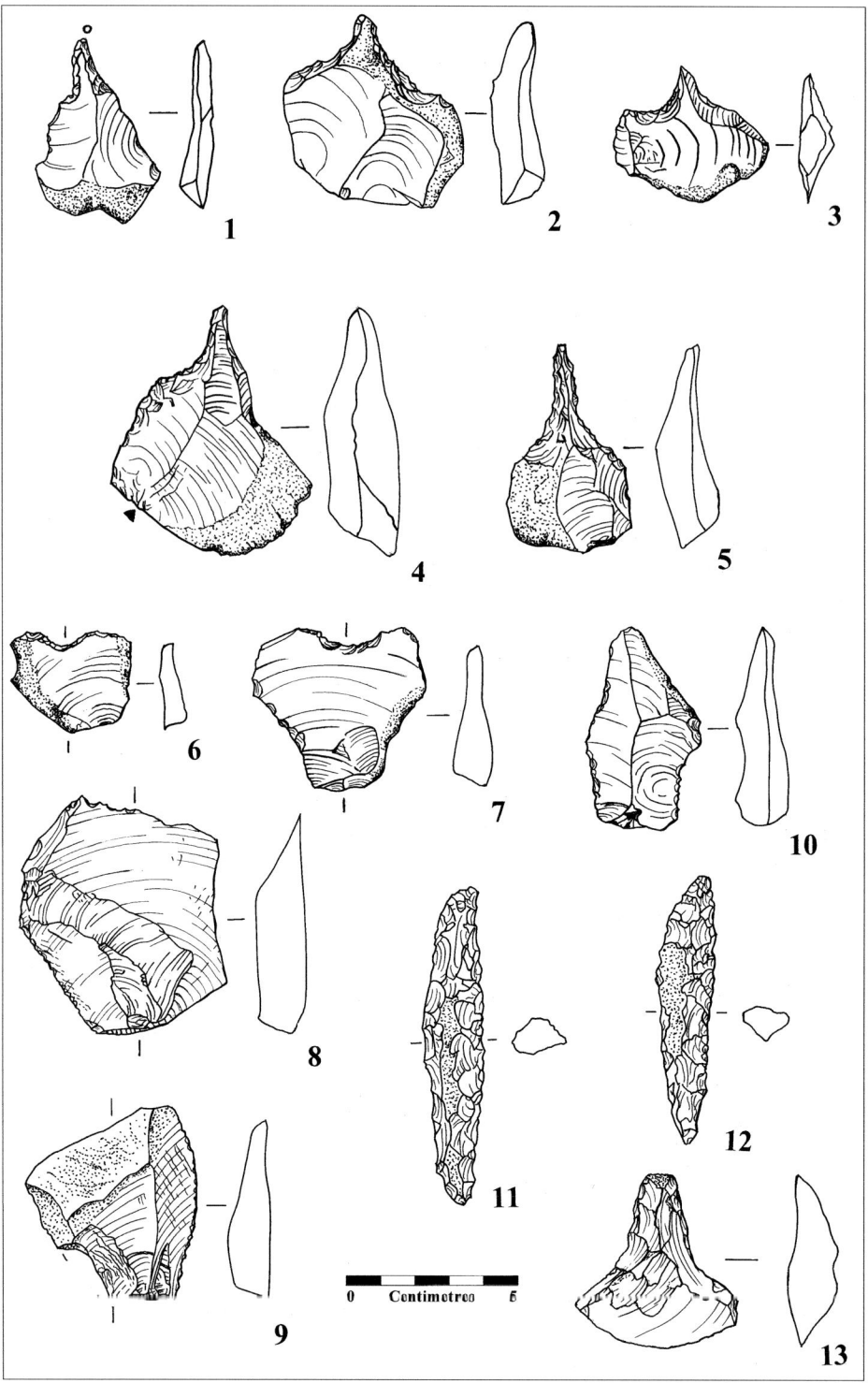

76 Later Bronze Age flintwork: 1-5) Piercers; 6-7) Notched pieces; 8-9) Cutting flakes; 10) Retouched flake; 11-12) Fabricators; 13) Chopper. From Crowlink, Grimes Graves and Blackpatch. *After Butler, Longworth* et al. *and Drewett*

these tools. Normally they have one unretouched lateral edge that was utilised for cutting. The opposite edge was either abruptly retouched or left in its natural (cortical or a steep unretouched) state.

RETOUCHED FLAKES

Retouched flakes and fragments quite often made up a significant proportion of the retouched pieces in later Bronze Age assemblages. They do not resemble any recognisable tool type, and were probably expedient tools manufactured for a one-off task and then discarded. The abrupt or semi-abrupt retouch was normally executed in small areas along one or both lateral edges of the blank (76).

FABRICATORS/RODS

Fabricators, probably utilised as strike-a-lights, are occasionally found. They were manufactured on long flakes or blades that had been flaked to produce a cylindrical piece of triangular or oval cross section. Frequently retaining some cortex on one side, they were heavily abraded through use at one or both ends (76). Rods also continued to be produced.

CHOPPERS

Bifacially or unifacially-worked chopping tools are occasionally found on later Bronze Age sites. Some of the better-made examples could be residual earlier pieces, but as they are found on so many sites it is possible that they were still being made as expedient tools. They were normally made on large flakes or nodules, with a narrow butt end broadening out to the cutting edge, thus forming a triangular shape. A number of flakes removed unifacially or bifacially from the cutting edge formed the chopper blade. Some later Bronze Age choppers are quite small (76). There was rarely any other additional flaking or retouch on these pieces, and little evidence of hafting.

FLINTWORKING IN THE LATER BRONZE AGE

The reduction in the number of different tool types used in the later Bronze Age, even when compared to the later Neolithic, is quite apparent. This was a process that had started in the early Bronze Age with copper-alloy axes, spears and daggers quickly replacing their flint predecessors. As more tools such as awls, saws and sickles were made from copper-alloy during the Bronze Age so further flint tools were made redundant. Analysis has shown that the mean number of tool types per site fell from seven in the later Neolithic to only three in the later Bronze Age (Ford *et al.* 1984).

Two examples of later Bronze Age sites will now be considered.

A later Bronze Age settlement site at Black Patch, Sussex
Black Patch was excavated between 1977 and 1979, and comprised a number of hut platforms and enclosures (Drewett 1982). Hut Platform 4 was fully excavated and revealed five round houses together with pits and fence lines. Radiocarbon dating put the site firmly in the later Bronze Age. The flint assemblage comprised 2,772 pieces of which 96 per cent was debitage. Length/breadth analysis of a sample of the flakes showed that the majority were broad and squat in shape. The cores were predominantly single platform (68 per cent) with smaller numbers of cores with two and three platforms. Thirty-two flint hammerstones were also found.

The main tool type present was the scraper, of which 49 were found. The majority of these were end scrapers, of which 63 per cent were short end scrapers. There was also a small number of side scrapers. Retouched flakes were the next largest category of tool present with 25 pieces, whilst there were also 7 notched flakes. A single awl and two fabricators completed this small assemblage. The small number of tools from this site is very apparent, as they make up only some 3 per cent of the assemblage. The limited range of tool types is also clear with only scrapers, notched flakes and retouched flakes being present in any numbers. Black Patch also produced a number of bronze artefacts, including a razor, a knife, a possible rapier blade and two awls. The bronze and flint artefacts from this site appear to confirm the trend, in that most cutting, chopping and piercing tasks appear to have been carried out using bronze tools, whilst flint tools were only being retained for scraping (scrapers and notched pieces) or expedient tasks (retouched pieces).

The flint industry from the Micheldever Wood Barrow
The excavation of an early Bronze Age barrow at Micheldever Wood, Hampshire produced evidence for a later Bronze Age flint industry (Fasham *et al.* 1978). The total flint assemblage comprised 16,030 pieces of which 10,539 were from the later Bronze Age industry. The raw material appeared to have been nodules scavenged from the existing barrow mound. The debitage made up 99 per cent of the assemblage, comprising mostly waste (chips, broken flakes and cortical lumps) and flakes, whilst 2.5 per cent were cores. There was a clear trend towards broader and squat flakes, with over 34 per cent being flakes where breadth exceeds their length. Although some 25 per cent of the flakes had blade-like proportions, only 2.4 per cent actually resembled blades.

The 255 cores comprised 99 with single-platforms, 40 with two-platforms, 47 with three or more platforms, together with 19 keeled and 50 that were unclassifiable. Single-platform cores with a relatively low number of flake scars per core, and a high per centage of remnant cortex dominated the cores. The tools made up only 1 per cent of the assemblage. Scrapers were the predominant type and were mostly on thick flakes with angular profiles and coarse abrupt retouch. Piercers were the other major tool type, and were mostly formed on irregularly-shaped flakes with a long thin point protruding from the body of the flake. One side of the point is concave, whilst the other is straight. Four of the piercers were made on core fragments.

This assemblage shows how in the later Bronze Age the flint raw material could be scavenged from existing man-made structures. Knapping was being carried out at the same location with the majority of the assemblage reflecting this industrial process. Although tools were being made at the site, the lack of many tools in the assemblage suggests that they were being taken elsewhere to be used. This form of exploitation and industry has been seen on a number of recently-excavated sites, for example the Crowlink barrow on the Sussex South Downs (Butler 2001c) (*colour plate 28*).

IRON AGE FLINTWORK – DOES IT EXIST?

One of the most controversial debates at present revolves around whether or not flintworking continued into the Iron Age. Suggested provenances for Iron Age flintwork have been proposed for some time (Curwen 1931). However, the lack of securely-dated flintwork in Iron Age contexts, without contamination by residual earlier flintwork, has been surprisingly lacking, and therefore most of the examples of Iron Age flintwork put forward have been dismissed: 'regular production and use of flint artefacts for everyday domestic activities declined and ceased altogether within the later Bronze Age' (Saville 1981).

Despite this, recent authors have attempted to show that flintworking continued into the Iron Age (Young *et al.* 1999). What is clear is that a number of Iron Age sites have produced groups of flintwork from pits and other features that could be contemporary with the Iron Age activity. What is not clear is whether this represents the premeditated knapping of flint to produce tools, or whether it results from the simple creation of a flake for an expedient cutting task. I have seen farmers working on the South Downs who would occasionally break a flint nodule to obtain a flake to cut baler twine, however this does not create a culturally-identifiable flintworking technology.

The proposed characteristics of an Iron Age flintworking technology are an extension of those found in later Bronze Age assemblages, namely (Young *et al.* 1999):

1 Utilisation of highly localised raw materials
2 Small assemblage numbers
3 Simple core/flake technology employing hard hammer, direct percussion
4 Lack of skill in knapping
5 A restricted range of tool types
6 Crude hammerstones

7 A predominance of secondary and tertiary flakes
8 Possible evidence for recycling of lithic material

The lack of skill in knapping would result in short squat flakes with a high instance of step or hinge terminations; thick, wide striking platforms; and obtuse striking angles. There would also be a high instance of chips and chunks, together with an irregular core morphology. Two examples of Iron Age sites with flintwork assemblages are:

Meare Village West, Somerset
The excavations in the early twentieth century and in 1979 at this Iron Age settlement produced an assemblage of over 1,400 pieces of worked flint (Smith 1981). An analysis of this material showed that 68 per cent were flakes and chips, 3 per cent cores, and the remaining 29 per cent tools and utilised flakes. It was also noted that 50 per cent of the assemblage had cortex remaining.

Length/breadth analysis showed that squarish flakes were preferred, and the majority of the blade-like flakes that were present were not true blades. There was some reuse of earlier pieces of worked flint, which could be identified by their heavy patination. The tools that could be assigned to earlier periods of prehistory (microliths, arrowheads etc.) were also heavily patinated. Around 15 per cent of the assemblage was made up of retouched and utilised flakes, many of which were also heavily patinated. Of the remaining tools, scrapers were the predominant type amounting to 10 per cent of the assemblage. The most common type of scraper was the side-and-end scraper (25 per cent), closely followed by the side scraper (21 per cent), whilst end scrapers made up only 11 per cent of the scrapers. Seventeen per cent of the scrapers were heavily patinated, although half of these had additional later retouch. The other major implement type was the knife of which 28 examples were found. Twenty-five per cent of the knives were heavily patinated, but again half of these have later additional retouch.

The flintwork from this site appears to be from two different phases, the first, represented by the patinated material is residual evidence of earlier prehistoric activity, and then a second phase, of unpatinated flintwork, that could be associated with the Iron Age settlement. This latter assemblage contains many of the expected characteristics listed above, such as utilisation of locally available raw materials, including the recycling of earlier lithic material, lack of knapping skill and a simple core-flake technology, together with a very restricted range of tool types.

Winnall Down, Hampshire
Another example of a possible early Iron Age flint assemblage comes from Winnall Down in Hampshire (Winham 1985). Here a sealed ditch deposit of early Iron Age date produced a small assemblage of almost 500 pieces of

Later Prehistoric Flintwork

worked flint. The majority of the material was waste fragments, chips and nodules, together with broad and squat hard hammer-struck flakes with obtuse flaking angles. There were also 14 cores and 10 core fragments. The tools comprised only six scrapers, but there were also 23 retouched flakes.

This small assemblage indicates that the flintworking was fairly *ad hoc*, with only one recognised tool type. This crude industry would certainly match the criteria expected for an Iron Age assemblage outlined above, although there was also Neolithic activity at the same site, so there may be problems with residual flintwork becoming incorporated into the later contexts.

ROMAN AND LATER FLINTWORKING

We can be certain that flintworking to create tools in any recognised form did not continue into the Roman period. Analysis of flintwork from a number of villas and other Roman sites in southern Britain has been quite clear in establishing that the only flintwork present is residual prehistoric material. The only exception is where flint has been used as a building material (*colour plate 29*). Occasionally in these cases knapped flakes from the shaping of nodules can be found in constructional contexts, whilst large numbers of accidentally knapped flakes occur in robber trenches. The latter appear to have been caused by the use of pickaxes and other tools to remove flint nodules from the walls. Frequently these flakes have mortar still adhering to them.

In the Medieval period, flint was still used as a building material, and occasionally used for strike-a-lights. In the early thirteenth century flint was used in its natural nodular form in roughly coursed walls. As whole nodules were used without modification, there was very little knapping taking place,

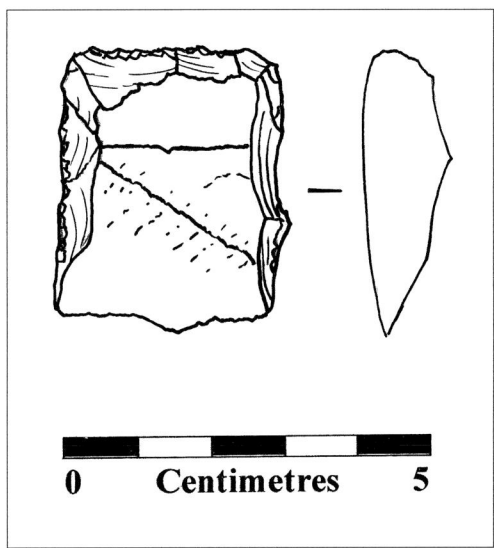

77 A nineteenth-century gunflint

and consequently very little flint debris discarded during the construction of these flint buildings. It is only later in the thirteenth century and more into the fourteenth century that flints tended to be laid in more regular courses and were roughly squared-off. Fourteenth century walls have neater coursing and less mortar visible than in earlier work, whilst the residual flakes from knapping the flint nodules were used for gallets from the fourteenth century onwards. Gallets would have been pushed into the mortar joints between the flint nodules thus reducing the amount of mortar required and giving added protection from the weather. Flint continues to be used as a building material today.

Few Medieval documents survive to indicate how flints were knapped for building walls, although it would require some skill to produce suitable squared nodules in quantity. Study of modern-day building flintknappers in Norfolk shows that a ton of finished nodules can be produced in some 4.5 to 5 hours (Whittaker 2001). The probable use of an iron hammer to knap the flint nodules for wall construction would have resulted in the debitage being very irregular. The debitage would have included flakes, fragments, chunks and shattered pieces, together with many pieces exhibiting little evidence of platform and bulbs of percussion but with negative facets and impact scars. The sparking qualities of flint also meant that it continued to be used into the early twentieth century for making gunflints (77). The Brandon flintknapping industry in the eighteenth and nineteenth centuries revolved around the manufacture of gunflints for muskets, both for military purposes and for sport (Forrest 1983).

10

ANALYSING PREHISTORIC FLINTWORK

One of the biggest problems encountered in producing reports on flintwork from archaeological excavations is the scepticism that many archaeologists have about using flintwork as a dating tool. On many occasions the smallest piece of pottery is triumphed as conclusive dating evidence and given copious description and prominence in the published report, whilst the flintwork is generally consigned to a secondary supporting role with a summary paragraph in the final report. Part of the problem is that because flintwork is very durable it tends to survive well in the archaeological record, whereas pottery (especially prehistoric pottery) does not. Therefore on many sites there will be residual flintwork from earlier activity that can become incorporated into later features, whilst the pottery will tend to only survive in primary contexts. Without careful consideration of the contextual data the residual flintwork can provide false dating evidence. The rest of the problem is historical, in that pottery and to some extent certain flint implement types (e.g. microliths, arrowheads and polished axes) have become established cultural indicators. However, it is only in recent years that the study of debitage and manufacturing technologies has meant that lithic specialists have been able to provide much more information. Other archaeologists have not yet caught onto this, and thus flintwork remains the poor relation. A detailed study of a good stratified flintwork assemblage can therefore provide not only dating evidence, but also information about activities that were being carried out on the site, together with aspects of trade, technology, social organisation and even ritual.

Having described the different flintworking technologies in the preceding chapters, I now want to look briefly at some of the methods a lithics specialist could use to analyse an assemblage of flintwork. The process is a circular one. Much of our understanding has come from the careful analysis of flintwork in the past, and this book represents the current state of our knowledge. The study of flintwork from new excavations uses that existing knowledge, applying tried and tested techniques of analysis, in an attempt to answer questions about the site and to increase our general knowledge of past human activity. For those who want to know more about flintwork analysis a quick look at the bibliography will provide more detailed text books on the subject (e.g. Andrefsky 1998, 2001), and what follows is an overview of some of the techniques used.

In trying to work out how our ancestors used flint we need to try and understand the strategies they were using. By knowing that their entire knapping strategy was geared towards the end result (i.e. the tool they were going to produce), but also understanding that the technology they used was influenced by the availability, size and quality of the raw material, we can begin to interpret the flint tools and waste that we find on excavations and in surveys. We can use that knowledge to explain how they were using the landscape, what they were doing and where they were doing it (Andrefsky 2001).

Much of what has been said about prehistoric flintwork in the preceding chapters is the result of using typology. This puts different tools into chronological sequences and periods based on their various attributes and their association with other artefacts and dating evidence. In recent years the use of scientific dating techniques has helped to date various types of flintwork more closely by association (Ashton *et al.* 1994). However, flint itself cannot currently be dated, unless it has been burnt, in which case the act of burning is dated, not the manufacture of the piece. Where an assemblage contains diagnostic pieces, it is normally fairly straightforward to apply a broad date to it. However, many archaeological sites produce huge quantities of debitage, but few tools or diagnostic pieces. Other sites frequently comprise more than one phase of activity, and where disturbed by later agricultural activity the assemblages can become mixed. To enable an understanding of these sites to be reached, alternative methods of dating or separating the flintwork into its different phases need to be found.

One way in which the flintwork from different periods of prehistory has been successfully classified has been by looking at the technological characteristics that can be seen in the debitage and tools (Schofield 1995). The technological characteristics involved are those that result from the manufacturing or knapping process, and can be seen on flakes and cores, other debitage and the implements. Therefore flint specialists today tend to be more interested in the debitage and technological aspects of flintworking rather than the resulting implements and tools *per se*. The replication of flint tools and ethnographic studies (Binford 1983) has also contributed to our understanding of the knapping process, the debitage that is produced, and how the different types of tool are made and may have been used.

FLAKES, TECHNOLOGY AND KNAPPING SEQUENCES

The most basic and common piece of flint debitage on a prehistoric site is probably the flint flake in all or any of its forms. Studying flint flakes and understanding the sequence of events that led to their creation can help us determine a number of things about the site from which it has come. We can understand how the flake was removed from its core, and the level of care that was taken in its removal, by looking at the flake's technological attributes (platform preparation, type of hammer etc.). This together with its shape and size can combine to determine the period in prehistory in which it was made. Furthermore the type of flake, its shape and distinctive features (e.g. the presence or absence of cortex) may be able to tell us when in the knapping sequence it was removed from a nodule or core, and what sort of tools were being produced at the site. I will give a few examples of this type of analysis:

Cortex

The amount of cortex that remains on the dorsal side of a flake is an indicator of when in the knapping sequence a flake was removed, and can indicate whether the raw material was being curated, as well as providing a possible guide to dating. It is also important to take into account other aspects of the flake's characteristics in making such determinations, including its size and other manufacturing traits. For example, in a knapping sequence connected with axe production, all of the primary flakes that are removed from the nodule will have some cortex on them. Those removed later in the reduction process (secondary flakes) have less cortex, whilst the final (tertiary) flakes will have no cortex. By looking at the flakes that result from this process and their other characteristics (e.g. soft or hard hammer-production), we can see the different knapping technology that was employed at each stage of the process. Furthermore, by analysing the distribution of each type of flake, it may be possible to tell where on a site the different stages of the reduction process took place, and determine whether any stages were absent, suggesting that they may have been carried out elsewhere (see Chapter 7).

The proportion of flakes with cortex on a non axe-producing site can also tell us about the curation of material. A predominance of cortical flakes would suggest that most flakes were primary and therefore cores were not being reduced much beyond the primary reduction stage. Alternatively if there is little cortex on the flakes they are likely to have come from a core that has been heavily worked. A comparison of the proportion of cortical/non-cortical flintwork from five sites in Wessex dating from the middle Neolithic period through to the middle Bronze Age showed an increase in the proportion of cortical pieces over this time, with the two middle Bronze Age sites having much higher proportions of cortical flakes (80 per cent and 75 per cent respectively) (Fasham and Ross 1978). This could be taken to demonstrate that during the middle Bronze Age there was less curation of raw material, with fewer flakes likely to be removed from each core, and therefore more of them having cortex.

However, the location of a site in relation to its raw material source may have had a crucial impact on the curation of the raw material. The closer the site is to the source of its raw material, the less likely people would have been to curate the flint, as they knew there were many more pieces that could be obtained relatively easily nearby.

Patination
The patination and staining on flintwork may help to determine the original source of the raw material. It can also be useful in dividing a mixed-period assemblage into its component parts, although this latter analysis would be combined with the study of the knapping technology used, and other characteristics of the pieces in the assemblage. At sites where different raw material sources were exploited in each period, or where a number of alternative sources were available, there may have been a preference for a raw material of a particular quality in one period. The flint obtained from these different sources may have distinctive colours of patination or staining, and thus can help to determine which components of the assemblage belong to a particular period.

Raw material and size of debitage
It has been established that over time flakes tend to get larger, and therefore heavier. It would therefore be expected that, given a common local and large-sized raw material, Bronze Age flakes would be larger and heavier than those from the Mesolithic period. More mobile communities such as Mesolithic hunter-gatherers were also more likely to carry small cores with them, thus resulting in small flakes, whilst more sedentary Bronze Age communities with access to a reasonable raw material source would use larger nodules and therefore produce larger flakes. Similarly if the raw-material nodules are small (for example river or beach gravel pebbles), the size of the flakes and any tools produced from them are also likely to be small. However, because the nodules are small there will be a greater proportion of primary cortical flakes associated with them. Associated with smaller raw material could be evidence of curation in the form of platform preparation and core rejuvenation, perhaps even in periods where it would otherwise not be expected.

The problem with size and weight in determining age and manufacturing processes is the size and availability of the raw material that was being used. If a nodule of flint has been transported a long way from its original source, it is likely that greater care will have been employed in getting the maximum number of flakes from it. So even on a Bronze Age site located some distance from a source of raw material, the flakes are likely to be small and have significant numbers of secondary and tertiary flakes. However, a similar site close to the source of raw material will have larger flakes that will be predominantly primary cortical flakes. There are many problems associated with the analysis of flint assemblages in some parts of the country where flint is not a common raw material (Saville 1982), and the general rules for identification of debitage and some implements from different periods should be applied with care.

Analysing Prehistoric Flintwork

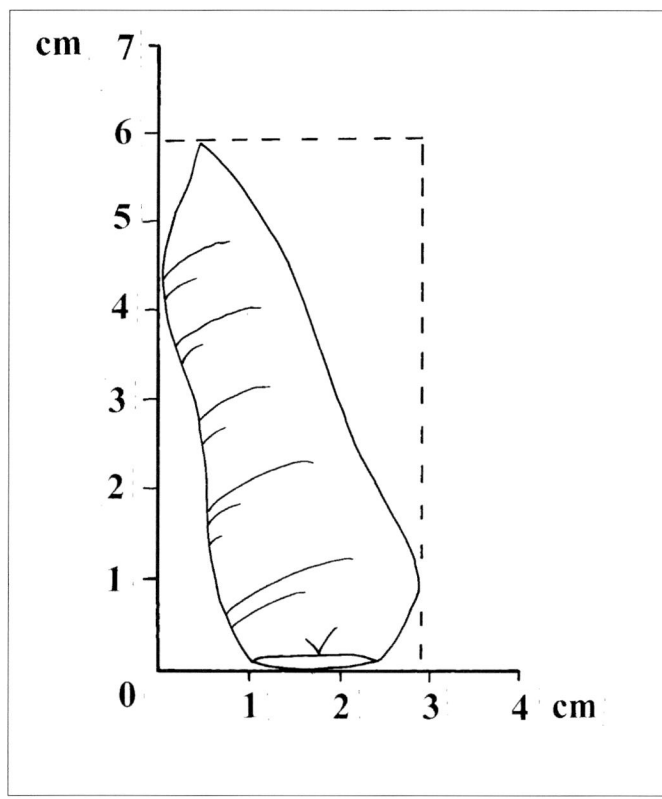

78 Example of the measurements of a flake for length/breadth analysis

Measuring flakes

A trend that has been noted is that over time the shape of flakes changed from long and thin to short and squat. Systems for the measurement of flakes were devised and have subsequently been used to confirm that this trend is a reality. The method outlined by Saville (1980) for measuring flakes is as follows (78):

Length: The maximum dimension at right angles to the striking platform (after Alexander *et al.*1960)
Breadth: The maximum dimensions at right angles to length
Thickness: Maximum thickness of piece from ventral to dorsal face

Having measured a sample of complete (i.e. unbroken) flakes using this method, the results can be explained in two different ways and then compared with assemblages from other sites. Firstly, the mean dimensions for the flakes from an assemblage can be compared, however these results can be affected by the size of the raw material. Secondly, the proportions of flakes of different dimensions (calculated by dividing the length of each piece by its width and called the length/breadth Index) can also be shown in table form (see below). The results of this analysis can then be compared with other sites, as the raw material size does not affect the results to a great extent. The following example

Prehistoric Flintwork

can illustrate such a comparison:

TABLE 4

	L/B INDEX	Streat Lane (Mesolithic)		Crowlink (Bronze Age)	
		NUMBER	%	NUMBER	%
Broad	< 0.5	0		0	
	0.6 – 1.0	18	18	40	40
Medium	1.1 – 1.5	19		45	
	1.6 – 2.0	21	40	13	58
Narrow	2.1 – 2.5	18		2	
	2.6 >	24	42	0	2
Total		100	100	100	100

This is an extreme example to demonstrate the point. The Streat Lane site is Mesolithic, producing bladelets, blades and flakes, and this is clear from the results displayed above with 42 per cent of the sample being narrow (i.e. having a length of twice or more than their width), whilst most of the remainder of the assemblage falls into the Medium category. However the Crowlink site has most of its flakes falling into the Medium category, whilst a significant proportion (40 per cent) is Broad (i.e. having a width greater than their length). Virtually none of the Bronze Age assemblage falls into the Narrow category.

The length/breadth analysis of debitage using this method can be very useful in determining the date of assemblages or phasing within a site, where there is little else to assist in its dating. However, as with most of the methods outlined here, it should not be used in isolation, but in conjunction with other characteristics of the flintwork, as it is always possible that variations in raw material or the type of tool that was being made at the site can affect the results.

Weight
When combined with other forms of analysis, the weight of individual flakes or groups of flakes may help in determining their place in the production process (or *chaîne opératoire*). Analysis has shown that primary flakes removed with a hard hammer tend to be larger and heavier than those removed further along in the reduction process (Butler 2001c). This applies not only in the production of implements such as axes, but also in the general reduction

of cores. Given a reasonable raw-material source that was being exploited through different periods, the size and weight of flakes increases over time, so flakes produced in later prehistory will be heavier than those from the earlier period.

CORES AND IMPLEMENTS

Many of the methods outlined above can also be used to analyse cores and implements. The presence or absence of cortex, weight and measurement of cores can assist in determining their dating and the manufacturing processes employed. Analysis of cores will normally involve counting the number of platforms, their relationship to one another, and whether there is evidence of platform preparation and rejuvenation. Sometimes the number of negative scars of flakes removed from each platform is counted, which may assist in determining the number of overall flakes removed. However, it should be remembered that normally the core represents the final stage in its life just prior to it having been discarded, and therefore this form of analysis may not produce any worthwhile results.

With implements, the main form of analysis is to divide up the different implement types based on their attributes, into their typological categories. Further analysis such as taking length/breadth measurements, weighing them, and establishing the presence or absence of cortex, can also be applied to flake tools. The measurement and weight of core tools can also be a useful indicator of raw-material size and production processes (Andrefsky 1998).

USE-WEAR ANALYSIS

Referred to as either use-wear or microwear analysis, this aspect of lithic research has been with us for over 40 years (Kooyman 2000). It works on the principle that wear and damage resulting from the use of a flint tool can be seen under a microscope, and by replicating that wear and damage, it can be determined what tasks the flint was used for in prehistory. Under a microscope minute striations, pitting and fracturing can be seen, together with a polish or what used to be called sickle-gloss. Only flintwork excavated from relatively undisturbed conditions is suitable for this analysis, and care needs to be taken during the excavation and finds processing stages to ensure accidental damage does not occur. Some researchers have claimed to be able to determine the type of material that was being worked by flint tools, for example wood, bone, grass or leather (Keeley 1977), whilst others have determined how the tool may have been used; such as scraping, boring and sawing. There is still some scepticism amongst archaeologists about use-wear analysis, and some problems, mostly theoretical and methodological, remain before it will become a widely accepted technique (Ashton *et al.* 1994). But use-wear analysis has highlighted that it is not only formal implement types that were used for various tasks in prehistory. Many unretouched flakes were also utilised for cutting, scraping and other tasks, and their possible use for these tasks may have been vastly understated. Given the large number of unretouched flakes that are recovered on excavations, it is clear that this form of analysis could be a useful method of determining the actual number of utilised pieces on a site. It can also help to establish a flake's true function, as it is clear that the retouched tools may only make up a small proportion of the overall number of pieces used as tools on some sites.

In a related form of analysis, researchers have established the presence of mammalian red blood cells, collagen, and hair fragments on lithic material from a cave site in Israel, suggesting that animal processing tasks were being undertaken at that site (Loy *et al*. 1992).

REFITTING AND REPLICATION STUDIES

The refitting of flintwork has become an important part of understanding the process by which flint tools were made, how debitage was disposed of and core reduction techniques. At its simplest, refitting can mean the fitting of a few flakes back onto their core (*79*). If the flakes and the core come from the same context, perhaps the fill of a pit or ditch, then this may indicate that this is debris from the same knapping episode. At its most complex is the complete refitting at Boxgrove of the flakes and other debitage to reform the nodule from which a handaxe was made. The ability to refit flakes enables the spatial patterning of discarded debitage to be determined, and this can tell us a lot about how prehistoric people not only produced tools, but also how they organised themselves and their working and living environments. For example: 'Knapping was probably carried out in a sitting or squatting position with most of the flakes being allowed to fall to the ground in front of the knapper from where useful flakes might later be selected for making into tools. Larger flakes and the core may have been discarded by being thrown away over the shoulder, or further away in front of them' (Binford 1983).

The experimental manufacture of flint tools also plays an important part in our understanding of prehistoric flintworking techniques. The replication of flint tools enables us to understand better the problems encountered by prehistoric flintknappers, and how they overcame them. It is possible to follow the different stages of the manufacture of a tool, replicating the types of debitage found on archaeological sites and experimenting with different flintworking techniques to see which most closely match the actual artefacts. Other forms of experimentation include the use of finished tools to carry out a variety of tasks to see to which they are most suited, for example the butchering of a deer with a handaxe (Pitts *et al*. 1997) or the chopping down of a tree with a Neolithic polished axe. All of these can provide us with more

Analysing Prehistoric Flintwork

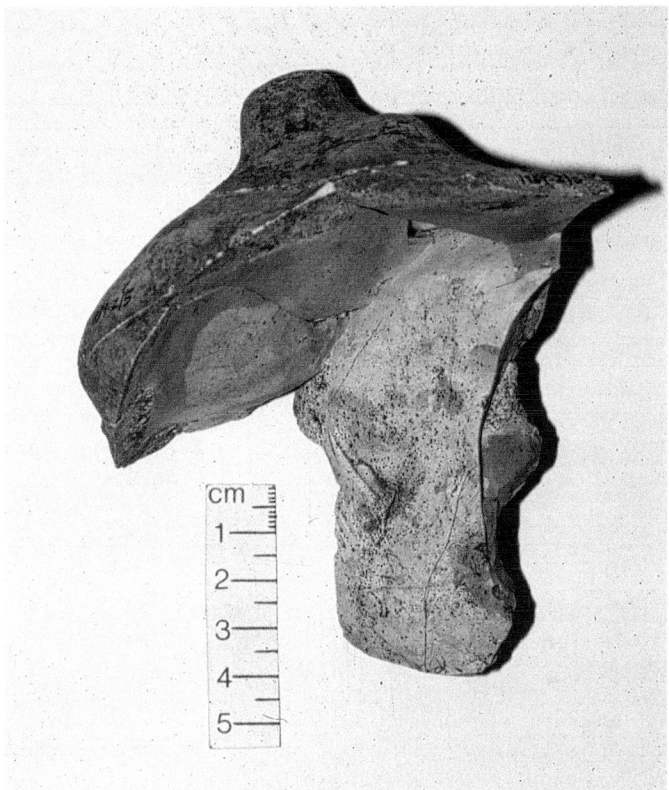

79 Four refitting flakes from the ditch of a round barrow at Pyecombe, Sussex

data on how prehistoric people may have made and used their tools, and enable us to interpret what we find on archaeological sites.

This is a brief guide to some of the methods used by lithics experts to analyse flintwork. There are many others, and variations on those mentioned, and it would take a number of books to cover all the different aspects of lithics analysis in detail. There are two recurring factors in the study of prehistoric flintwork assemblages. The first is the size and availability of the raw material, and the second is the end product i.e. the type of tool that was being produced. These two things dominate the techniques used by prehistoric flint workers, and also, therefore, our study of worked flint.

GLOSSARY OF TERMS

ABRASION
This describes the wearing away of the edge of the platform on a core by friction, usually with a coarse stone (e.g. sandstone), to facilitate the removal of flakes. It can also be used to describe the damage on the working edge of a tool from use, or the wear caused by friction with its handle.

ABRUPT RETOUCH
Steep retouch (generally about 90°) on the edge of a tool, normally to form a scraping edge or to blunt a piece to facilitate hafting or handling (*18*).

ANVIL
A block of hard stone either placed on the ground, held by a second person, or steadied by other means, against which a core can be struck to remove a flake.

ARRIS
See Ridge.

ASSEMBLAGE
A group of finds (e.g. the worked flint) from a site, or from a feature on a site.

BACKED
An edge that has been blunted by continuous abrupt retouch or semi-abrupt retouch to facilitate hafting or handling of the piece.

BASE
The part of a tool at the opposite end to the presumed working edge.

BIFACE
An implement, generally round or oval, which has been flaked over both surfaces, and has sharpened edges. Also used as a general term for Palaeolithic handaxes.

BIFACIAL
A piece from which removals have been made over both surfaces or faces, from the same edge.

BIPOLAR CORE
A blade or bladelet core with two opposing platforms (*30*).

BLADE
This is a flake that has a length of more than twice its width. A true blade will also have

more or less parallel lateral edges, and parallel ridges that result from previous similar blade removals from the same core (*14*).

BLADELET

A blade whose width is less than 12mm (*14*).

BLANK

A piece from which an object is knapped, flaked or retouched, for example this could be a flake or bladelet.

BULB OF PERCUSSION

A conchoidal shape that forms on a flake radiating from the point at which the percussion or pressure was applied; generally the platform (*12*).

BULBAR SCAR

Occasionally a small secondary flake (or chip) is produced at the moment a flake is separated from the core, normally from the front of the bulb of percussion.

BURIN

A flake or blade that has been modified by the removal of a narrow splinter (spall) from a break, unmodified surface or a prepared surface (*19*). There are a number of sub-types; for a full description see Barton 1992 and Inizan et al. 1992.

BURIN SPALL

The waste piece(s) removed during the final production of a burin (*28*). These generally have a triangular section, and may have evidence of prior preparation.

BUTT

This is the proximal end of a flake, with the remnant of the platform (*12*). Where the flake is a first flake, the butt may be cortical. The butt may exhibit evidence of platform preparation on its dorsal side.

CHAÎNE OPÉRATOIRE

A term used to explain the series of predetermined stages, and goals for each of those stages, in the production of stone tools (*5*).

CHIP

A small waste piece that is removed as a by-product of flaking, preparation or retouching. It will normally be less than 10mm in size, and may have all the attributes of a flake (platform, bulb etc.).

CONCHOIDAL FRACTURE

The technical term for the way in which flint breaks when it is struck.

CONJOINING

The matching and fitting together of pieces (normally flakes or other debitage) in order to demonstrate that they are associated.

CORE

A piece or nodule of raw material from which flakes, blades or bladelets have been removed (*11*).

CORE REDUCTION

The process by which flakes are removed from a core.

CORE TOOLS
Tools that are made from the remnant nodule or core. i.e. the primary purpose of removing flakes is to shape the nodule to form the tool, therefore all the flakes are primarily intended as waste. Typical core tools include axes and picks.

CORTEX
The outer skin on a nodule of raw material.

CORTICAL
Denotes the presence of cortex. The extent of cortex remaining on the dorsal surface of a flake can be expressed by the terms: wholly cortical, partly cortical etc., or can be expressed as percentages.

CRESTED BLADE
The first blade or bladelet removed from a core that has been prepared by cresting. It will have a triangular cross section, with uni- or bidirectional removals originating from the central ridge (*31*).

CRESTING
The use of alternate (bifacial), or occasionally unifacial, flaking to create a ridge on the face of a core running away at 90° from the platform, to act as a guide in the removal of the first blade (crested blade). It can also be used to prepare the platform of a core or blank, prior to the removal of a spall or flake.

DEBITAGE
Waste material produced during the knapping process; includes flakes, blades, bladelets and chips, as well as cores and all types of core rejuvenation pieces.

DENTICULATION
A line of successive notch removals along the edge of a flake or blade, producing a saw-like edge (*44*).

DIRECT PERCUSSION
The act of striking a core or other piece directly with a hammer to remove a flake.

DISTAL END
The opposite end of the flake to the proximal end; i.e. the end directly opposite the platform and bulb of percussion (*12*).

DORSAL SURFACE
The side or face of a flake opposite to the ventral surface, and that would have been on the outer surface of the core prior to its removal (*12*). It will normally have either cortex or negative scars from previous removals on its surface.

ÉPERON
A method of platform preparation used in the Late Upper Palaeolithic that results in a projecting spur (*éperon*) on the edge of the platform, which allows blades to be detached with greater precision (*28*).

Glossary of Terms

FACETS

The negative scars left on a piece after the removal of a flake.

FACETTED

The removal of a number of small flakes from the surface of a platform to prepare or change the angle of the platform. It is also used to define the flattened straight lateral edges of some Neolithic polished axes, which were initially shaped by facetting.

FICRON

A form of Palaeolithic handaxe (*22*). From the French for the tip of a punt-pole (British Museum 1950).

FIRST FLAKE

The first flake removed from a nodule, and which will normally be fully cortical. It can also be referred to as a primary flake.

FLAKE

General term for all fragments that have been removed from a core (*14*). It may be intended for manufacture into a tool, or may simply be debitage. Some types of flakes can be subdivided into blades or bladelets.

FLAKE TOOLS

Tools that are made from flakes, blades or bladelets.

FLAKING

The action of removing flakes.

FLAKING ANGLE

The angle at which the platform was struck by the hammer. This angle can determine the morphology of the flake that is removed (*10*).

FLANC DE NUCLÉUS

A core rejuvenation flake that removes the exhausted flaked face of a core, thus allowing flaking to continue from the same platform (*31*). It can be removed either from the side of the core at 90° to the old platform, or by placing a blow on the platform some way back from its exhausted edge.

FRAGMENT

A piece of debitage that has been broken off or removed. It will have one or more attributes of the original complete flake, but will be incomplete. The term can be qualified if sufficient of the original piece is present; e.g. blade fragment.

HAMMER

An implement used to strike a core or flake for knapping or retouching. A hard hammer is used to describe a pebble or stone hammer, whilst a soft hammer could be antler, wood, bone or soft stone (*colour plate 6*).

HINGED

Any removal of a flake where the distal end bends sharply and is prematurely removed from the core. This can be as a result of an incorrect flaking angle, or due to a flaw in the raw material (*10*).

IMPACT POINT
The point at which a blow is applied to remove a flake. The bulb of percussion derives from the impact point.

IMPLEMENT
General term for any piece intended as a tool or weapon (see Tool).

INDIRECT PERCUSSION
Where a punch is used between the hammer and the core (*16*).

INVASIVE RETOUCH
An acute form of retouch, generally at an angle of 10° or less, which extends across the surface of a piece, and is normally used to create a cutting edge on a piece.

JANUS FLAKE
A flake with a bulb of percussion on both its dorsal and ventral sides. This can result when a core platform is struck, and the blow removes an additional flake from the bulb of percussion of the main flake being removed, and which can sometimes remove the entire bulb. The resulting additional flake will then have its own bulb on the ventral side and the bulb from the original flake on the dorsal side.

KNAPPING
A general term that describes the intentional fracturing of flint, and frequently used to describe the process used to shape a tool.

LENTICULAR
Usually used to describe the section of an axe. i.e. shaped like a lentil or a biconvex (two-convex-sided) lens (*59*).

LEVALLOIS
A method used to produce a particular type of flake whose form is predetermined by the special preparation of the core prior to its removal (*24*).

LINGULATE
Tongue-shaped, sometimes used to describe the shape of an axe (*22*).

LIP
A very slight projection, which can be felt and sometimes seen on the edge formed by the platform and bulb of percussion (*15*). It is associated with soft hammer-produced flakes, but can sometimes also be produced with a broad hard hammer.

NEGATIVE REMOVAL OR SCAR
The scar, normally on a core or on the dorsal side of a flake, or from retouching, left by the removal of a flake.

Glossary of Terms

NOTCH
A small concave area created by retouch on the edge of a flake (*19*).

OGEE POINT
A point with an S-shaped curve on each side, meeting at the point (*22*).

OVERHANG
A projection left on the edge of a platform, which overhangs the negative removal on the core, after the removal of a flake. Removal of the overhang by abrasion can assist in the more effective removal of subsequent flakes from the platform (*13*).

PATINATION
A sheen that forms on the surface of flint. The colour of the patination will depend upon the surrounding soil and minerals that are absorbed by the flint.

PLATFORM
See striking platform.

PLATFORM PREPARATION
Although this term could be applied to any form of work carried out on a piece prior to flaking or knapping, it is normally applied to the abrasion of the edge of the platform on a core to remove overhangs prior to the removal of a flake. The small negative removal scars produced by this action can be seen on the dorsal edge of the butt of a flake subsequently removed from the platform (*13*).

PREFORM
An interim stage in the production of an axe, between the roughout and the finished flaked axe (*57*). This stage normally involves the removal of any remaining cortex and the shaping of the axe into its final form, prior to sharpening or polishing.

PRESSURE FLAKING
Unlike direct percussion, this method of flaking relies on the application of gradual pressure with a special tool to remove a flake (*18*). It can be used to remove a flake from a core, or for retouching.

PRIMARY FLAKE
Used to refer to any flake that has been removed from a nodule during the initial removal of the cortex, and will therefore be fully or partially cortical on its dorsal side. See first flake.

PROXIMAL END
The end of a flake that contains the butt and bulb of percussion (*12*).

PUNCH
An object placed between the hammer and the striking platform of the core for indirect percussion (*16*).

REJUVENATION
This term is generally applied to preparing the platform of a core for flaking when the condition of the existing platform means that no further flakes can be removed. This normally involves the removal of the existing platform whilst at the same time creating a new platform to allow continued flaking.

RETOUCH
The modification or alteration of a piece to make a tool (*18*). Normally this takes the form of flakes or chips being intentionally removed from its edge, and therefore shows as a series of regular negative flake scars (the retouch) on the edge. It can usually be distinguished from edge damage, which does not have the same regularity. Retouch is not always used to create a working edge, sometimes it is used to modify an edge to facilitate its hafting or handling.

RIDGE
The distinctive ridge formed at the intersection of two negative scars on the dorsal side of a flake, the surface of a biface or face of a core. Also called the arris.

RIPPLES
The effect of the shock wave travelling through the flint after it has been struck can show as a series of ripples on both the flake and the negative scar. These can be of assistance in determining the direction of the removal.

ROUGHOUT
The initial stage in the production of an axe or biface (*57*). It will normally still have some cortex present, but will have started to take the general form of the proposed axe.

SECONDARY FLAKE
A flake removed from a core or axe after the primary flakes have been removed, and normally having a small amount of cortex on the dorsal side.

SHOULDER
A regular line of removals on the butt, which continues to the lateral edge of the flake or blade, and then around the corner and partly down one lateral edge.

STRIKING PLATFORM
The flat, natural or prepared surface on a core, which is struck by a hammer or punch to remove flakes.

TANG
A projection formed by two flanking notches or shoulders. Normally formed to assist the hafting of the tool e.g. Barbed-and-tanged arrowhead (*68*)

TERTIARY FLAKE
A flake removed from a core or axe after the secondary flakes have been removed. Tertiary flakes will not have any cortex on the dorsal side, and are frequently removed with more care than primary or secondary flakes.

Glossary of Terms

TESTED NODULE
A nodule of raw material from which one or two flakes have been removed to determine whether it is of suitable quality for continued knapping.

THERMAL FLAKE
The name given to any flake formed by natural processes, such as frost fracturing. Although formed naturally, these are sometimes retouched and utilised as tools (*colour plate 7*).

TOOL
A piece intended for utilisation as a tool or weapon. (see Implement)

TRUNCATION
A line of regular continuous abrupt retouch truncating either the proximal distal or lateral part of a flake, blade or bladelet, and forming two angles with the edges of the blank (*44*).

VENTRAL SURFACE
The front face of a flake, normally exhibiting the bulb of percussion (*12*).

BIBLIOGRAPHY

Alexander, J. and Ozanne, P. C. and A., 1960, 'Report on the investigation of a round barrow on Arreton Down, Isle of Wight', *Proceedings Prehist. Society.* 26, 263-302.

Aldhouse-Green, S., Scott, K., Schwarcz, H, Grûn, R., Housley, R., Rae, A., Bevins, R. and Redknap, M., 1995, 'Coygan Cave, Laugharne, South Wales, a Mousterian Site and Hyaena Den: a Report on the University of Cambridge Excavations', *Proceedings Prehist. Society* 61, 37-79.

Andrefsky, W., 1998, *Lithics: Macroscopic approaches to analysis*, Cambridge University Press: Cambridge.

Andrefsky, W. (ed.), 2001, *Lithic Debitage: Context, Form, Meaning*, The University of Utah Press: Salt Lake City, USA.

Ashmore, P.J., 1996, *Neolithic and Bronze Age Scotland*, Historic Scotland/ Batsford: London.

Ashton, N., 1988, 'Tranchet adze Manufacture from Cliffe, Kent', *Proceedings Prehist. Society* 54, 315-333.

Ashton, N., Dean, P. and McNabb, J., 1991, Flaked flakes: what, where and why?, *Lithics* 12, 1-11.

Ashton, N.M., McNabb, J. and Parfitt, S., 1992, Choppers and the Clactonian: A Reinvestigation, *Proceedings Prehist. Society* 58, 21-28.

Ashton, N. and Andrew, D. (ed.), 1993, *Stories in Stone*, Lithic Studies Society Occasional Paper 4: London.

Ashton, N.M., Bowen, D.Q., Holman, J.A., Hunt, C.O., Irving, B.G., Kemp, R.A., Lewis, S.G., McNabb, J., Parfitt, S.A. and Seddon, M.B., 1994, Excavation at the Lower Palaeolithic site at East Farm, Barnham, Suffolk: 1989-1992, *Journal of the Geological Society* 151.

Ballin, T.B., 2000, Classification and description of lithic artefacts: A discussion of the basic lithic terminology', *Lithics* 21, 9-15.

Ballin, T.B., 2002, 'Later Bronze Age flint technology: A presentation and discussion of post-barrow debitage from monuments in the Raunds area, Northamptonshire', *Lithics* 23, 3-28.

Barber, M., Field, D. and Topping, P., 1999, *The Neolithic Flint Mines of England,* English Heritage: London.

Barton, R.N.E., 1990, The *en éperon* technique in the British Late Upper Palaeolithic, *Lithics* 11, 31-33.

Barton, R.N.E., 1992, *Hengistbury Head, Dorset, Volume 2: The Late Upper Palaeolithic and Early Mesolithic Sites*, Oxford University Committee for Archaeology, Monograph No 34: Oxford.

Barton, R.N.E., 1997, *Stone Age Britain*, English Heritage/ B.T. Batsford: London.

Barton, R.N.E., 1998, 'Long Blade Technology and the Question of British Late Pleistocene/Early Holocene Lithic Assemblages', in N. Ashton, F. Healy and P. Pettitt (eds), *Stone Age Archaeology. Essays in honour of John Wymer*, Lithic Studies Society Occasional Paper 6, 158-164.

Barton, R.N.E. and Bergman, C.A., 1982, 'Hunters at Hengistbury: some evidence from experimental archaeology', *World Archaeology* 14, 237-248.

Bell, M., 1990, *Brean Down excavations 1983-1987*, English Heritage Archaeological Report no. 15: London.

Binford, L.R., 1983, *In Pursuit of the Past; Decoding the Archaeological Record*, Thames and Hudson: New York, USA.

Bishop, B., 2002, A *Bout Coupé* Handaxe from Enfield in the Lower Lea Valley, *Lithics* 23, 43-47.

Bordes, F., 1961, *Typologie du Paléolithique Anchen et Moyen*, Delmas: Bordeaux, France.

Bordes, F., 1968, *The Old Stone Age*, World University Library: London.

Bradley, R., 1970, 'The Excavation of a Beaker Settlement at Belle Tout, East Sussex, England', *Proceedings Prehist. Society.* 36, 312-379.

British Museum, 1950 *Flint Implements: An Account of Stone Age Techniques and Cultures*, The Trustees of the British Museum: London.

Brossler, A., Early, R. and Allen, C., 2004, *Green Park (Reading Business Park) Phase 2 Excavations 1995 – Neolithic and Bronze Age Sites*, Thames Valley Landscapes Monograph 19, Oxford Archaeology.

Butler, C., 1989, 'An Early Mesolithic Site and Later Flintwork from Hassocks, West Sussex', *Sussex Archaeological Collections* 127, 230-235.

Butler, C., 1991, 'The Excavation of a Beaker Bowl Barrow at Pyecombe, West Sussex', *Sussex Archaeological Collections* 129, 1-28.

Butler, C., 1998, 'Mesolithic Streat', *Sussex Past and Present* 84, 6.

Butler, C., 1999, 'A Fieldwalking survey at Mill Lane, Clayton, West Sussex', *Sussex Archaeological Collections* 137, 175-181.

Butler, C., 2001a, 'A Mesolithic and later prehistoric flintworking site at East and West Hills, Pyecombe, West Sussex', *Sussex Archaeological Collections* 139, 7-25.

Butler, C., 2001b, 'The Flint', in C. Greatorex, 'Evidence of prehistoric ritual traditions', *Sussex Archaeological Collections* 139, 27-73.

Butler, C., 2001c, 'Horned scrapers and other prehistoric flintwork from Alfriston, East Sussex', *Sussex Archaeological Collections* 139, 215-223.

Butler, C., 2001d, 'A polished flint arrowhead from Tilgate Lodge, West Sussex' *Lithics* 22, 37.

Butler, C. and Holgate, R., 2002, 'The Flintwork' in 'Excavations at Redhill' by Barber, L. and Bennell, M., in *Downland Settlement and Land Use*, D. Rudling (ed.), English Heritage: London.

Campbell, J.B., 1971, *The Upper Palaeolithic of Britain*, D. Phil. thesis, University of Oxford.

Care, V., 1979, 'The Production and Distribution of Mesolithic Axes in Southern Britain', *Proceedings Prehist. Society* 45, 93-102.

Clark, J.G.D., 1927, Some Hollow Scrapers from Seaford, *Sussex Archaeological Collections* 68, 273-276.

Clark, J.G.D., 1932a, 'Discoidal polished flint knives – their typology and distribution', *Proceedings Prehist. Society of East Anglia* 5, 40-54.

Clark, J.G.D., 1932b, 'The date of the plano-convex flint-knife in England and Wales', *The Antiquaries Journal* 12, 158-162.

Clark, J.G.D., 1934a, 'The Classification of a Microlithic Culture: The Tardenoisian of Horsham', *Archaeological Journal* 90, 52-77.

Clark, J.G.D., 1934b, 'Derivative forms of the petit tranchet in Britain', *Archaeological Journal* 91, 34-58.

Clark, J.G.D., 1934c, 'The curved flint sickle blade of Britain', *Proceedings Prehist. Society of East Anglia* 7, 67-81.

Clark, J.G.D., 1960, 'Excavations at the Neolithic site at Hurst Fen, Mildenhall, Suffolk', *Proceedings Prehist. Society* 26, 202-245.

Clark, J.G.D., 1970, *The Mesolithic Settlement of Northern Europe*, Greenwood Press, New York: USA.

Clark, J.G.D., 1971, *Excavations at Star Carr* (Second edition), Cambridge University Press.

Clark, J.D.G. and Rankine, W.F., 1939, 'Excavations at Farnham, Surrey (1937-8): the Horsham culture and the question of Mesolithic dwellings. Schedule of Mesolithic sites in the Farnham District', *Proceedings Prehist. Society* 5, 61-118.

Clarke, D.L., 1976, 'Mesolithic Europe: the economic basis', in G. de G. Sieveking *et al.* (ed.), *Problems in economic and social archaeology*, 449-81, Duckworth: London.

Clough, T.H.McK. and Cummins, W.A., 1979, *Stone Axe Studies*, CBA Research Report 23: London.

Clough, T.H.McK. and Cummins, W.A., 1988, *Stone Axe Studies: Volume 2*, CBA Research Report 67: London.

Coulson, S.D., 1986, The *Bout Coupé* Handaxe as a Typological Mistake, in S.N. Collcutt (ed.), *The Palaeolithic of Britain and its nearest neighbours: Recent Trends*, University of Sheffield, 53-54.

Curwen, E. and Curwen, E.C., 1926, 'Harrow Hill Flint Mine Excavation 1924-5', *Sussex Archaeological Collections* 67, 103-38.

Curwen, E.C., 1931, 'Excavations in the Trundle', *Sussex Archaeological Collections* 72, 100-149.

Darvill, T., 1989, 'The Circulation of Neolithic Stone and Flint Axe: A case study from Wales and the Mid-West of England', *Proceedings Prehist. Society* 55, 27-43.

Dawson, B. 1998, *Flint Buildings in West Sussex*, West Sussex County Council.

David, A., 1998, 'Two Assemblages of Later Mesolithic Microliths from Seamer Carr, North Yorkshire: Fact and Fancy', in N. Ashton, F. Healy and P. Pettitt (eds), *Stone*

Age Archaeology. Essays in honour of John Wymer, Lithic Studies Society Occasional Paper 6, 196-204.

Drewett, P.L., 1978, 'Neolithic Sussex', in *Archaeology in Sussex to AD 1500*, CBA Research Report 29, 23-29.

Drewett, P.L., 1982, 'Later Bronze Age downland economy and excavations at Black Patch, East Sussex', *Proceedings Prehist. Society* 48, 321-400.

Durden, T., 1995, 'The production of specialised flintwork in the later Neolithic: a case study from the Yorkshire Wolds', *Proceedings Prehist. Society* 61, 409-432.

Edmonds, M., 1995, *Stone Tools and Society*, B.T. Batsford: London.

Evans, J., 1897, *The Ancient Stone Implements of Great Britain, Second edition*. Longmans and Co: London.

Ellaby, R., 1987, 'The Upper Palaeolithic and Mesolithic in Surrey', in J. and D.G. Bird (eds), *The Archaeology of Surrey to 1540*, 53-69, Surrey Archaeological Society: Guildford.

Fasham, P.J. and Ross, J.M., 1978, 'A Bronze Age Flint Industry from a Barrow Site in Micheldever Wood, Hampshire', *Proceedings Prehist. Society* 44, 47-67.

Field, D., 1982, 'Two flint Daggers from Kingston', *Surrey Archaeological Collections* 74, 207-8.

Field, D., 1989, 'Tranchet Axes and Thames Picks: Mesolithic core tools from the West London Thames', *London and Middlesex Archaeological Society Transactions* 40, 1-26.

Field, D. and Woolley, A.R., 1984, 'Neolithic and Bronze Age ground stone implements' from Surrey: morphology, petrology and distribution. *Surrey Archaeological Collections* 75, 85-109.

Finlay, N., 2000, 'Microliths in the making', in R. Young (ed.), *Mesolithic Lifeways: Current Research from Britain and Ireland*, Leicester Archaeology Monographs 7, 23-31.

Flanagan, L.N.W., 1966, 'The Petit-tranchet Derivative Arrowhead and the Irish Neolithic', in J. Filip (ed.), *Actes du VIIe Congrès Internatuional des Sciences Préhistoriques et Protohistoriques Vol. 1*, 523-7.

Ford, S., Bradley, R., Hawkes, J. and Fisher, P., 1984, 'Flint-working in the Metal Age', *Oxford Journal of Arch.* 3, 157-173.

Forrest, A. J., 1983, *Masters of Flint*, Lavenham Press Ltd: Lavenham.

Gabel, G., 1976, 'St. Catherine's Hill: a Mesolithic site near Guildford', *Research Volume of the Surrey Archaeological Society* 3, 77-102, Surrey Archaeological Society: Guildford.

Gallios, R. W., 1965, *The Wealden District*, British Geological Survey, Fourth edition.

Gardiner, J.P., 1988, *The composition and distribution of Neolithic Surface Flint Assemblages in Central Southern England*. Unpublished Ph.D. thesis, University of Reading.

Gardiner, J.P., 1990, Flint procurement and Neolithic axe production on the South Downs: a re-assessment, *Oxford Journal of Archaeology* 9:2, 119-40.

Green, H.S., 1980, *The Flint Arrowheads of the British Isles*, BAR British Series 75, Oxford.

Harding, P., 1989, 'An experiment to produce a ground flint axe', in G. de G,. Sieveking and M. Newcomer (eds), *The Human uses of Flint and Chert*, 37-42. Cambridge University Press.

Harding, P., 2000, 'A Mesolithic site at Rock Common, Washington, West Sussex', *Sussex Archaeological Collections* 138, 29-48.

Healy, F., Heaton, M. and Lobb, S.J., 1992, 'Excavations of a Mesolithic Site at Thatcham, Berkshire', *Proceedings Prehist. Society* 58, 41-76.

Holden, E.W. and Bradley, R.J., 1975, 'A Late Neolithic site at Rackham', *Sussex Archaeological Collections* 113, 85-103.

Holgate, R., 1988, *Neolithic Settlement of the Thames Basin*, BAR British Series 194, Oxford.

Holgate, R., 1991, *Prehistoric Flint Mines*, Shire Publications Ltd: Princes Risborough.

Holgate, R., 2003, 'Late Glacial and Post-glacial Hunter-gatherers in Sussex', in D.Rudling (ed.), *Archaeology of Sussex to AD 2000,* CCE University of Sussex.

Holgate, R., and Butler, C., Forthcoming, The Neolithic Flint Mines in Sussex: The results of recent fieldwork.

Inizan, M.-L., Roche, H. and Tixier, J., 1992, *Technology of Knapped Stone*, CREP, Meudon, France.

Jacobi, R., 1978, 'The Mesolithic of Sussex', in P.L. Drewett (ed.), *Archaeology in Sussex to AD 1500*, CBA Research Report 29: London.

Jacobi, R., 1986, The Contents of Dr. Harley's Show Case, in S.N. Collcutt (ed.), *The Palaeolithic of Britain and its nearest neighbours: Recent Trends*, University of Sheffield, 62-68.

Jacobi, R., 1997, 'The Creswellian in Britain', in J-P. Fagnart, and A. Thévenin (eds), *Le Tardiglaciaire en Europe du Nord-Ouest*, Éditions du CTHS: Paris, France.

Jacobi, R. and Tebbutt, C.F., 1981, 'A Late Mesolithic Rock Shelter site at High Hurstwood, Sussex', *Sussex Archaeological Collections* 119, 1-36.

Jochim, M.A., 1998, *A Hunter-Gatherer Landscape: Southwest Germany in the Late Palaeolithic and Mesolithic*, Plenum Press: New York, USA.

Keeley, L.H., 1980, *Experimental Determination of Stone Tool Uses*, University of Chicago Press: London.

Kooyman, B.P., 2000, *Understanding Stone Tools and Archaeological Sites*, University of Calgary Press: Canada.

Lhomme, J.P. and Maury, S., 1990, *Tailler le Silex*, A.D.D.C., Périgueux: France.

Longworth, I., Herne, A., Varndell, G. and Needham, S., 1991, *Excavations at Grimes Graves, Norfolk 1972-1976,* Fascicule 3, British Museum Press: London.

Lord, J.W., 1993, *The Nature and Subsequent Uses of Flint*.

Loy, T.H and Hardy, B.L., 1992, 'Blood on 90,000-year-old stone tools', *Antiquity* 66, 250.

Luedtke, B.E., 1992, *An Archaeologist's Guide to Chert and Flint*, Archaeological Research Tools 7, University of California: Los Angeles, USA.

McNabb, J., Felder, P.J., Kinnes, I. and Sieveking, G., 1996, 'An archive report on recent excavations at Harrow Hill, Sussex', *Sussex Archaeological Collections* 134, 21-37.

Malone, C., 2001, *Neolithic Britain and Ireland*, Tempus Publishing Ltd: Stroud.

Manby, T.G., 1979, 'Typology, materials, and distribution of flint and stone axes in Yorkshire', in T.H.McK. Clough and W.A. Cummins (eds), *Stone Axe Studies*, CBA Research Report 23, 65-81.

Martingell, H. and Saville, A., 1988, *The Illustration of Lithic Artefacts: A Guide to drawing stone tools for specialist reports*, Lithic Studies Society and AAI and S.

Mercer, R.J., 1981, *Grimes Graves, Norfolk. Excavations 1971-72 Volume I*, doe Archaeological Reports II, HMSO, London.

Neeley, M.P. and Barton, C., 1994, 'Late Pleistocene microliths in southwest Asia', *Antiquity* 68, 275-88.

Olausson, D.S., 1982, 'Lithic technological analysis of the thin butted axe', *Acta Archaeologica* 53, 1-88.

Palmer, S., 1977, *The Mesolithic Cultures of Britain*, Dolphin Press: Poole.

Palmer, S., 1999, *Culverwell Mesolithic Habitation Site*, BAR British Series 287, Oxford.

Piel-Desruisseaux, J-L., 2002, *Outils Préhistoriques*, Fourth edition, Dunod: Paris, France.

Pitts, M. and Roberts, M., 1997, *Fairweather Eden*, Century: London.

Priestley-Bell, G., 2002, 'The Worked Flint' in *Heathend Sandpit, Duncton*. unpublished report. Archaeology South East: Ditchling.

Rankine, W.F., 1960, 'Further Excavations at a Mesolithic Site at Oakhanger, Selborne, Hants', *Proceedings Prehist. Society* 26, 246-62.

Reynier, M.J., 1994, 'A statistical analysis of ten early Mesolithic sites in south east England', in N. Ashton and A. David (eds), *Stories in Stone*, Lithic Studies Society Occasional Paper 4, 199-205.

Reynier, M.J., 1998, 'Early Mesolithic Settlement in England and Wales: Some Preliminary Observations', in N. Ashton, F. Healy and P. Pettitt (eds), *Stone Age Archaeology. Essays in honour of John Wymer*, Lithic Studies Society Occasional Paper 6, 174-184.

Robertson-Mackay, R., 1987, 'The Neolithic Causewayed Enclosure at Staines, Surrey: Excavations 1961-63', *Proceedings Prehist. Society* 53, 23-128.

Robins, P., 2002, 'A Late Neolithic flint hoard at Two Mile Bottom, near Thetford, Norfolk', *Lithics* 23, 29-32.

Robinson, P., 1986, 'An Introduction to the Levallois Industry at Baker's Hole (Kent), with a Description of Two Flake Cleavers', in S.N. Collcutt (ed.), *The Palaeolithic of Britain and its nearest neighbours: Recent Trends*, University of Sheffield, 20-22.

Russell, M., 2000, *Flint Mines in Neolithic Britain*, Tempus Publishing Ltd: Stroud.

Russell, M., 2001a, *Rough Quarries, Rock and Hills*, Bournemouth University School of Conservation Sciences Occasional Paper 6, Oxbow Books: Oxford.

Russell, M., 2001b, *The Early Neolithic Architecture of the South Downs*, BAR British Series 321.

Saville, A., 1980, 'On the Measurement of Struck Flakes and Flake Tools' *Lithics* 1, 16-20.

Saville, A., 1981, 'Iron Age Flintworking – Fact or Fiction?', *Lithics* 2, 6-9.

Saville, A., 1982, 'Carrying Cores to Gloucestershire: Some thoughts on Lithic Resource Exploitation', *Lithics* 3, 25-28.

Saville, A., 2002, 'Lithic artefacts from Neolithic causewayed enclosures: character and meaning' in G.Varndell and P. Topping (eds), *Enclosures in Neolithic Europe*, Oxbow Books: Oxford.

Schofield, A.J. (ed), 1995, *Lithics in Context: Suggestions for the future direction of Lithic Studies*, Lithic Studies Society Occasional Paper 5, London.

Smith, A.J., 1981, 'The Flint' in J.M. Coles (ed.), *Somerset Levels Papers 7*.

Smith, C., 1992, *Late Stone Age Hunters of the British Isles*, Routledge: London.

Smith, I.F., 1965, *Windmill Hill and Avebury; Excavations by Alexander Keiller 1925-1939*, Oxford University Press.

Smith, R.A., 1919-20, 'The Chronology of Flint Daggers', *Proceedings of the Society of Antiquaries, Second Series,* 32, 6-22.

Stafford, M., 1998, 'In search of Hindsgavl: experiments in the production of Neolithic Danish flint daggers', *Antiquity* Vol. 72, No. 276, 338-349.

Timms, P., 1980, Flint Implements of the Old Stone Age, Shire Publications Ltd: Princes Risborough.

Topping, P., 2004, 'The south downs flint mines: towards an ethnography of prehistoric flint extraction', in J Cotton and D Field (eds), Towards a New Stone Age: Aspects of the Neolithic in South East England, 177-190 CBA Research Report: York.

Van Peer, P., 1992, *The Levallois Reduction Strategy*, Monographs in World Archaeology 13, Prehistory Press: Wisconsin.

Vemming Hansen, P., 1981, Neolitisk bopladsflint, *Kontaktstencil* 19, 23-37.

Wainwright, G.J. and Longworth, I.H., 1971, *Durrington Walls: Excavations 1966-1968*, Reports of the Research Committee of the Society of Antiquaries of London 29.

Wainwright, G.J., 1979, *Mount Pleasant, Dorset: Excavations 1970-1971*, Reports of the Research Committee of the Society of Antiquaries of London 37.

Wenban-Smith, F.F., 1998, Clactonian and Acheulian Industries in Britain: Their Chronology and Significance Reconsidered, in N. Ashton, F. Healy and P. Pettitt (eds), *Stone Age Archaeology. Essays in honour of John Wymer*, Lithic Studies Society Occasional Paper 6, 90-97.

Whittaker, J. C., 1994, *Flintknapping: Making and understanding stone tools*, University of Texas Press: Austin, USA.

Whittaker, J. C., 2001, 'Knapping Building Flints in Norfolk', *Lithic Technology* 26, No 1, 71-80.

Wickham-Jones, C.R. and Holden, T.G., 1999, 'The Opportunistic Exploitation of Flint at Easter Hatton, Aberdeenshire', *Lithics* 20, 23-29.

Winham, R., 1985, 'The Flint', in P. Fasham, *Prehistoric Settlement at Winnall Down, Winchester: Excavations of MARC3 Site R17 in 1976-1977*.

Woodcock, A.G., Kell, D.B. and Woolley, A.R., 1988, 'The petrological identification of stone implements from south-east England', in T.H. McK Clough and W.A. Cummins (eds), *Stone Axe Studies*, vol. 2, CBA Research report 67, 21-33.

Woodman, P.C., 1992, 'Excavations at Mad Mans Window, Glenarm, County Antrim:

problems of Flint Exploitation in East Antrim', *Proceedings Prehist. Society* 58, 77-106.

Wymer, J.J., 1962, 'Excavations at the Maglemosian Sites at Thatcham, Berkshire, England', *Proceedings Prehist. Society* 28, 329-361.

Wymer, J.J., 1977, *Gazetteer of Mesolithic sites in England and Wales*, CBA Research Report 22: London.

Wymer, J.J, 1999, *The Lower Palaeolithic Occupation of Britain*, Wessex Archaeology and English Heritage.

Young, R. and Humphrey, J., 1999, 'Flint use in England after the Bronze Age: Time for a Re-evaluation?', *Proceedings Prehist. Society* 65, 231-242.

INDEX

Numbers in **bold** refer to illustrations, whilst *italics* refer to an entry in the glossary.

Acheulian **colour plate 11**, 64, 66
Adzes 55
   Duggleby type 145
   Early Neolithic **56**, 132
   Hassocks. *See* Hassocks adze
   Mesolithic **42**, 103
   Tranchet. *See* Tranchet adze
Amesbury archer **colour plate 27**, 177
Anston Cave 76
Anvil 88, *202*
Arrowheads **colour plate 16**
   Barbed-and-tanged **68-69**, 39, 162, 164, 175
   Chisel **66-67**, 158
   Hollow-based **67**, 162
   Leaf-shaped **48-49**, 25, 119, 122
   Oblique **66-67**, 158, 160
   Petit tranchet **66-67**, 94, 158
   Polished **69**, 123, 164
   Ripple-flaked **66-67**, 160
   Transverse 158, 176
   Triangular **67**, 160
Awls **19**, 53
   Early Neolithic **54**, 126
   Later Bronze Age 185
   LNeo/EBA 168
   Mesolithic **44**, 110
Axe thinning flakes **colour plate 22**, **58**, 42, 64, 139, 153
Axes 55
   Flaked **colour plate 20**, **61**, 103, 145

Ground *See* Polished Axes
Handles **colour plate 19**, 55, 103, 142
Neolithic **colour plate 17**, **57-61**, 139, 142
Polished **7**, **60**, 119, 139, 142, 145
Scandinavian **61**, 147
Seamer 145
Stone 148

Backed *202*
Backed blades
   Angled 79
   Curve 79
   Final Upper Palaeolithic **29**, 79
   Straight **29**, 79
   Upper Palaeolithic **28**, 76, 78
Backed knives **19**, 54
   Early Neolithic **54**, 129
   Mesolithic 112
   Middle Palaeolithic **25**, 70
Backed pieces **27**, 73
Ballyclare *See* Barbed-and tanged arrowhead
Beakers 155, 162, 172, 177
Bec *See* Piercer
Beedings 73
Biface 62, *202*
Black Patch 188
Blade segments 113
Bladelets **14**, 35, 40, *203*

Final Upper Palaeolithic 78
Mesolithic 24, 83, 88
Blades **14**, 35, 40, *202*
 Early Neolithic 121, 122
 Later Bronze Age 181
 LNeo/EBA 157
 Mesolithic 84
 Upper Palaeolithic 72, 76
Borer *See* Piercer
Boxgrove **colour plates 9–10**, 57, 64, 200
Bronze tools 39, 172, 175, 187
Bruised blades **29**, 79
Bulb of percussion **12**, 32, 38, 43, *203*
Bullhead flint **colour plate 3**, 21
Burin **19**, 51, *203*
 Break 53, 74
 Busked **27**, 74
 Dihedral **19**, 53, 74, 78, 109, 132
 Spall **28**, 51, 53, 74, 108, *203*
 Truncation **19**, 53, 74, 78, 109, 132
Burins
 Early Neolithic **55**, 131
 Final Upper Palaeolithic **29**, 78
 Mesolithic **44**, 108
 Middle Palaeolithic 70
 Upper Palaeolithic **27–28**, 74, 76

Causewayed enclosures
 Staines 131, 137
 Windmill Hill 137
Chaîne opératoire **5**, 23, 198, *203*
Chert 16
Chips 41, *203*
Chisels **59**, 134, 145
Chopper-cores **21**, 62
Choppers
 Later Bronze Age **76**, 187
 LNeo/EBA 170
 Mesolithic **46**, 113
Clactonian 62, 66
Clactonian notch **25**, 60, 70
Clay-with-flints 18, 21, 100, 117, 139, 151
Cleavers **22**, 62

Middle Palaeolithic **26**, 70
Combination tools
 Early Neolithic 127
 LNeo/EBA **71**, 168
 Upper Palaeolithic **27**, 74, 78, 79
Conchoidal, **8**, 16, 27, *203*
Conygar Hill *See* Barbed-and tanged arrowhead
Copper-alloy tools *See* Bronze tools
Core rejuvenation **47**, 32, 78, 84, 86, 88, 121, 157, *208*
Core tablets **31**, 78, 84, 88, 121
Core tools 55, 174, *204*
Cores **colour plate 5**, **9**, **11**, 28, 41, 199, *203*
 Bipolar **30**, 72, 88, 121, *202*
 Coned *See* Pyramidal
 Cube-shaped **47**, 121, 122
 Discoidal **47**, **65**, 121, 136, 157
 Early Neolithic **47**, 30, 121, 136
 Final Upper Palaeolithic **29**, 78
 Keeled **47**, 121, 136, 157
 Later Bronze Age **74**, 181
 Levallois 66, 157
 LNeo/EBA **65**, 155
 Lower Palaeolithic **21**, 62
 Mesolithic **30–31**, 30, 84, 86
 Pyramidal **30**, 86, 88
 Tortoise 66, 157
 Upper Palaeolithic 72, 76
Cortex 20, 23, 33, 38, 83, 100, 121, 139, 155, 181, 195, *204*
Crested blade **31**, **47**, 72, 84, 88, 121, *204*
Cresting 72, 78, *204*
Creswellian 76, 78
Crowlink **colour plate 28**, 189, 198
Cutting flakes 54
 Later Bronze Age **76**, 185
 Mesolithic 112

Daggers **73**, 172, 175
Debitage 41, 194, 196, *204*
 Building 191
 Early Neolithic 122

219

Final Upper Palaeolithic 78
Iron Age 189
Later Bronze Age 181, 182, 188
LNeo/EBA 157, 175, 176
Mesolithic 84, 116, 117
Deepcar 96
Denticulates
Early Neolithic **55**, 130
Final Upper Palaeolithic 81
LNeo/EBA 168
Mesolithic **44**, 110
Middle Palaeolithic **25**, 70
Denticulation *204*
Durrington Walls 175

En éperon **28**, 76, *204*

Fabricators **19**, 56
Early Neolithic **55**, 132
Later Bronze Age **76**, 187
LNeo/EBA **71**, 174
Mesolithic **44**, 110
Feather termination **10**, 35
Ficron **22**, 62, *205*
Finglesham 118
Fire-fractured flint 27
Flaked flakes **23**, 66
Flakes 12, **14-15**, 32, 35, 40, 194, 197, *205*
Early Neolithic 121, 122
Iron Age 190
Later Bronze Age 179, 181
Levallois 66, 68, 157, 158
LNeo/EBA 157
Lower Palaeolithic **21**, **23**, 60, 64
Measurement **78**, 176, 197
Mesolithic 86
Primary 33, 108, 122, 151, 181, 195, 196, 198, *207*
Secondary 33, 121, 190, 195, 196, *208*
Tertiary 33, 190, 195, 196, *208*
Upper Palaeolithic 72
Flanc de nucléus **31**, 86, *205*
Flint

Characteristics **4**, 19
Formation **1**, 15
Raw material **colour plate 1**, 17, 20, 23, 27, 49, 55, 60, 66, 72, 76, 83, 99, 114, 121, 138, 139, 155, 179, 181, 188, 189, 194, 195, 196
Sources **colour plate 2**, **3**, 17
Flint mines **63**, 148
Ballygalley Hill 149
Blackpatch 148
Church Hill 148
Cissbury 148
Den of Boddam 149
Grimes Graves **colour plate 21**, 149, 150, 170, 179
Harrow Hill **colour plates 23-24**, **62**, **64**, 148, 152
Long Down 148
Martin's Clump 149
Food Vessels 172
Fragments 40, 157, 179, 185, 192, *205*
Frost fracturing **colour plate 7**, 43
Fyfield Down **colour plate 18**, 142

Galleting 27, 192
Gough's Cave 76
Gravers *See* Burin
Green Low *See* Barbed-and tanged arrowhead
Grooved Ware pottery 155, 158, 160, 172, 175
Gunflints **77**, 192

Hammers **colour plate 6**, 28, 37, 195, *205*
Hard 37, 44, 55, 60, 62, 84, 122, 139, 157, 181, 189, 298, *205*
Metal 37, 192
Soft 37, 44, 55, 64, 84, 122, 140, 157, *205*
Hammerstones 28, 37, 88, 157, 181, 189
Handaxes **20-23**, 60, 62
Bout Coupé **26**, 62, 66, 72
Coygan-type *See Bout Coupé*

Hassocks Adze **42**, 103
Heat treatment 46
Hengistbury Head 78, 98, 110
Hermitage Rocks 98, 116
Hinge fracture **10**, 33, 38, 84, 157, 179, 190, *205*
Horsham points **38-39**, 92, 96, 98
Hoxne 64
Hurst Fen 49, 135

Iron Age flintworking 189

Janus flakes 32, *206*

Kent's Cavern 76
Kettlebury 98
Kilmarnock *See* Barbed-and tanged arrowhead
Knives 54
    Backed *See* Backed knives
    Discoidal **72**, 170, 177
    Early Neolithic 129
    Later Bronze Age 185
    LNeo/EBA **72**, 170
    Mesolithic **46**, 112
    Plano-convex **72**, 172, 177
Krukowski microburin **34**, 89

Laurel Leaf **54**, 130
Levallois **24**, 66, *206*
Limpet scoops 114

Meare Village West 190
Mèche de foret **44-45**, 110
Micheldever Wood 188
Microburins **33-34**, 88, 116, 117
Microdenticulates **44**, 109
Microliths **32-39**, 24, 81, 83, 88, 90, 96, 116, 117, 118
    Deepcar type 96
    Horsham type *See* Horsham points
    Star Carr type 96
Microwear 64, 89, 110, 174, 199

Natural flint flakes 43

Nodular flint **2**, 15, 18
Notch *207*
Notched pieces **19**, 54
    Early Neolithic **55**, 132
    Final Upper Palaeolithic 81
    Later Bronze Age **76**, 185
    LNeo/EBA **71**, 170
    Mesolithic **46**, 112
    Middle Palaeolithic 70

Obsidian 16
Oldowan 60
Ovates
    Early Neolithic 130
    LNeo/EBA **71**, 170
    Lower Palaeolithic **22**, 62, 64
Overshoot **10**, 34

Patination 20, 43, 45, 190, 196, *207*
Picks 55
    Early Neolithic 132
    Mesolithic **42**, 103, 115
Piercers **19**, 53
    Early Neolithic **54**, 126
    Final Upper Palaeolithic **29**, 79
    Later Bronze Age **76**, 185
    LNeo/EBA **71**, 168
    Mesolithic **44-45**, 110
    Upper Palaeolithic **27-28**, 74, 77
    Zinken 79
Platform preparation **13**, 30, 33, 41, 62, 72, 84, 88, 121, 122, 136, 157, 195, 199, *207*
Points
    Cheddar **28**, 76
    Creswellian **28**, 76
    Curve-backed **29**, 79
    Final Upper Palaeolithic **29**, 78
    Font-Robert **27**, 73
    Jermanovice 73
    Leaf-shaped **27**, 73
    Levallois **25**, 68
    Middle Palaeolithic **25**, 68
    Mousterian **25**, 68
    Penknife **29**, 79

Shouldered **29**, 78, 94
Tanged **29**, 73, 78, 94
Upper Palaeolithic **27-28**, 73, 76
Polissoir **colour plate 18**, 142
Portland chert 21
Preform 55, *207*
  Mesolithic **40**, 100 117
  Neolithic **57**, 139, 152
Pressure flaking **17**, 37, 38, 45, 172, *207*
Punch **16**, 37, 38, 72, 84, *207*
Pyecombe 18, 117, 151, 178

Rackham 176
Radley 178
Refitting **79**, 64, 200
Replication **6**, 200
Retouch **18**, 44, *208*
  Abrupt 44, *202*
  Invasive 45, *206*
  Semi-abrupt 45
Rods
  Early Neolithic **56**, 134
  Later Bronze Age 187
  Mesolithic 110
Roughout 55, *208*
  Mesolithic **40**, 100, 117
  Neolithic **57**, 130, 139, 152, 170, 173
  Palaeolithic 64

Scrapers **colour plate 8**, **19**, 49
  Button **70**, 168
  Carinate **27**, 74
  Concave *See* Hollow
  Disc **53**, 126
  Discoidal 51, 167
  Double ended **52**, 50, 78, 105, 125, 167
  Early Neolithic **50-53**, 125, 136
  Edge-ground 167
  End **19**, 50, 74, 76, 78, 105, 125, 167, 182
  Final Upper Palaeolithic **29**, 78
  Hollow **19**, 51, 105, 125, 167, 183

Horned **75**, 51, 183
Horseshoe **51**, 50, 125, 167
Invasively retouched **70**, 168, 175, 178
Later Bronze Age **75**, 182, 188
LNeo/EBA **70**, 166, 176
Lower Palaeolithic **23**, 64
Mesolithic **43**, 104, 108
Micro **43**, 105
Middle Palaeolithic **25**, 68
Nosed **27**, 50, 74, 125
Quina type **25**, 70
Side **19**, 50, 68, 105, 125, 167, 183
Side-and-end **53**, 51, 105, 125, 167
Thumbnail *See* Button
Upper Palaeolithic **27-28**, 74, 76
Seamer Carr 88
Segment **46**, 113
Serrated blades *See* Denticulates
Shattered pieces 42
Sheet flint See Tabular flint
Sickles **colour plate 26**, **73**, 132, 172
Star Carr 96, 112
Starch fracture **colour plate 7**, 43
Step fracture 34, 38, 84, 190
Streat Lane **colour plate 13**, 27, 108, 198
Strike-a-lights 17, 56, 187, 191
Striking platform 28, 32, 37, *208*
Sutton *See* Barbed-and tanged arrowhead

Tabular flint **2**, 15, 18
Tanged points **29**, 73, 78, 94
Tested nodule 31, *209*
Thames Pick 104
Thatcham 117
Thermal flakes **colour plate 7**, 43, 125, 136, *209*
Tranchet adzes **colour plate 12**, **40-41**, 18, 83, 86, 99, 115, 117, 118, 119
Tranchet sharpening flake **40**, 56, 64, 70, 100, 103, 118
Tribrachs 174
Truncated pieces

    Final Upper Palaeolithic 81
    Mesolithic **44**, 109
    Upper palaeolithic 74, 76, 77
Truncation *209*
Use-wear *See* Microwear
Utilised pieces
    Early Neolithic 134

    Mesolithic 112

Waisted core tools **56**, 103, 174
West Kennet 142
Winnall Down 190

Y-shaped tool **56**, 134

If you are interested in purchasing other books published by The History Press,
or in case you have difficulty finding any of our books in your local bookshop,
you can also place orders directly through our website

www.thehistorypress.co.uk